Contents

Introduction

Take a good look at the table of contents in this book and try to imagine what the world would have been like if these great lefties had never lived. Try to imagine the Italian Renaissance without Leonardo, Michelangelo and Raphael, science without Isaac Newton or Marie Curie, the American novel without Mark Twain, the computer without Alan Turing or Bill Gates, baseball without the Babe. And that's before we even begin to consider the left-handed statesmen, soldiers, rulers and conquerors whose effect upon the shape of history has been so enormous.

Left-handers have a disproportionate presence in the history of the world. Looking at the table of contents, you could be forgiven for thinking they would have been cherished throughout history as a source of special gifts and insights. But sadly, despite all they have brought to human progress, this is mostly not true. Throughout history, left-handers have been discriminated against. They have been burnt as witches, refused as marriage partners, had their hands tied behind their backs when they tried to write with the left hand, and beaten into orthodoxy. Faced with these obstacles, many lefties have submitted, and have spent their lives trying to pass as righties, which makes the achievement of the people in these pages even more impressive.

Discrimination against the left-hander is one of the deepest prejudices there is. The proto-Indo European language, spoken before 3000 BC, and from which ancient languages such as Sanskrit, Greek and Latin as well as most European vernaculars are derived, had a word for 'right', but not one for 'left', apparently because of the taboos associated with that side of the body. When subsequent languages developed a word for left, the connotations were usually appalling. In Latin, the word for left is *sinistre*, from which our word 'sinister' is derived, while the word for right is *dexter* from which we get dextrous. In Greek, *skaios* means both left-handed and ill-omened or awkward. In Hindi, following the proto-Indo European, left hand is *Ulta Haanth*, which simply means the wrong hand, while in French,

OPPOSITE: SCIENTIST ISAAC NEWTON (1643–1727), DISCOVERER OF THE UNIVERSAL LAW OF GRAVITY, THE LIGHT SPECTRUM AND THE REFLECTING TELESCOPE.

6

A Left-Handed

History of the World

First published in 2007 by Pier 9, an imprint of Murdoch Books Pty Limited

Murdoch Books Australia	Murdoch Books UK Limited
Pier 8/9	Erico House, 6th Floor
23 Hickson Road	93–99 Upper Richmond Road
Millers Point NSW 2000	Putney, London SW15 2TG
Phone: +61 (0) 2 8220 2000	Phone: +44 (0) 20 8785 5995
Fax: +61 (0) 2 8220 2558	Fax: +44 (0) 20 8785 5985
www.murdochbooks.com.au	www.murdochbooks.co.uk

Chief Executive: Juliet Rogers
Publishing Director: Kay Scarlett

Commissioning Editor: Hazel Flynn
Project Manager: Colette Vella
Editor and Photo Researcher: Ariana Klepac
Concept and Design: Peter Long
Production Controller: Maiya Levitch

Text and design copyright © Murdoch Books Pty Limited 2007

All images copyright © Getty Images, with the exception of images on pages 136 and 142 which are copyright © APL/Corbis.

National Library of Australia Cataloguing-in-Publication Data

Wright, Ed, 1968- .
A left-handed history of the world
Bibliography.
Includes index.
ISBN 9781740458108 (pbk.).
1. Left- and right-handedness - History. 2. Left and right (Psychology). I. Title.
152.335

A catalogue record for this book is available from the British Library.

Printed by 1010 Printing International Ltd. in 2007. PRINTED IN CHINA.
Reprinted 2007, 2008.

A Left-Handed History of the World

Ed Wright

PIER 9

it is *gauche*, which has crossed over into English with the meaning of clumsy, especially in social circumstances. The word for right in French is *droit* which also means law. In German, it's worse: *recht* means right-handed, the law and also correct, while *links* means both left-handed and weak. In English, people are right and have rights, while others are left behind. The etymology of 'left' is from the Friesian (a region on the North Sea Coast of Holland and Germany) *luf* meaning weak and worthless, while the Old English *lyft* once combined with *ädl*, meaning disease, to form the word for paralysis. It's no wonder then that left-handers are more likely than their right-handed friends to be dyslexic. This also may be part of the reason why so many of the great left-handers have starred in non-linguistic domains, such as maths, sciences, technology and the visual arts.

Around 10 per cent of the population is left-handed. This seems to be fairly constant across history and culture although, in places where discrimination against the left-hander is particularly strong (in the conformist culture of Japan, for example, which reports 5 per cent of the population as left-handed), people are less likely to own up to left-handedness, while many natural lefties will buckle under the pressure and switch. Given the historical discrimination against lefties in virtually all cultures (the ancient Incas, who thought left-handers lucky, were an exception), it's hard to know how many great lefties are missing to history, their handedness switched, concealed or not recorded at all and thus assumed to be right. While the figure is around 10 per cent of the population, men—of whom 12 per cent are lefties—are 50 per cent more likely to be left-handed than women, of whom only 8 per cent are lefties. One theory for this is that left-handedness is caused by the exposure of the foetus to excess testosterone in the womb.

Left-handers tend to be nature's risk-takers. This is also perhaps why left-handers have a disproportionate presence in the annals of human achievement: they take more risks, and sometimes they pull them off. It might be the physical risk of battle, found in lefties such as Alexander the Great or Napoleon; or intellectual risks, as in the case of philosopher Friedrich Nietzsche, who found that when he looked into the abyss of meaning, it looked back at him. Historically, these kinds of risk-taking have tended to be more of a male preserve, which makes the short career of Joan of Arc so spectacular. Possibly this is because males are not as vital to the perpetuation of society. Perhaps it's because for women, childbirth is enough of a risk in itself.

In the primate family, only humans are restricted to 10 per cent left-handers, and there is no conclusive evidence to suggest why. Other members of the primate family can be left- or right-handed, the ratio is roughly equal. It has been suggested that right-handed dominance has something to do with the way language is run from the left hemisphere of the brain. Another possible explanation is that the development of more intricate tools—scissors, for instance—privileged one hand over the other. It does, however, seem likely that this proportion has remained fairly constant throughout the history of humankind. But why? One theory that has arisen to explain this is that left-handers have ensured their evolutionary survival by the advantage of surprise in hand-to-hand combat. Put simply, most people expect to be attacked with the right hand and are not as competent in defending themselves against the left. If too many people become left-handed, however, then this advantage of the unexpected would obviously be diminished.

To a certain extent this theory can be used to explain the disproportionate presence of left-handed players in sports such as tennis, baseball and cricket. The play of a left-hander is more difficult to predict because the angles are different. It can also be argued that if left-handers have enjoyed this advantage in a physical sense, their minds have evolved to maintain it in a mental or abstract sense. In other words, the left-hander's ability to surprise is not just limited to hand-to-hand combat or sports. This can be seen in the careers of people like Alexander the Great or Napoleon, left-handed military geniuses who profited by their power to outwit the enemy through surprising strategies on the battlefield. Furthermore, it can be said that this capacity of the left-hander to use surprise translates to the deployment of unorthodox stratagems in other areas of life. As the philosopher Walter Benjamin once said, 'All the decisive blows are struck left-handed'. Many, if not all, of the great left-handers in this book have made unorthodox moves. They have been agents of major changes that have astonished and transformed their worlds and altered the course of human history.

You may have heard the expression, 'Only left-handers are in their right minds'. This is because the left side of the body is controlled by the right-side of the brain. In neurological terms, left-handers tend to be what is termed 'right-hemisphere dominant'. Studies have shown that the right and left hemispheres of the brain perform different cognitive functions.

The right hemisphere, for instance, has primary responsibility for managing the visual and spatial aspects of sensory perception. Architecture, for example, is a profession renowned for having a large number of left-handers. Possessing enhanced visual and spatial faculties can be an asset in fields ranging from the visual arts (Leonardo, Michelangelo and Raphael), industrial design (Henry Ford), sports (Babe Ruth, Martina Navratilova and John McEnroe), or on the battlefield (Napoleon, for instance, who had an amazing ability to visualise maps). This faculty is also connected to the ability for abstract visualisation that often generates mathematical genius. More than a quarter of the people featured in this book were brilliant at maths: Leonardo, Newton, Napoleon, Carroll, Curie, Turing and Gates. Another link often conjectured is one between mathematical thought and music. Recent research into phenomena such as synesthesia has shown that both these gifts may be related to an enhanced visual-spatial faculty in the mind. It is no surprise then that many of the great left-handers featured here are scientists, visual artists, mathematicians and musicians.

The hemispheric functioning of the brain, however, is more complex than simply right and left dominant. This is particularly the case with

MANY, IF NOT ALL, OF THE GREAT LEFT-HANDERS IN THIS BOOK HAVE MADE UNORTHODOX MOVES. THEY HAVE BEEN AGENTS OF MAJOR CHANGES THAT HAVE SURPRISED AND TRANSFORMED THEIR WORLDS AND ALTERED THE COURSE OF HUMAN HISTORY.

left-handers. As Chris McManus argues in his book, *Right Hand, Left Hand,* while almost all right-handers have the same type of left-hemispheric dominance, the situation with left-handers is more diverse. For example, while 95 per cent of right-handers have language dominance in the left hemisphere, only 70 per cent of left-handers do. McManus argues that left-handers, on average, have greater cerebral variability than right-handers. In other words, lefties are risk-takers in neurological terms too. The brains of left-handers have a built-in tendency to be different: more reason why they can be expected to be harbingers of change and disturbers of the status quo.

This innate difference of left-handers is accentuated by the fact that they have to operate in a world that doesn't fit them. Some, frustrated by the dictates of society, become rebels, while others seek sanctuary by devoting their genius to largely solitary pursuits, where their unique minds are allowed to reign free. Other left-handers, however, adapt to a world where things are often the wrong way round. While this may be an impediment in the operation of can openers, scissors and circular saws, it means that the left-hander's mind is more fully trained in adaptation than the right-hander's. We learn through imitating those around us. Most of us learn by imitating right-handers. For a lefty, this learning demands translation or adaptation; an extra cognitive step. Lefties have to concentrate harder to work out what to do. Perhaps this is the reason why there are so many left-handed actors. This extra step may also be the generator for the lateral thinking found so often in the left-handers in this book.

TRAITS AND EXPLANATIONS LIST

In analysing the personalities and achievements of the great lefties, some traits seem to stand out as being left-handed. Not all the subjects have them but, as you will see in individual chapters, each of the lefties here has a combination of them. In many cases the latent talent is brought out and amplified by the circumstances of individual life. These traits are not exclusive to lefties, but these left-handers have been gifted with them to a prodigious extent. They are also suggestive rather than conclusive. As you read this left-handed history of the world, look to the lefty links in the margins and you will see obvious and surprising connections between the various protagonists, as well as information about many of the other great lefties who have shaped our destiny.

INTUITIVE There seems to be a special kind of intuition, an awareness that shows in the reading of situations and the solution of problems. It's an ability to leap through the stages of conventional thought to penetrate to the core of a question and come up with unexpected answers that surprise those around them. Sometimes it's a battle tactic (Alexander), other times it's a deep affinity with mathematical structures (Newton), or the ability to rewire the received wisdom on a subject in an unorthodox but effective

OPPOSITE: TENNIS PLAYER
MARTINA NAVRATILOVA, WINNER
OF 18 GRAND SLAM SINGLES TITLES
AND 40 DOUBLES TITLES.

manner (Ford). Left-handed intuition can also be the result of that extra step in the lefty's learning process; the necessity of having to adapt right-handed information produces an enhanced awareness of the self.

EMPATHETIC While some left-handers turn their intuition towards themselves, or abstract it into mathematical or musical terrains, others use it to achieve a knowledge of others. This skill is often found in the kind of left-hander who tries to join the hierarchies of right-handed society. Alexander had it when he wanted to, as did Julius Caesar. Bill Clinton is another lefty renowned for it, as was Charlie Chaplin. Often this empathy can be camouflage for the ruthless ambition lurking beneath.

VISUAL-SPATIAL ABILITY With the right hemisphere of the brain usually dominant, in terms of visual-spatial perception, great left-handers are often vested with superior skills in this area. As I have argued above, this ability is also related to having gifts for mathematics and music. Perhaps the most neurological of all the lefty traits, this ability has artistic, scientific and military applications.

LATERAL THINKING Lateral thinking is the ability to make unortho-dox connections. It also has the quality of metaphor; being able to see one thing in terms of another. We have seen that left-handers' brains have more variety in the way they are wired. It can also be argued then that left-handers have more variety in the ways that they think. This ability to see one thing in terms of another is evidenced by the way Isaac Newton, for instance, could visualise the general movement of heavenly bodies in the action of an apple falling from a tree in an orchard. Or how Alexander could look at his men's leather tents and transform them into a flotilla of rafts that enabled his army to cross a river and conquer the opposition.

Two kinds of lateral thinking stand out strongly as markers of left-handed genius: adaptive and transformational. The first is based in the necessity of adapting and learning how to operate in a right-handed world. This means that the left-hander can often have a chameleon-like quality, an ability to change as circumstances demand. Transformational thinking is perhaps an emphasised version of this gift. These types of lateral thinking are, for instance, one reason why so many actors are left-handed, since the ability to become someone else begins with mimicry then becomes self-transformation.

On another level, the desire for transformation is enhanced by the fact that the left-hander exists in a world that doesn't quite fit them. At its most extreme this manifests itself as the creative-destructive impetus of compul-sive conquerors such as Alexander or Napoleon, who seize control and then embark on the impossible quest of remaking the world. It can be said that the left-hander is innately an agent of change. Indeed it may even be our evolutionary function in terms of the survival of the species.

OPPOSITE: LUDWIG VAN BEETHOVEN COMPOSED SOME OF THE WORLD'S GREATEST MUSICAL WORKS, DESPITE BEING STONE DEAF FOR MUCH OF HIS LIFE.

HOT-TEMPERED There's no use trying to hide it. Many left-handers have ferocious tempers. From Alexander to Super Brat John McEnroe, the whole spectrum of anger is on show from childish tantrums and bravery in battle to cold-blooded fury. It may have something to do with the discrimination lefties face in life, or the extra obstacles they have to overcome. Or it may have something to do with the theory that the genes for left-handedness can be triggered by exposure to excess testosterone in the womb.

SOLITARY One approach, when you don't fit in, is to pretend as much as possible that the rest of the world doesn't exist. Beethoven, Nietzsche, Michelangelo, Newton, Turing, Carroll and Joan of Arc all belong to the category of lefty solitaries, while others such as Leonardo and Bill Gates show a tendency.

ICONOCLASTIC As argued above, great left-handers are innately agents of change, who eschew traditions and laws and march to the beat of their own lefty drum. Many left-handers abhor the confinement of social or intellectual structures and thus derive satisfaction from knocking them down so their own individuality has space to flourish.

SELF-TAUGHT If you ever thought failing school would be the end of you, then this book will help you to think again. Some of the greatest minds in history showed little aptitude in their schooling while others, such as Alan Turing, got in trouble for ignoring the curriculum in favour of more complex mathematics. Still others, such as Mark Twain, Henry Ford, Joan of Arc and Charlie Chaplin, hardly had an education at all. What many of them do have in common, though, is an emphasis on learning by doing, rather than through reading books. Experience is valued above theory. This trait can be found in Leonardo's attitude to nature, Marie Curie's preference for experiments over theory, Mark Twain's use of real American speech in his books and Jimi Hendrix's guitar playing, to name but a few.

EXPERIMENTAL A combination of the iconoclastic, experiential, self-teaching and lateral thinking aspects of the left-hander, rather than observing the rules, these left-handers operate on the principle, 'What if …?', then try it out. This trait is linked to the left-hander's inborn tendency to operate as an agent of change.

FANTASIST The variability of the lefty mind can be a hit and miss affair. Uniqueness in itself is no guarantee of success. Not all conceivable changes exist within the realm of possibility. However, what is possible changes from generation to generation, and left-handers, with their powers of seeing beyond the status quo, are often at the cutting edge of making the seemingly impossible come true. In other cases, fantasy provides a mirror for looking at ourselves: it is literally the left hand looking at the right.

OPPOSITE: FOUR OF THE LAST SEVEN US PRESIDENTS HAVE BEEN LEFTIES, INCLUDING THE 42ND US PRESIDENT, BILL CLINTON, WHO SERVED FROM 1993–2001.

Ramses the Great

EGYPT HAD 13 PHARAOHS BY THE NAME OF RAMSES, BUT ONLY THE left-handed, redheaded Ramses II is remembered as Ramses the Great. Taking over from his father, Seti I, in 1279 BC, this pharaoh of the nineteenth Dynasty fought bravely against the Hittites, most notably at the famous battle of Kadesh, and expanded the territory of the Nile Kingdom. With the Hittites, Ramses also concluded the world's first recorded peace treaty, which bore many of the similar conditions seen in modern counterparts. His 67-year reign was phenomenal, given that the average lifespan of an Egyptian at the time was 30–40 years, and the consequent political stability brought enormous prosperity to the Nile Kingdom. With this wealth Ramses built some of the most amazing monuments known to all antiquity. He also managed to sire an enormous number of children—between 100 and 400—to the many wives in his harem. Because he lived to such an old age, many of Ramses' children pre-deceased him. It was his thirteenth son, Merenptah, who eventually inherited the throne. Ramses' reputation as a great pharaoh has endured for thousands of years. In 1976, when his mummy was taken from Egypt to Paris to be treated for fungal growth, it was met by a full French military guard of honour at the airport.

EARLY RAMSES Ramses II was the third of the nineteenth Dynasty pharaohs whose origins were from Egypt's military elite. The dynasty was founded when the last Pharaoh of the eighteenth Dynasty, Horemhèb, who had no sons of his own, chose his military commander, Ramses I, as his successor. One of the reasons he did this was because Ramses I had a son, Seti, who could in his turn take over, thus enhancing the stability of the regime. Ramses I only lasted two years before his son, who was co-regent, took over. Following in the family tradition, Seti introduced his son Ramses II to military life from an early age. According to the hieroglyphs—and it must be remembered that the official records of the

Ancient Egyptians were prone to boasting—Ramses II showed considerable prowess on the battlefield and was a military commander by the age of 10. When he was 14, Seti appointed him co-regent and when Seti died in 1279 BC Ramses, still in his early twenties, became Pharaoh.

KING RAMSES II From the outset Ramses was a proactive Pharaoh. One of the first challenges he faced was the incursions of the Shardana sea pirates (from the coast of Turkey) who were causing major problems for Egypt's Mediterranean trade. In only the second year of his reign, Ramses cleverly placed his navy, backed up by troops, at strategic positions along Egypt's Mediterranean coast. He allowed the pirates to attack, drawing them into a false sense of security. Then he counter-attacked and the pirates were completely surprised. After capturing them, Ramses showed typically left-handed lateral thinking. Instead of slaughtering the pirates or sending them off to work in the harsh slavery of the Nubian gold mines, he incorporated them into his own army (presumably their wives and children were held hostage to assure loyalty) where their straight swords, horned helmets and round shields proved a significant asset in a number of battles, including Kadesh. In the next few years of his reign, Ramses proved a smart military strategist by building a series of forts (next to wells and thus self-sustaining) northwest of modern Alexandria to protect Egypt from bands of Libyan marauders whose influence in the region was growing.

BATTLE OF KADESH The most famous battle of Ramses' military career was undoubtedly the Battle of Kadesh and it illustrated both the advantages and disadvantages of the Pharaoh's mercurial left-handed temper. Early in his reign, Seti had made some strong territorial gains in Syria, at the expense of the Hittites who were based in Turkey. However, by the time Seti died, the Hittites had regained this territory, including the prized city-state of Amurru (in Lebanon) and the fortified hill town of Kadesh (in Syria) where much treasure was kept.

In the fifth year of his reign, Ramses set out with an army of 20,000 men, split into four divisions—named after the Egyptian gods Amun, Re, Ptah and Seth—to recapture this territory. They marched up the coast of Canaan and through the Bekaa Valley in southern Syria, approaching Kadesh from the south. As they approached Kadesh, the Egyptian Army discovered two Bedouins lurking about who, when questioned, informed Ramses that the army of the Hittite King, Muwatallis, was still about 190 kilometres to the north. Thinking he had gained the advantage, Ramses set off with his Amun division towards Kadesh. Not expecting to encounter significant opposition, the other three divisions lagged behind as Ramses and his elite division raced off to set up camp on the northwestern edge of the city.

Unfortunately for Ramses the rush of blood associated with his hot, left-handed temper prevailed over his strategic intuition—a feature of left-handed military leaders throughout history. Shortly after Ramses

PREVIOUS PAGE: DETAIL OF RAMSES' FACE FROM THE STATUE OF THE PHARAOH AT LUXOR, SITE OF THE ANCIENT CITY OF THEBES.

and his division pitched camp, Ramses' forces captured a further two Hittite spies. The truth that was beaten out of them revealed that the first two spies had been plants designed to trick Ramses into a false sense of security. The Hittite army, numbering around 37,000 soldiers, was hiding behind Kadesh, ready to launch a surprise attack. Ramses urgently tried to get word to his other divisions and sent the non-combatant parts of the expedition, including a number of his wives, away to safety.

The warning came too late. As the Re division approached the royal camp, they were attacked and virtually decimated by 2500 of the famously formidable Hittite chariots. Having broken the Egyptian line, the chariots then turned towards the Egyptian camp and Amun division fell into serious disarray. At this point things looked bleak for the Egyptians. It was likely that Ramses would become the first Egyptian pharaoh to be captured in battle: a major disgrace. But rather than submit to this, Ramses mounted his chariot and led his household troops in a series of counter-charges that confounded the Hittites, who were already counting the spoils of victory. Ramses fought fiercely, inspiring his troops, who were further aided by the arrival of troops from the Syrian coast, including the former Shardana sea pirates. The Hittites, surprised by the ferocity of these attacks, fell into disarray and those who weren't slaughtered were forced to swim across the Orontes River to where the main part of the army was camped in relative safety. The two armies ceased fighting for the evening and by the time they lined up against each other the next day, it seemed the only possible result would be a stalemate after much bloodshed. A truce was declared. Even though Ramses had been out-strategised, his bravery and the divine fury of his left-handed rage on the battlefield saved the day against an army almost twice the size of his own. However, it must also be noted that he had failed in his chief objective of capturing Kadesh.

PEACE TREATY After Kadesh, an uneasy peace reigned between Egypt and the Hittites until the death of the Hittite King, Muwatallis. Muwatallis' youngest son, Mursili III, inherited the throne, but was unpopular and only managed to reign for seven years before he was deposed by his uncle Hattusili III. Mursili was exiled to Syria, then Cyprus, before seeking refuge at the Egyptian court, where he tried to cause as much mischief as possible for his uncle. Ramses refused Hattusili's repeated requests for his nephew's extradition. For a while it looked as though war between the two empires was going to break out as a result. However, the military resources of both countries were concerned with more pressing campaigns, involving actual territory rather than pride: the Egyptians were fighting against the Libyans and the Hittites against the Assyrians. Instead of war, diplomats for both sides met over a period of two years and the result was the world's first known peace treaty.

When we think that the Egyptian and Hittite empires were fighting over territory which today belongs to Israel, Lebanon and Syria, the ability to abandon enmity in favour of peace seems extremely impressive, given that

LEFTY LINKS

1. Ramses II conquered the Shardana sea pirates then incorporated them into his army. The pirates who encountered Julius Caesar, another formidable left-hander of the ancient world, were not so fortunate. After being captured by them, then released upon payment of a ransom, Julius Caesar tracked them down to their island lair, defeated them, took their treasure and had them all executed.

2. A similar kind of hot-tempered desperation to Ramses' behaviour at the Battle of Kadesh was shown by Joan of Arc. Against the odds, she led her army by inspiration to victory at Orleans. However, the next time she attempted this she was captured and handed over to the English, who set in motion the processes which led to her being burnt at the stake.

3. After he signed the peace treaty with the Hittites, Ramses reigned for a further 46 years, a period predominantly marked by prosperity and peace. Although he had a strong martial streak in his personality, Ramses tempered it in order to achieve harmony and wealth for his land. As such, his reign bears considerable resemblance to the nineteenth-century British monarch Queen Victoria, who loved a good war but reigned through mainly peaceful prosperity for 63 years.

4. Ramses II belonged to the very exclusive club of left-handed redheads. Other members include Napoleon I, Nicole Kidman, Robert Redford, Mark Twain, John (Johnny Rotten) Lydon, and possibly the King of the Franks and Holy Roman Emperor Charlemagne.

00586537

RAMSES' LEFTY TRAITS

LATERAL THINKING Ramses' capacity for lateral thinking is evidenced by his involvement in the world's first known formal peace treaty. Also, his strategy of claiming the monumental glories of previous pharaohs by changing the inscriptions and defacing the statues to take on his own image can be considered lateral—a sign of the left-hander's innate facility for transformation.

HOT-TEMPERED This seems to be Ramses' defining left-handed trait. It is reflected in his battle strategy, and in his rashness and haste when building his prosperity.

ICONOCLASTIC This lefty trait is most notable in Ramses' tendency to disfigure statues of previous pharaohs and change their likenesses and inscriptions to his own. A number of his temples are also notable for the fact that his statues have been carved on the same scale as the gods. Even though all the pharaohs were divine, this was still a departure from the norm.

EXPERIMENTAL Ramses experimented with peace treaties, new modes of building monuments as well as military strategies such as the system of forts he built across the northwest borders where the Libyan tribes were a threat.

PREVIOUS PAGES: FOUR COLOSSAL STATUES OF RAMSES AT THE ENTRANCE TO THE GREAT TEMPLE OF ABU SIMBEL.

OPPOSITE: DEPICTION OF KING RAMSES II OFFERING TO THE GOD RA, FROM THE INTERIOR OF THE TEMPLE OF ABU SIMBEL.

this is a region of the world that holds long grudges and seems obsessed with the notion of 'an eye for an eye'. It took considerable lateral thinking from the two kings to come up with a document that, despite continuing tensions between the two nations, enabled them to co-exist peacefully for the next 40 years of Ramses II's reign.

The treaty consisted of 18 articles. The first article was a non-aggression pact. The next two established a mutual alliance that either party would go to the aid of the other in the face of invasion by a third power. A further three articles promised that the kings would go to each other's aid, or their sons' aid, should there be an internal attempt to overthrow the crown or its intended heir. The next 10 articles constituted the world's first extradition treaty, whereby fugitives from one regime would not be allowed to live in the other; rather they would be captured, treated civilly and then handed back to their place of origin and whatever fate awaited them. The final two articles cited the authority of 1000 gods from both countries as witnesses, guarantors of the treaty and sanction against breaking it:

> They who do not observe the words that are in this silver tablet, the great gods of the country of Egypt as well as the great gods of the country of Hatti will exterminate their houses, their country and their servants.

Although Egypt was forced to give up its claims to Kadesh and Amurru, the treaty established a valuable right of travel and trade for Egyptians within the Hittite territories, giving them free access to the Mediterranean port of Ugarit. The terms of peace were highly advantageous to the ensuing prosperity of Ramses II's reign, more so than if Ramses had persisted in his attempts to acquire Hittite territories. This is an example of lateral thinking on the part of Ramses.

The peace wasn't always easy, however. To begin with, the continued presence of Mursili in Egypt was problematic: the Hittites believed the extradition treaty should be retrospective, while Ramses did not. After Ramses had sent prized Egyptian doctors to the Hittites he complained that he had only received one lame servant in return. Yet 13 years after the treaty had been signed it was reinforced when the Hittite king offered one of his beautiful daughters to Ramses, who developed such a taste for them (and their sizeable dowries), that he married two more. The royal wedding strengthened the treaty considerably so that when a king of Asia Minor, Mira, approached Ramses in the hope of forming an alliance against the Hittites, Ramses rebuffed him saying, 'Today there is fraternity between the great King of Egypt and the King of Hatti …'.

MAN OF MONUMENTS One of the main activities of an Egyptian pharaoh was the building of monuments. Because he was Pharaoh for over 60 years, Ramses built many of them. Part of the reason why he remains so well known to history is because of the sheer weight of the monuments he left behind. Yet curiously, even though his presence in the ruins is large

compared to most pharaohs, much of the construction was shabby and the masonry wasn't nearly as fine as in the reign of his father, Seti. The left-handed temper and rashness that saw Ramses deceived and isolated from his troops at the Battle of Kadesh also seemed to be at work in Ramses' attitude towards his monuments. Like Alexander the Great, Ramses the Great was a man on a mission in a hurry—perhaps because he had no reason to expect to live as long as he did. Also, it took a long time to build monuments and, for this reason, Egyptian pharaohs generally began building their tombs as soon as they were throned. For Ramses, the urge to monumentalise himself was insatiable. In his reign, he not only constructed some of the greatest monuments in antiquity, but an entire capital city, Piramses, which was, unsurprisingly, named after himself.

Egyptologists frequently note that, for Ramses, it was case of quantity over quality. In order to make possible his lust for monuments, he made extensive use of the slave labour he captured in his military campaigns. For the inscriptions and images in his temples, Ramses traded in the delicate and time-consuming raised relief—whereby images were lifted clear of the background—for the much quicker process of sunken relief, where the images were carved into the stone. Another reason for the adoption of this technique was that it was harder to change an image once it had been carved. Ramses had good reason to think of this. Not only was he a prolific builder, he was also a repurposer of monuments built by pharoahs who had gone before him. Again, this kind of shortcut displays the predisposition for impatience that went with his hot-headed, left-handed temperament. One of his tricks was to get his stonemasons to work on statues of his predecessors, chipping away at them until the statued ended up being an image of Ramses instead. This is about as close to the concrete definition of iconoclastic as you can get.

In other areas of self-immortalisation, Ramses showed a willingness to experiment. His most striking monuments include the twin temples dedicated to Ramses and his favourite wife, Nefretari, at Abu Simbel on the banks of the Nile, near the border between Egypt and Nubia. The most extraordinary feature of the temple was the four enormous statues of himself. Ramses used the unusual technique of carving these directly into the cliff face as opposed to the imported slabs of granite which were usually the material for such endeavours. Each one was over 20 metres high and the whole complex took more than 20 years to build. It was an experiment which had a lasting effect. The statues at Abu Simbel would become the inspiration for the statues of great American presidents carved into the rock at Mount Rushmore, which were also roughly the same size as those of Ramses built 3000 years earlier. Despite Ramses' reputation for hasty workmanship, many of the works he commissioned are still identifiable today.

OPPOSITE: ONE CAN STILL SEE THE BASIC FEATURES OF RAMSES THE GREAT FROM LOOKING AT HIS MUMMY, WHICH WAS DISCOVERED IN 1871 AND IS NOW PRESERVED IN CAIRO'S EGYPTIAN MUSEUM.

Alexander the Great

356–323 BC

SHORT AND LEFT-HANDED BUT IMMENSELY STRONG, BOTH PHYSICALLY and mentally, Alexander the Great is probably the most formidable conqueror and most charismatic warrior statesman the world has ever seen. A great hand-to-hand fighter and master military technician, his political decisions were often strikingly original. Between his coronation as King of Macedonia at the age of 20 and his death at the age of 32, he acquired control over an unparalleled domain, which stretched from Afghanistan, India and Uzbekistan in the east, through Iran (then Persia), Iraq, Kuwait, (Mesopotamia), Syria, Egypt, Turkey, Bulgaria (Thrace), and breached the Danube in the north. In his own times, he was king of over half the known world, stretching over 500 million hectares. His army fought for 12 years without losing a single battle. It marched more than 32,000 kilometres and defeated adversaries with much larger armies and killed more than 200,000 enemy soldiers and 250,000 civilians.

One of Alexander's most significant weapons was the original angles produced by his brilliant and ruthless left-handed mind. While bravery and unity were important, the ability to outthink the enemy was perhaps Alexander's greatest talent. Wherever he went, he left people bewildered to the extent that, throughout the Middle East, he almost ceased being considered a human, becoming a force of nature whose terrifying brilliance is still invoked in bogeyman tales used to frighten children into obedience, while his Macedonian compatriots considered him not just a king, but a god.

EARLY ALEXANDER Alexander's ability to see what others didn't was crucial to his success and reputation from a very early age. A famous instance of his burgeoning prowess, recorded by the eyewitness Marsyas of Macedon, was Alexander's taming of the horse, Bucephalas. The horse had been sold to Alexander's father, Philip, King of Macedonia, who became angry when Bucephalas proved to be wild and unmanageable, and

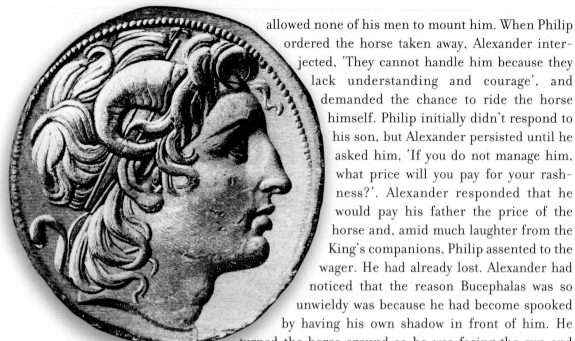

A DETAIL VIEW OF A GOLD MEDAL SHOWING ALEXANDER THE GREAT WEARING AN ELEPHANT SCALP. ALEXANDER MADE HIS PUSH INTO THE INDIAN SUBCONTINENT IN 326 BC.

allowed none of his men to mount him. When Philip ordered the horse taken away, Alexander interjected, 'They cannot handle him because they lack understanding and courage', and demanded the chance to ride the horse himself. Philip initially didn't respond to his son, but Alexander persisted until he asked him, 'If you do not manage him, what price will you pay for your rashness?'. Alexander responded that he would pay his father the price of the horse and, amid much laughter from the King's companions, Philip assented to the wager. He had already lost. Alexander had noticed that the reason Bucephalas was so unwieldy was because he had become spooked by having his own shadow in front of him. He turned the horse around so he was facing the sun and encouraged him gently before taking a flying leap and mounting him. When Philip noticed his son's success he allegedly said, 'My boy, seek a kingdom to match yourself. Macedonia is not large enough to hold you.' While it was a brave thing to mount the horse, it was Alexander's ability to see things differently from everyone else, his capacity to get under the skin of the horse and intuit what was bothering it, that proved the deciding factor.

The tale of taming Bucephalas, while showing Alexander's bravery and brilliance, is primarily one of empathy. It's a quality more commonly associated with women than men. However, empathy is a faculty often concentrated in lefties. Why? The dissonance between lefties' sense of themselves and their surroundings often has the psychological effect of causing alienation. Because of this the lefty has to learn how to adapt more than the righty. This involves learning the thinking of people (or horses) who think differently to oneself, in the same way perhaps that a migrant develops knowledge when trying to adapt to a new society. This capacity for empathy, born from alienation, is what enabled Alexander to solve a problem that his father's best horsemen couldn't. It would also give him a powerful political advantage over the Persians, in places such as Egypt and Babylon, because he understood and was tolerant towards their local religions and, through this, managed to bring their inhabitants onside. Alexander's ability to escape the prejudices of his own culture was undoubtedly helped by the fact that, unlike many of the left-handers in these pages, Alexander had one of the best educations anyone could hope for. His personal tutor was the great philosopher, Aristotle, who complemented his physical prowess with strategical smarts and insight into the human condition.

PREVIOUS PAGE: BY THE END OF HIS 11-YEAR REIGN, AT 32 YEARS OF AGE, ALEXANDER HAD BECOME RULER OF HALF THE KNOWN WORLD.

GETTING ONE OVER THE GETAE

Few battles illustrate the unorthodox genius of Alexander's practical thinking as clearly as his victory over the Getae at the Danube. With his father Philip's assassination in 336 BC, Alexander became King of Macedonia at the age of 20. His ultimate ambition was to take on the Persians, but he had the foresight to realise that if he embarked on such a long-distance mission, it was necessary to annihilate all of Macedonia's neighbouring threats first. After quelling internal Macedonian dissent, he headed north into Thrace (modern day Bulgaria), vanquishing the Triballian and Illryian peoples who had revolted when they heard of the death of Philip. When chasing the remnants of their armies, he found himself on the southern shores of the River Danube in present day Romania. Across the river were the Getae, a tribe of sun-worshippers who had allied themselves with Alexander's enemies. They'd known of Alexander's approach for weeks and had assembled a large army—approximately 4,000 cavalry and 10,000 infantry—to repel any Macedonian attempt to cross the river.

The Getae were used to defending their turf: over the years they'd repelled invasions by a range of marauders including Scythians, Persians and Celts. They were confident that Alexander would take time to get across the Danube as, from their experience, the usual solution was to build a bridge. All they had to do was wait and attack the point where Alexander attempted to do this. With the combination of a strong force and the river against him, the Getae thought Alexander would be sensible, and consider the Danube as the natural limit of his campaign. If he didn't, they were confident that much of his army would be fish food by the time they got across. All they had to do was wait and see which option he took.

Alexander was in a quandary. The more he looked at the river and the Getae army on the opposite shore, the more he wanted to cross it and defeat them. The obvious answer was to build a bridge, but he knew that if he did that the chances of defeat were high. The stakes were high too. If a second-rate military power like the Getae were proved able to defeat him, he would lose the aura of invincibility he was acquiring, and that would make his passage into Asia to defeat the Persians far more difficult.

Perhaps he should turn around. They were fairly close to the Black Sea, and the Danube, having flowed over 2400 kilometres from its German origins, had grown wide. More importantly, Alexander's men, coming from the mountainous regions of Macedonia, couldn't swim.

Still, there had to be another way. One thing Alexander had noticed was that along the banks of the river were a number of canoes which the locals used mainly for fishing. He sent his men out to requisition every one they could find. However, when they came back it soon became clear that although the boats were useful, there simply weren't enough of them to get the army across in sufficient numbers to take on 14,000 Getae.

It wasn't looking promising and most military leaders in this position would have given up. Not Alexander. Now he had seen the Danube, he needed

LEFTY LINKS

1. Alexander's tutor was the great philosopher Aristotle. In various sources it has been asserted that Aristotle was also left-handed. However, the evidence is inconclusive.

2. As with many left-handers, direct evidence for Alexander's left-handedness is difficult to find. Handedness has rarely been remarked upon in history. The Hebrew *Book of Jossippon*, however, mentions Alexander talking of the superiority of the left hand and of how 'kings stemming from the tribe of kings are left-handed'.

3. The rage which powered Alexander's path of conquest, and was also the seed of his destruction, fits the model of the Dionysian principle, as expounded by the left-handed philosopher Friedrich Nietzsche.

ALEXANDER'S LEFTY TRAITS

INTUITIVE Alexander's passage of conquest and mode of battle were largely intuitive endeavours.

EMPATHETIC Alexander was able to empathise with his soldiers which, for the most part, earnt him their loyalty. He was also understanding of other cultures, and even of his horse.

VISUAL-SPATIAL ABILITY This skill was particularly necessary in the planning and execution of battle plans, especially those involving hand-to-hand combat.

LATERAL THINKING Alexander had this in spades, and it was primarily this quality that enabled him to continually outwit his enemies. His transformative capacity to see his army's tents as potential river-crossing vessels against the Getae was crucial to the victory, as well as the reputation he began to accumulate throughout the Ancient World.

HOT-TEMPERED Alexander had a combination of the left-handed and Balkan propensity for violent rage. In one incident he killed his friend Clitus with a spear after a drunken quarrel. In January 332, the citizens of Tyre, in what is now Lebanon, offered to surrender to Alexander, but their religion didn't allow him to sacrifice in their temple. Enraged, Alexander decided to lay siege to the town. When his troops forced their way into the city, they slaughtered 6000 troops. Alexander then ordered that 2000 civilians be crucified on the beach.

EXPERIMENTAL Alexander experimented with new tactics in battle. Yet he was also interested in social experiments. For instance, he tried to blend Greek and Persian society through intermarriage and put troops from different races together in his army. In addition to carnage, he also founded more than 70 cities, including Alexandria in Egypt which, with its famous library, was to become the cultural capital of the Ancient World.

PREVIOUS PAGES: PAINTING BY JEAN-SIMON BERTHELEMY OF ALEXANDER THE GREAT CUTTING THE GORDIAN KNOT.

to cross it. It was part of the incessant drive within him, a combination of curiosity and conquest. With dusk approaching, and a decision yet to be made, his army began to unpack their tents for the night.

As he walked among his men while they were setting up their tents, Alexander had an idea. Macedonian tents of the day were made from leather, and leather was waterproof. What if you sealed a tent . . . better still, filled it with straw and sealed it watertight? Would it float? If Alexander's men hadn't revered him so completely—when he took a tent and stuffed it with straw, then told one of his men to see if he could float on it in the river—they might have mutinied. Instead, that night, through the genius of their commander and his army's faith in him, the Macedonians safely crossed the river, unknown to the Getae, via a scraped-together assortment of canoes and tents.

Alexander had chosen a deep cornfield to land in, which gave the Macedonians excellent cover. Early the next morning, he sent his troops in to attack. The Getae were so amazed that Alexander had managed to cross the great river without building a bridge that they scattered on the first cavalry charge. The Macedonians chased them towards their town. Instead of defending it, the Getae gathered their women and children, then fled. Alexander decided to let his army plunder the town. He then ruthlessly razed it to the ground, so it could no longer be used as a focal point for further revolt.

Alexander's victory of the Getae was a classic case of conquering the enemy with the power of the unexpected. In an era without radar, combustion engines, aerial reconnaissance or long-range artillery—let alone guided missiles—one furthermore beholden to omens, portents and the capricious wills of multiple deities, the power of surprise cannot be underestimated. But how was this surprise achieved? And what might it have to do with lefty thinking?

ALEXANDER THE GREAT LEFTY Today's left-handers know that the world hasn't been designed for their use. Every time they pick up a pair of scissors or a can-opener they have to adapt them. Whereas a right-hander feels things to be natural, that the world has been created to fit their needs, for the lefty, experience has a permanent dissonance. While this can be annoying, in creative terms, it's a bonus. At one level, the lefty is always translating the world, and from this constant activity of translation comes the desire to transform it.

These forces were clearly at work in Alexander's defeat of the Getae. To begin with, he won the battle because he refused to bow to the accepted wisdom that a bridge was needed. Left-handers have less investment in the status quo because it simply hasn't been designed for them. In Alexander's case, this attitude grew to become one of the hallmarks of his character. His encounter with the philosopher, Diogenes the Cynic, is a classic example. Diogenes was famous for his indifference towards the collective vanity of society. When Alexander, as ruler of most of the known world, asked Diogenes what he could do for him, Diogenes told him he could stop blocking his sunlight. Alexander was so impressed by this lack of respect for the status quo that he replied that if he hadn't been Alexander, he would have liked to have been Diogenes—the unkempt philosopher, who in today's society would be categorised as a tramp.

Lacking respect for the status quo is perhaps why a higher proportion of lefties end up in prison but, when combined with daring and talent, it sparks originality, something Alexander had in spades. In the battle against the Getae, the most obvious manifestation of this originality is the use of tents stuffed with straw to float his men across the Danube. This adaptation of something to suit a new purpose for which it wasn't designed, belongs to the same branch of thinking as the lefty's perpetual challenge of reorienting and translating the world. The primal scene of the lefty's realisation that the world doesn't fit, generates a powerful motivation to alter and invent things. By adapting a familiar object for an unfamiliar purpose, Alexander was able to have his men in position to surprise the Getae when they charged out from the cornfield that morning. The transformation of tents into rafts, something only Alexander visualised, was the pivotal moment in the victory.

LEFT RIGHT OUT Alexander's original goal was to conquer Persia and revenge the injury to the Greeks of the Persian King Xerxes' invasion some 150 years before. In October 331 BC, Alexander succeeded when he defeated Darius, King of Persia, at the Battle of Gaugamela, with enormous cost of life to both sides. Darius fled back to the capital, Persepolis, where Alexander crowned himself King of the Persians for the first time. He acquired so much treasure that it took 500 camels and more than 2000 pairs of mules to carry it out. He also captured Darius' wife, universally considered the most beautiful woman in the Persian kingdom, and was able, if he so chose, to assemble the most ravishing personal harem the world had ever known. Xerxes' magnificent palace was also his to inhabit and, with the Persians' talent for luxury renowned, he could have lived a life which most people could only dream about.

Yet Alexander's dreams were of a different order. Instead of enjoying the spoils of victory, he got drunk one night with his friends and gave them permission to burn Xerxes' palace to the ground. He then spent the next five years camped out in some of the most inhospitable regions of the world, such as Afghanistan, in preparation for battle with whatever army happened to venture into his orbit. In the process he would alienate himself from his most loyal comrades, watch many of his soldiers die, kill his best friend with own hand, stain his brilliance with paranoia and essentially conquer his way into an early grave. Why?

While the story of Bucephalas illustrates how the lefty's alienation is capable of inspiring empathy, it can also inculcate a special kind of rage,

A ROMAN MOSAIC DEPICTING
ALEXANDER THE GREAT
ENGAGED IN BATTLE WITH
DARIUS III, KING OF PERSIA (IN
THE CHARIOT), AT ISSUS.

an unquenchable fire of anger levelled almost against being itself. The rightness of the world we know is an arbitrary thing. There is no good reason why a left-oriented world wouldn't work just as well. Intelligent lefties feel this keenly. It's frustrating: their limbs work perfectly well, yet they are stigmatised, because the right-handers, knowing the ground-lessness of their advantage, have historically resorted to the kind of wrong-headed discrimination evidenced by the characterisation of the lefty as evil and clumsy in languages all over the world.

It is indubitable that Alexander suffered from this rage. Warfare provides an outlet in which this kind of rage becomes a celebrated activity. It takes a remarkable amount of energy to try to conquer the

world, because why would someone bother if they actually liked it? Alexander needed enemies to feed his rage. Whenever he stopped fighting, his rage would inevitably begin to eat him from within, making him unreasonably suspicious. He turned his friends into enemies and imagined them plotting against him, while his inability to quit conquering caused his men—many of whom had families in Macedonia—despite their reverence for his military genius, to become disgruntled with their lot. Yet while in that rage were the seeds of his own destruction, it was the fuel for an unparalleled achievement. When Alexander died at the age of 32, he was undefeated king of over half the known world. Arguably no single person, left- or right-handed, has ever been as powerful.

Julius Caesar

In 69 BC Julius Caesar, serving as a Quaestor (Lieutenant Governor) in Spain, was approaching his 31st birthday. In a moment of leisure he was reading a history of his great left-handed predecessor, Alexander the Great, when Caesar suddenly burst into tears. When his friends asked him what was wrong he replied, 'Do you think I have not just cause to weep when I consider that Alexander at my age had conquered so many nations, and I have all this time done nothing that is memorable?'.

By the time of his death, 25 years later, Julius Caesar was the greatest of Romans, a man who fought brilliantly with lefty cunning and honour against his military and political adversaries. His name 'Caesar' would later mutate to become *czar* in Russian and *kaiser* in German. The most formidable conqueror since Alexander the Great, he would be remembered for the phrase *veni, vidi, vici* ('I came, I saw, I conquered'). His conquest of Gaul resulted in 800 conquered cities, 300 subdued tribes, 1 million men sold into slavery and another 1 million dead in the battlefields. Gaul would remain loyal to Rome until the fall of the Western Empire 500 years later. Julius Caesar's political legacy was also considerable and included the consolidation of the Roman Empire and improving the lot of the poor. After little more than a year of full power, he was assassinated, and it is interesting to wonder what he might have achieved if he had survived.

While he was weeping in Spain, however, his reputation was that of a profligate youth gifted with a silver tongue to match the silver spoon of his aristocratic birth. Alexander was a spur to his ambitious and ruthless mind. By the time Caesar's life was over he would have displayed much of the left-handed valour of his hero, and the world would know that the two of them had much in common, not least the lefty advantage of being able to outwit their opponents on the battlefield with unorthodox methods.

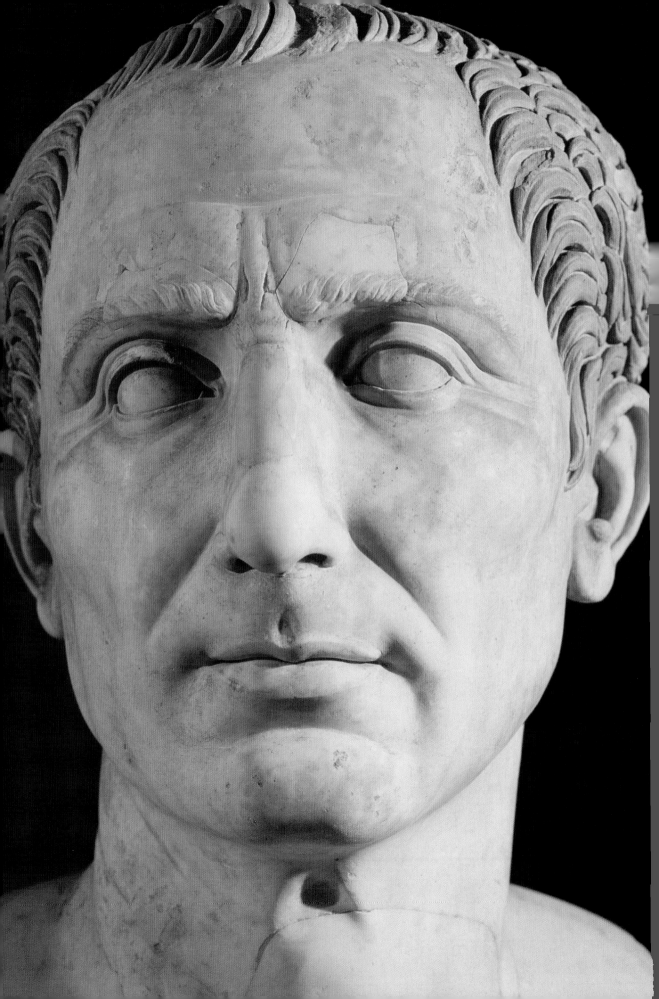

CONQUERING THE PIRATES

Although he didn't take an army into battle until relatively late in life, from an early age Caesar displayed the combination of tactical brilliance and unconventionality which are the hallmarks of the left-handed conqueror. The first major instance of this on record was when he set off for Rhodes in 75 BC to study oratory and was captured by pirates.

Most people when captured tend to be overwhelmed by their fear. They obey the power dynamics and become compliant towards the people who are holding the swords over their heads. The pirates were Cicilians, renowned in their time for being among the most bloodthirsty people in the world, as likely to kill someone as soon as look at them. All the more reason then to hope for their mercy. Not Caesar. Rather than huddle and hope, he attacked from a position of utmost weakness using strategies learnt in his study of oratory. When the pirates demanded a ransom of 20 talents, he ridiculed them, offering to give them 50 instead because the pirates had failed to understand his status. Having sent most of his fellow travellers away to raise the ransom, he was left alone with the pirates. Yet instead of capitulating to their demands, he continued to disrespect them spectacularly.

When he wanted to sleep, he ordered them to make no noise. He wrote poems and speeches which he delivered to his piratical audience. If they didn't appreciate them, he called them illiterate and barbarous to their faces. He threatened to execute them. This went on for 38 whole days. Rather than kill him for his insolence (they were wealthy enough not to need the 50 talents) the pirates were captivated by Caesar's brave display and attributed his trash talking to simplicity and boyish playfulness. Not only was this brave, it was also classic left-handed thinking, the kind which uses reverse psychology to throw the enemy off balance. Caesar could have waited passively to be ransomed. Instead, with trust in his intuitions, he bravely abused his captors, despite their reputation for ruthlessness and violence. This unconventional approach had the unlikely consequence of Caesar earning his captors' almost affectionate respect. He had subverted the natural order of his predicament.

When his ransom was paid and the pirates released him, Caesar went straight to the port of Miletus where he took command of a number of ships and went back and surprised the pirates at the island where they had been holding him hostage. His small force captured most of them and he also secured their treasure, most of which he gave to Junius, Governor of Asia, in exchange for the right to determine the fate of the pirates. Having established a semi-friendly bond with Caesar, the pirates were surprised to hear him give the order for their crucifixion.

UNDERDOG SMARTS

A notable tendency in lefties is that because they have been a suppressed minority, they often ally themselves with the underdog. In Caesar's day, the main political division in Rome was between

PREVIOUS PAGE: BUST OF JULIUS CAESAR. THE ROMANS WERE KEEN ON THE 'VERISTIC', OR REALISTIC PORTRAIT, RATHER THAN THE IDEALISED GREEK FORM.

those who conservatively advocated the continued rights of the aristocracy and the populists who courted the support of the everyday people. Although of aristocratic birth, Caesar established his political power base by gaining popularity with his soldiers and the plebeians (commoners) of Rome.

Winning over the people was largely a matter of 'bread and circuses'. Caesar became known for his largesse. As Plutarch observed:

> He was unsparing in his outlays of money, and was thought to be purchasing a transient and short-lived fame at a great price, though in reality he was buying things of the highest value at a small price. We are told, accordingly, that before he entered upon any public office he was thirteen hundred talents in debt. Again, being appointed curator of the Appian Way, he expended upon it vast sums of his own money; and again, during his aedileship, he furnished three hundred and twenty pairs of gladiators, and by lavish provision besides for theatrical performances, processions, and public banquets, he washed away all memory of the ambitious efforts of his predecessors in the office. By these means he put the people in such a humour that every man of them was seeking out new offices and new honours with which to requite him.

Caesar's actions went against the grain since most Roman politicians' idea of office was to cement their own financial gain. While being laughed at by many in his own class for his profligacy, he managed to earn the support of the people, something which would protect him against his political enemies. Again, Caesar showed that lefty capability for achieving one's goals by turning the established way of doing things on its head.

Caesar's counter-intuitive lefty thinking is also evidenced by Dio Cassius's observation that, 'He showed himself perfectly prepared to serve and flatter everybody, even ordinary people . . . and he did not mind temporarily grovelling'. Again we are confronted with a man whose natural stigma as a lefty, combined with his aristocratic pedigree, provided him with the ability to understand and operate easily within the full social spectrum. Lefty thinking ensured that Caesar wasn't captive to his pride or social position and, as a consequence, his ambition had full rein to operate in the most strategically advantageous manner. His skills in oratory were paralleled by his skills as an actor. Throughout his life Caesar would be able to transform his personality to meet the demands of a given situation while never losing sight of his own goals.

GALLING THE GAULS

One of Caesar's great strengths as a military commander was his ability to inspire the loyalty of his men. This loyalty was partly based on his populist sensibility and his reputation for generosity in sharing the spoils of victory with his army. Yet, it was also because he had sufficient empathy with his men to understand what they wanted from their leader. It was a form of charisma he shared with

LEFTY LINKS

1. Alexander the Great was a powerful source of inspiration and emulation for the young Caesar. Caesar chastised himself for having achieved nothing by the age of 31, by which time Alexander had conquered most of the known world. It would be another 10 years before Caesar would lead his first military campaign, at which age Alexander had been dead for almost a decade.

2. Caesar was not the only left-handed Roman emperor, although he was by far the greatest. Other lefty emperors included the talented and troubled Tiberius (42 BC–37 AD) who ended his life in paranoid, decadent isolation on the isle of Capris, and Commodius (161–192), who is widely considered one of the worst Roman emperors of all. He believed he was the reincarnation of Hercules, and used to fight as a gladiator, where he would arm the disabled with sponges then put them to the sword. A psychopath and hedonist, he was running the empire into the ground until he was murdered in his bath by a wrestler called Narcissus. Both Tiberius and Commodius were afflicted by the left-hander's increased disposition towards mental illness.

Alexander and Napoleon, whose soldiers also out-performed other armies through their loyalty to their commander.

Despite being an epileptic and having the soft white skin of the pampered classes, Caesar amazed his troops with his powers of endurance. In the first Gallic War against the Helvetii, in what is today known as Switzerland, after some initial victories Caesar was surprised by his enemies and forced to retreat to a place of defensible refuge. At this stage, he was presented with a horse, presumably as a means of making a prudent escape. But Caesar preferred to remain with his troops. Even more exceptional was that, once he had made the decision to fight, he refused to use the horse. He earnt the awe and loyalty of his men by arguing that the horse was better left for pursuing the enemy after the battle had been won. He then marched off on foot at the head of his army to confront the enemy. The whole campaign could have turned at that point, yet Caesar's ability to look from the outside in and force his will upon the action was crucial. The ensuing battle lasted from morning till midnight with the Romans eventually triumphing. Through his unconventional entirely intuitive action, Caesar turned his army into a powerfully coherent force.

Although Caesar showed a complete lack of mercy to the pirates who had captured him but treated him well, his attitude towards the Gauls, once he had vanquished them, was entirely different. The Gauls had razed much of their own land and cities with the intention of denying Caesar's army supplies. Yet once he had defeated them, instead of slaughtering or selling them into slavery, he made them resettle their own land under the banner of Rome. This clever strategy showed great flexibility and foresight, and none of the bloodlust for revenge, which often erupts in the aftermath of such fiercely fought battles. It ensured a vacuum wasn't created that would entice the Germans over the Rhine to try and colonise Gaul, while giving the Romans a buffer zone against other yet-to-be conquered Gauls. Just as importantly, it gave Caesar a power base from which to continue his conquests, safe from, but still reasonably close to the political whirligig of Rome.

DEFEATING POMPEY Caesar displayed many of the identifiable qualities of the left-handed conqueror and he therefore had the ability to surprise his enemy with left-handed thought. In the Roman army at the time, soldiers were taught the difference between left and right by their correspondence with the hands holding shield and sword respectively, and orders to change direction were often given using these words. With such regimentation and the technological constraints of the day, the movement of armies was slower and more conventional than today. Having a talented and charismatic commander was an asset, even more so if he was left-handed. Forced to translate the right-handed organisation of the army into his left-handed mind, the left-handed commander was more capable of

OPPOSITE: A STATUE OF JULIUS CAESAR DRESSED IN ARMOUR, C.50 BC.

THE RIGHT-HANDED SHAKE

When people put out their right hands to shake when greeting, they are following a custom established by Julius Caesar. The handshake originated as a guarded method for establishing trust between strangers. By taking hold of each other's hands, the shakers are ensuring that they aren't going to be punched or stabbed. But why would a left-handed Roman emperor enshrine the right-handed handshake as the primary way for men to greet each other? Easy. Because it keeps the left hand free to attack while the right-hander's strong arm is too busy being polite. Unfortunately, it was no use in preventing Caesar from eventually being stabbed in the back.

arriving at novel military strategies which had the dual advantage of inspiring his own men and vanquishing the enemy through the power of sheer surprise.

Caesar's first taste of true power came as a consequence of his victories in Gaul when he became part of the First Triumvirate with Crassus, the richest man in Rome and the celebrated General Pompey. It was an alliance cleverly put together by Caesar. His attempts to win popularity with the people had put him into debt which Crassus was able to help him out of, while Caesar surprised his political enemies by concluding an alliance with Pompey and sealing it with the successful marriage of his daughter, Julia, to the older general. But when Crassus was killed in an ill-advised military campaign against the Parthians and Julia died in childbirth, the alliance dissolved and it wasn't long before Pompey and Caesar were at war in the struggle for control of Rome.

The civil war was a protracted one, fought throughout the Roman Empire. Battles were waged in Gaul, Africa, Greece and Italy itself between two leaders with exemplary military records. The crucial moment came in Greece in 48 BC. Caesar had followed Pompey's army across the Adriatic, but was outnumbered by more than three to one. The two enemies ended up camped either side of a stream near a place called Dyrrhachium, where they attempted to deprive each other of supplies. Caesar mounted a siege and built a fortified wall 27 kilometres long around Pompey's army and also succeeded in blocking his supply of fresh water. Pompey's army was unable to breach the wall until two of Caesar's soldiers, who had been caught stealing, managed to escape to Pompey's camp where they informed him of the weakest point. Pompey's army breached the wall and set up a camp outside it, from which they were able to attack Caesar's smaller army. Caesar was forced to retreat. Yet having enforced the retreat, Pompey hesitated in prosecuting the advantage. The moment was lost and Caesar was able to resupply his army. Caesar stated, 'Today the victory had been the enemy's had there been any one among them to gain it'. Put another way, if Caesar had been in charge of Pompey's army, the Civil War would have been over.

The subsequent battle of Pharsalus in August 48 BC effectively ended the civil war and demonstrated Caesar's clear strategical superiority to his vacillating enemy. Caesar was again outnumbered, yet after several days of jockeying for position, he taunted Pompey so brilliantly that pride forced Pompey to take up a position on level ground. Pompey's army was arranged with his right wing protected by the river. In the centre were Syrian and African troops. Pompey gambled by stacking his left flank with his entire cavalry, archers and slingers as well as a legion of infantry. Outnumbering Caesar's cavalry seven to one, Pompey was confident of outflanking Caesar's right and winning the war with minimal loss of life.

Caesar, however, saw this as a chance to counter Pompey's one-dimensional plan. He thinned his infantry out to match the length of

Pompey's numerically superior lines at considerably less depth. His infantry were ordered to hold firm and were not expected to break through the enemy's ranks. He put his much smaller cavalry on the right to counter Pompey's cavalry. The relative numerical weakness was a huge risk, yet Caesar gambled that Pompey would focus his attack at this point precisely because of this. He further reduced his main infantry lines by removing 3000 of his best men, who he put in a semi-concealed position behind his cavalry and right flank infantry.

Caesar, and not Pompey, ordered the initial advance and the battle began slowly as a series of infantry skirmishes until Pompey finally unleashed his cavalry. His horsemen hit Caesar's cavalry hard, and almost broke through. Pompey ordered his archers and slingers, who were behind the cavalry, to assist in the assault with heavy blanket covering fire. At this point Pompey must have felt his success was almost assured. Yet, just as Caesar's cavalry were beginning to retreat, he ordered his reserve infantry to launch their surprise assault. Using their javelin-like pila, Caesar's 3000 infantry attacked the 7000 Pompeian cavalry with direct orders from Caesar to aim for the faces of the riders. Why? Caeasar had noticed the men in this unit were young, particularly good looking and vain, and would therefore value their faces. Caesar's plan was a resounding success and the cavalry was routed. As Pompey's cavalry fled, they exposed the archers and slingers. Caesar then turned to attack Pompey's exposed left flank, which crumbled. Pompey panicked. Although he still had a strong numerical superiority, he had no back-up plan. Unlike Caesar in Gaul, he retreated to his camp while his army was decimated. When defeat became clear, instead of committing suicide as an honourable Roman was supposed to do, he abandoned his army to the enemy and fled. The civil war was effectively over.

The battle of Pharsalus was fundamentally a war of left versus right. The right-handed Pompey relied on conventional logic and numerical superiority. Caesar, on the other hand, used the left-handed qualities of surprise and intuition, by holding his infantry back and intuitively adopting the unorthodox tactic of attacking the enemy cavalry's faces rather than their horses, to cause panic.

As a left-hander forced from birth to interpret a world that doesn't fit, Caesar had that crucial extra degree of thinking, giving him the ability to intuit Pompey's tactics and come up with his own novel and successful strategy. The importance to history of this left-handed moment cannot be underestimated. This victory of Caesar set up a system of inherited imperial power which would help make the Roman Empire the undisputed leading power in the Ancient World.

CAESAR'S LEFTY TRAITS

INTUITIVE Caesar's behaviour in situations such as his kidnapping by the pirates illustrates how he was capable of using his instincts to get out of a jam.

EMPATHETIC Like Alexander the Great and Napoleon, Caesar was able to put himself in the shoes of his soldiers which, combined with his bravery, earnt him fearsome loyalty.

VISUAL-SPATIAL ABILITY In Caesar's defeat of Pompey he displayed the ability common to all great military commanders to visualise a battlefield, anticipate the enemy's strategy and then devise a plan to outwit them.

LATERAL THINKING Very few generals would have thought of using the vanity of his enemies against them, and conceive a novel mode of attack to rout a numerically superior army.

EXPERIMENTAL Caesar was prepared to gamble with new tactics on the battlefield and always tried to fit his strategy to a specific context.

Joan of Arc

1412–31 THERE ARE FEW MORE ASTONISHING FIGURES IN HISTORY THAN THE late-medieval, cross-dressing, virginal, lefty saint and French military commander, Joan of Arc. She was born a simple peasant girl in a period when France was in thrall to the Hundred Years War. Guided by divine voices Joan surmounted almost impossible societal hurdles, in a world riven by class and chivalric codes, to lead her army to a series of important victories which changed the balance of the war. She was captured in battle, sold to the English, convicted of heresy in a medieval show-trial and eventually burnt at the stake. She was only 19 years old. Not long after her death, when the Dauphin Charles she had fought for became legitimate King of France, she was rehabilitated by the church in a reverse trial. The reversal was taken to the extreme in 1920 when the Catholic Church made her a saint.

HEARING VOICES As a child, Joan was remembered by her fellow villagers for being helpful, friendly and devout. When she was 12 years old, she said she was visited by the Archangel Michael, the protective angel of France, who told her that her fate was to lay siege to the town of Orleans and, by doing so, help the Armagnac claimant to the throne, the Dauphin Charles, to become King of France. The Armagnac faction, with whom Joan was allied, was at war with the Burgundians, who were also French but allied with the British. Known as the Hundred Years War, skirmishes and battles between these forces took place across the countryside. Towns and farms were often pillaged by poorly supplied troops from both sides of the battle.

The Archangel Michael told Joan to listen and follow the advice of St Catherine and St Margaret, virgin martyrs who were popular in the Middle Ages. These days if someone goes about telling people they have heard the voice of an angel, they are usually diagnosed with

1. It's easy to underestimate how complete the Christian worldview actually was in medieval Europe. Christian symbolism almost unfailingly viewed the left as evil, secondary or inferior. The devil, for instance, was depicted with his left hand outstretched, while passages from the Bible, such as the following from Matthew 25, show a clear preference for the right: 'Then shall the king say unto them on his right hand, come ye blessed of my father, inherit the kingdom prepared for you . . . Then shall He say also unto them on the left hand, depart from me ye cursed into everlasting fire. Prepare for the devil and his angels.'

As Rowena and Rupert Shepherd point out in *1000 Symbols*, in Christianity 'the right side of the body represents the first stage of Creation, daytime, consciousness, Adam, Man and active power. The left represents the second stage of Creation, Earth, matter, Eve, Women and receptivity.' Left-handed people were treated with considerable suspicion in the Middle Ages, and were more vulnerable to being charged with ecclesiastical crimes, such as heresy and witchcraft, which were often trumped up—as in the case of Joan's trial—to preserve the interests of those in control of the status quo. If you were in the wrong place at the wrong time, merely being left-handed made you more prone to being burned at the stake for being either a heretic or a witch.

2. It is interesting to note here that left-handers are more prone to schizophrenia than their right-handed counterparts. This is perhaps the downside of the heightened powers of sensitivity and empathy left-handers often exhibit. Some research has shown that left-handers tend to have greater schizoid tendencies than right-handers and furthermore, those with schizoid tendencies that don't deteriorate into schizophrenia tend often to be better lateral thinkers than those without Some of the more conspicuous schizoid personalities among the lefties in these pages include Lewis Carroll, Nietzsche and Jimi Hendrix.

3. One of Joan's biggest fans was fellow lefty Mark Twain.

schizophrenia, treated with drugs or worse, and shunted to the margins of society. In fact, being a left-hander, Joan was actually statistically more vulnerable to schizophrenia. However, in the Middle Ages, prophets and visionaries who claimed to be in contact with God were fairly common, and there was certainly not the same stigma attached to the idea of paranormal experience as there is today. Unlike most contemporary schizophrenics, Joan was very fond of her voices and claimed they brought her warmth and joy. With the exception of some moments before her execution, Joan felt herself to be in the permanent presence of the divine and it was this certainty that enabled her to act with the kind of total conviction necessary to bring others into her orbit and achieve her goals. The voices accompanied Joan throughout her adolescence. They advised her to maintain her virginity in order that she would be able to serve a higher purpose. In her seventeenth year, this higher purpose was revealed when she was told that her role would be to assist the Dauphin Charles to be crowned King of France.

An amazing aspect of Joan's personality was her ability to persuade men in positions of authority to adopt her cause. The first person she had to convince of her mission was her local lord, Robert de Baudricourt. As an illiterate peasant girl of 17, it was surprising that he even deigned to see her when she turned up in her traditional red peasant's dress with the request to raise an army. De Baudricourt was a notorious philanderer and people were also surprised that Joan escaped with her virginity intact, especially since it is on record that she had very attractive breasts.

Joan's manner of approach threw de Baudricourt off guard. Without granting the deference she was supposed to pay to his social position, she introduced herself by saying:

I have come from my Lord so that you may tell the Dauphin to be brave and and keep going in his war against his enemies. Before mid Lent the Lord will help him. My Lord who the kingdom actually belongs to, wants the Dauphin to be King and to rule this kingdom. The Dauphin will be made king despite his enemies, and I have been chosen to take him to the coronation.

WINNING OVER THE KING If Joan's success in winning over de Baudricourt was a major coup, her achievement in winning over the eventual King of France was nothing short of phenomenal. By all accounts Charles was a fairly unspectacular candidate to benefit from the religio-political miracle Joan was selling. He was weak-chinned, squinty-eyed and stumpy-legged with a reputation for vacillation and over-dependence upon those who surrounded him. When Joan arrived, the Dauphin and his advisers were initially reluctant to meet her. She was forced to wait for more than two days outside the castle at Chinon before they let the drawbridge down. Once they did, they set a test for her. Gathering

300 elaborately dressed courtiers, they demanded that Joan look through them and select the King. Using her lefty intuition, she was able to look beyond the false symbolic hierarchy of appearance and spot the moderately dressed Charles as the genuine article.

Once she had achieved this feat, Joan was granted an audience with Charles. What she then accomplished was amazing: she persuaded Charles to give her the Kingdom of France. The deed was witnessed by four of the King's secretaries. Soon after she gave the Kingdom to God. Then, having done this, she re-invested Charles with the Kingdom, acting under the authority of God. For an illiterate peasant girl with no schooling, this was brilliant and complicated stuff.

A final test saw Joan being examined by a learned bunch of ecclesiasts, including the Archbishop of Reims and the Royal Confessors, whose job it was to determine whether her mission was divinely inspired. As Joan would later discover, the line between divinity and heresy could be extremely subjective and she certainly wasn't the first person to be burned on falsified charges. The ecclesiasts decided Joan was the fulfilling of a prophecy that a virgin would save France. Joan was given a suit of armour, a sword and set off towards the enemy with a retinue of 4000 men.

JOAN WARRIOR VIRGIN

The argument that left-handers are made by having extra testosterone is backed up by Joan's cavalier behaviour on the battlefield. Her fury and eagerness to fight were on display from the very beginning at the Battle of Orleans. The commander of the French forces was the Bastard of Orleans, aka Dunois, the illegitimate son of the Duke of Orleans who was a captive of the English. When Joan arrived in late April 1429, the English had laid siege to the city of 30,000 people for six months and the citizens' capacity to resist was beginning to fade. Joan arrived ready to attack, but the mistrust of some of the experienced military saw her sidelined as part of a plan to help supply the city through its one remaining accessible gate. They didn't tell Joan, however, of the secondary role they intended her to play and when she found out she went crazy, telling the bastard, who was at least half royal, that if anyone tried to con her like that again, she'd cut off their head. Dunois merely replied that he was sure she would.

The immense chutzpah of her dealings with her superiors was compounded by her bravery in the battle. After a series of successful skirmishes, in which Joan had a significant impact, the Battle of Orleans began in earnest on 7 May 1429. When the army charged, Joan was at the forefront. At noon, she was hit above the left breast by an arrow which buried itself six inches into her. She had already told her confessor this was something her voices had foretold. Joan pulled the arrow out herself and, after allowing her wound to be dressed with animal fat, she rested a while before rejoining the battle, which greatly boosted the morale of the French troops. At 8 pm, the horn for retreat was blown, but Joan ignored it. She was on foot, part of an

MAID WITH TESTOSTERONE

Around the time she went to see de Baudricourt, Joan self-consciously adopted the nickname, La Pucelle, or the Maid. She did this both to emphasise her virginity and to deny her femininity. The closest women usually came to being in the army was as camp-following prostitutes. Joan also adopted the wearing of male clothes since it was harder to be sexually assaulted while wearing them, but also because it distinguished her from the other women and enhanced her capacity to be accepted as one of the boys.

Joan was without doubt a prototype tomboy, passionate, hot-headed, idealistic and rash. It has long been known that men are twice as likely to be left-handed as women. Some scientists have claimed that a cause of left-handedness is exposure to extra testosterone in the womb that favours the development of the right hemisphere of the brain. This might explain Joan's alpha male approach to life. It also casts light on a possible cause for the kind of testosterone-fuelled rage found in many of the great left-handers in this book: Alexander, Caesar, Napoleon, John McEnroe and Michelangelo, to name but a few.

Joan was also renowned for her temper. When the powerful Duke Charles of Lorraine, hearing of Joan's powers, summoned her to cure him, she went and lectured him that she could do nothing for his health, but he should give up his mistress and go back to his wife. Surprised and chastened, the duke made her a gift of some money and a horse.

PAGE 45: JOAN OF ARC AT THE CORONATION OF THE DAUPHIN AS KING CHARLES VII IN REIMS CATHEDRAL, ACCOMPANIED BY HER SQUIRE, CHAPLAIN AND PAGES.

FOLLOWING PAGES: JOAN OF ARC ARRIVES AT CHINON CASTLE TO MEET THE DAUPHIN DURING THE HUNDRED YEARS WAR.

assault that involved crossing a moat and scaling the walls to the city. The soldier next to her, who was carrying her standard, collapsed with exhaustion and passed it on to a soldier who wasn't under Joan's command. When Joan saw this, she was enraged and rushed up through a torrent of stones that was being slung by the English, to take hold of the standard herself. All the other soldiers saw the standard blown by the wind so that it pointed in the direction of the enemy—an omen of victory. The troops headed back into battle and by the morning the English had decamped and, with victory hers to savour, Joan became known for the first time as the Maid of Orleans.

DOWNFALL With the English having retreated from the Loire Valley, Charles was crowned King of France in the cathedral city of Reims, just as Joan had predicted. In keeping with her impetuous character, she agitated for an immediate attack against the English and Burgundian forces that were holding Paris. She was probably right, yet Charles was vacillating and his chief adviser strongly favoured a diplomatic end to the war. Charles signed a 15-day truce, which was merely a ploy for the enemy to bring in new troops and better organise their defence.

Joan's fortunes declined markedly in her second series of campaigns. After a number of unsuccessful skirmishes, her army was temporarily disbanded and Joan was stuck at court, whose ornate and stultifying manners clashed with her impatient spirit. Like Leonardo da Vinci, Joan was a person who preferred nature over culture and, like Alexander the Great, she treasured the glory of battle over the trappings of luxury.

When, in 1430, Charles finally decided a diplomatic solution was impossible, the army marched towards Paris. In the interim, however, the army had been underfed and underpaid and had lost much of its enthusiasm for the fight. After an all-night ride, Joan attempted to persuade her 300 men to take on 6000 Burgundians at the town of Soissons. Drastically outnumbered, she made assault after assault until her men were too exhausted to fight any more. Those who could retreated, but Joan continued to fight until she was surrounded and knocked off her horse by a Picardy archer. She was then sold to the English, tried for heresy and burned at the stake and she was still only 19 years old.

Joan of Arc's success had been brief but phenomenal. She lacked the training of other great commanders, but not the courage. When Charles eventually took Paris in 1437, he organised for the rehabilitation of Joan's reputation and she remains one of the great enigmas of history, the left-handed peasant girl who came from nowhere, guided by angelic voices, to lead the French army into one of the greatest victories it had ever known. As Winston Churchill was later to remark in *The Birth of Britain*:

Joan was a being so uplifted from the ordinary run of mankind that she finds no equal in a thousand years.

JOAN OF ARC'S LEFTY TRAITS

INTUITIVE Joan's whole life was based on gut instinct guided by divine voices and acted out with tremendous temerity.

EMPATHETIC Joan had the ability to see into people, especially important men, which made it possible for her to achieve her unlikely strategies.

HOT-TEMPERED Joan's rage in battle was astonishing, while she was almost as fierce with those who crossed her path. It was as if she was channelling the wrath of her God.

ICONOCLASTIC Joan was so iconoclastic that no other woman has yet been able to fully follow her example. Of all the people in this book, she is probably the most unique. Her iconoclasm also cost her her life as she was burned at the stake for heresy.

SELF-TAUGHT It's arguable that Joan even educated herself. A peasant girl with no formal schooling, she was able to outwit members of the nobility with pure instinct and the strength of her conviction in her guiding voices.

FANTASIST Joan harnessed her imagination and probable schizoid character to become one of the greatest figures in history.

OPPOSITE: BEFORE GOING IN TO BATTLE, JOAN OF ARC HAD HER STANDARD PAINTED WITH AN IMAGE OF CHRIST IN JUDGMENT AND A BANNER MADE BEARING THE NAME OF JESUS CHRIST.

Leonardo da Vinci (handwritten signature)

1452–1519

WHO WOULD HAVE THOUGHT THAT THE GREATEST MIND IN WESTERN civilisation would have been an illegitimate, gay, vegetarian lefty? No name in history is more synonymous with genius than Leonardo da Vinci, who was all of these things. In addition to creating the world's most famous painting, the _Mona Lisa_, Leonardo (as he is best known) had an unbounded natural curiosity. His notebooks contained ideas for inventions and techniques centuries ahead of his time, in fields as diverse as engineering, anatomy, aviation, aerodynamics, hydraulics, military technology and art. Of all the Italian 'renaissance men', Leonardo was the most outstanding; a polymath whose vast talent traversed the boundaries of art and science like few others ever have.

While his homosexuality and illegitimacy gave Leonardo the freedom from the masculine conventions of career and family to pursue his creativity, his left-handedness had a crucial impact on his personality and productivity. In many ways, he was the quintessential left-hander, the outsider whose sheer brilliance, original thinking and enhanced visual-spatial skills took him to the centre of his world. With his fellow artists Michelangelo and Raphael, Leonardo forms one of the most fascinating lefty clusters of history. Without these three, the Italian Renaissance, a crucial period in the development of Western civilisation, would have been far less interesting.

EARLY LEONARDO Leonardo was born to an unmarried peasant girl called Caterina. His father, who recognised Leonardo as his son, but did not marry his mother, was Ser Piero da Vinci, a young lawyer who later became prominent in Florentine circles.

Leonardo's childhood was spent in the rustic environment of Vinci (his surname literally means 'from Vinci') a small town outside of Florence, where his father's family had its country estates. Because he was illegitimate, Leonardo didn't receive much formal education. It wasn't until

later life that he learnt Latin, the language of academic knowledge—and when he did, he taught himself. His lack of formal schooling is evidenced by the fact his natural mode of writing was left-handed mirror writing. In Leonardo's notebooks the letters are written backwards, while words and sentences read from right to left on the page. He could use regular script, but only did so when he was writing letters for other people to read.

In a schoolroom Leonardo may have been encouraged to write and think in a conventional ('right-handed') way. Instead, his genius was allowed to flower independently. He spent much of his childhood wandering through the countryside, usually accompanied by his pet dogs, training his eye by observing the Tuscan landscape and its native flora and fauna. The natural world was his schoolroom, and what he learnt here would pay great dividends in his later artistic and scientific work.

Even as a child, Leonardo was obsessed with drawing. He showed considerable aptitude for music too, but the visual arts were his mainstay. Putting pen to paper was the primary way he could understand the world and work his way through the design problems of his many inventions. Many great left-handers, from painters to military commanders and baseball players, have enhanced visual-spatial skills, since this faculty is usually concentrated in the right hemisphere of the brain, which controls the left side of the body.

Leonardo strongly believed in the importance of seeing the world for himself rather than reading about it. For him, the eye was the most important organ and it offered the best chance to penetrate nature's secrets. It is often said that the eyes are the window to the soul, but in Leonardo's case the eyes were a window to the world. As he wrote in his notebook:

> The eye is commander of astronomy; it makes cosmography; it guides and rectifies all the human arts; it conducts man to various regions of the world; it is the prince of mathematics; its sciences are surest; it has measured the height and size of the stars; it has disclosed the elements and their distributions; it has made predictions of future events by means of the course of the stars; it has generated architecture, perspective and divine painting. Oh excellent above all other things created by God . . . it triumphs over nature in that the constituent parts of nature are finite, but the works that the eye commands of the hands are infinite, as is demonstrated by the painter in his rendering of the numberless forms of animals, grasses, trees.

PAINTING At the age of 14 Leonardo was apprenticed to the Florentine painter Andrea del Verrocchio. At the time, Italian painting was on the cusp of a major technical transformation: the replacement of tempera paints with those based on oil. Tempera paints were created by mixing colour pigment with egg yolk. They were fast drying, which meant their capacity for depth and detail was limited. The technique of making paint

OPPOSITE: LEONARDO'S PAINTING TECHNIQUE OF SFUMATO CAN BE SEEN IN THE HAZY BACKGROUND LANDSCAPE IN THE *MONA LISA*.

PAGE 53: A SELF-PORTRAIT IN SANGUINE (RED CHALK), DRAWN AROUND 1512 WHEN THE ARTIST WAS 60 YEARS OLD.

LEFTY LINKS

1. Leonardo's greatest connections with other lefty geniuses in history are undoubtedly with Michelangelo and Raphael, both of whom he knew. In their personalities, Leonardo and Michelangelo were chalk and cheese rivals, mainly because of the latter's paranoid competitiveness—though Leonardo was capable of being dismissive in his opinions of other artists. Raphael shared and extended upon Leonardo's reputation for urbanity and grace, but lacked his all-round genius.

2. Leonardo's intuitive genius for mechanical design is perhaps most noticeable in the equally self-taught brilliance of automobile pioneer Henry Ford, while his belief that nature operated according to mathematical laws was furthered by Isaac Newton.

3. Another characteristic Leonardo shared with Henry Ford was vegetarianism. An eccentric lifestyle choice for a fifteenth-century Florentine, it's a trait shared with other lefty greats including Paul McCartney and Mahatma Gandhi.

4. One of the most significant aspects of Leonardo's notebooks was the use of mirror writing. This is very rare in real life, but gets a famous fictional outing at the beginning of *Through the Looking Glass*, written by lefty fantasist Lewis Carroll.

using oil had begun with Flemish painters, such as Jan van Eyck, and was known to the Italian painters, but they generally used it only as a surface glaze. Leonardo was one of the first to use oils as his primary medium. The longer drying time helped him to achieve the level of detail he required and allowed him to create a stronger sense of depth by adding layers of paint. Throughout his life he was always open to new ways of doing things, and his willingness to depart from the known often delivered excellent results.

His creativity was liberated by his technical experiments with oils. His depictions of people and nature, honed by his anatomical investigations, were richly realistic. Looking at a Leonardo painting, you see how much accurate detail there is in the natural settings of their backgrounds. Leonardo was a perfectionist. In painting, for instance, he pioneered techniques, such as sfumato (fine shading), in which he applied a haze to objects in the background of the picture. This mimicked the effect of looking into the distance in Tuscany's distinctive light, and gave his work a sense of depth that other painters had not yet been able to achieve.

Leonardo had a strong dislike of people who bolstered their own views by quoting the experts who had gone before them. He believed they were the owners of second-hand knowledge when it was knowledge gained from direct experience that counted:

No one should ever imitate the style of another because he will be called a nephew and not a child of nature with regard to art.

This attitude is again typical 'right-brain thinking'. Eschewing the accepted wisdom that artists were beholden first and foremost to tradition, Leonardo championed originality, a quality which was both a marker of both genius and great art. But what is accepted wisdom now was radical then, which made him an iconoclast—another characteristic lefty trait.

According to one of his early biographers, Giorgio Vasari, Leonardo's talent was formidable from the outset. So good was the apprentice's work on one of Verrocchio's paintings that the latter apparently retired from painting when he saw it. But Leonardo's gift was coupled with a renowned tendency not to finish what he had started.

A typical example was the altarpiece Leonardo was commissioned to paint for the monks of S. Donato a Scopeto in Florence, the work which became known as *Adoration of the Magi*. Leonardo was expected to take around two years to complete it, with an agreed outside limit for the job of three years. As payment he would receive a stake in some land that had been bequeathed to the monks. The initial agreement was made in March 1481. In early 1482, much to the chagrin of the monks, Leonardo packed his bags and headed to Milan with the painting only partly finished. It was never delivered. He left what he had completed with a friend for safe-keeping and it eventually ended up in the Medici Collection as an unfinished work, and is now in the Uffizi Gallery. (The monks were forced to approach a lesser but more reliable artist, Filippino Lippi, to get their

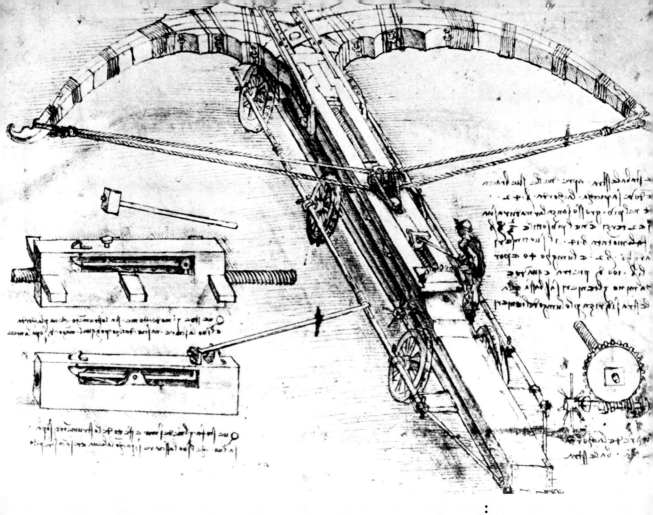

SKETCHES FROM LEONARDO'S NOTEBOOK, C.1499, FOR A GIANT CATAPULT-LIKE MACHINE.

altarpiece; Lippi also saved the day for the Florentine government when Leonardo failed to deliver an altarpiece it had commissioned.) In Milan, Leonardo was commissioned to make a massive bronze sculpture of a horse in honour of Francesco Sforza. He got as far as making the clay model. However, he dallied at the point of casting the bronze, distracted by scientific experiments and a foray into directing pageants. He delayed so long that war broke out with the French, the metal was diverted for military purposes and the clay model was destroyed when the invading army used it for archers' target practice.

Right-handed thought tends to prefer a step-by-step process—completing one thing before beginning another. In contrast, left-handers are known for their divergent (rather than convergent) thought patterns. In some, this produces a superior capacity to multi-task. Leonardo, however, was a victim of his own incessant curiosity and perfectionism, as well as the often conflicting demands of his patrons. He would frequently become sidetracked by other ideas and projects. While painting a fresco, for instance, he would have a brainwave concerning a pet project, such as flight, and he would abandon the painting to pursue the new idea. His low completion rate demonstrates the risks of divergent thinking. It's unlikely that he completed more than 20 paintings in a 46-year career—in a way he had too much genius for one person to be able to effectively manage.

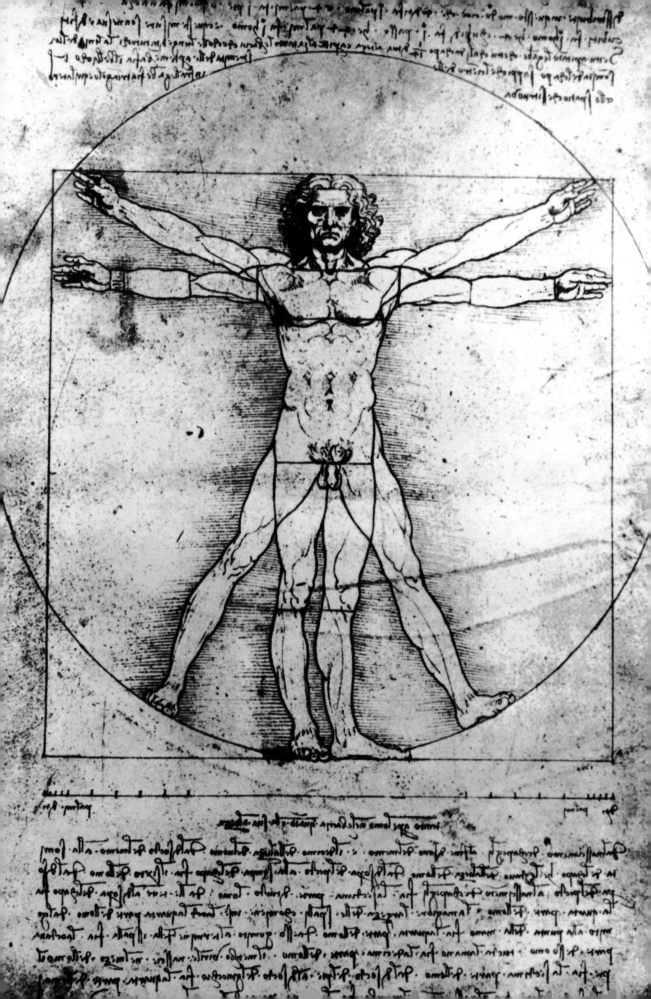

THE NOTEBOOKS The greatest insight into the way Leonardo thought can perhaps be gained from looking at his copious notebooks, which are full of sketches, inquiries and observations as well as jokes, shopping lists and accounts. In these books there are meditations on the many things that intrigued that mighty brain, including art, engineering, flying, architecture, philosophy and mathematics. Leonardo often had a notebook hanging from his belt and would stop in the street to sketch observations or note down ideas. Paper was expensive, so the pages were cluttered, filled to their corners with drawings and writing that revealed the man's eclectic brilliance.

Leonardo was prone to signing his notebooks *disscepolo para sperientia*, which can be translated to mean a disciple of either experience or experiment. It is an indicator that he had forsaken Christianity as the organising principle of his life. His refusal to accept tradition for tradition's sake meant that he had traded in what he regarded as the abstract values of Christianity, in favour of the kinds of truth that can be observed with the eye. In this, he was a forerunner of the Age of Reason (or Enlightenment) with its belief in science and the power of the human mind to penetrate the mysteries of nature.

LEFT WING One of Leonardo's great obsessions was the idea of human flight. In the notebook now known as the *Codex Atlanticus* he wrote:

A bird is a machine working according to mathematical laws. It lies within the power of man to reproduce this machine with all its motions, but not with as much power ... Such a machine constructed by man lacks only the spirit of the bird, and this spirit must be counterfeited by the spirit of man.

The possibility of flying occupied large periods of Leonardo's time. As a lefty, he was fascinated by flying because of the seeming impossibility of achieving it. To fly would surmount the ultimate frontier. The man who flew would no longer be subject to the conventions of his society on earth.

Leonardo's flying designs included a pyramid-shaped parachute, which was built in 2000, then tested from 3,050 metres by English skydiver Adrian Nicholas. It worked. He also designed a vertical flying machine that anticipated the helicopter, but his most notable flying machine was the *ucello*, or 'great bird'. For this, Leonardo put his amazing observational, anatomical and drawing skills to work figuring out how birds actually flew, then attempted to adapt his findings into the design of a machine that would allow humans to fly. Here again he was assisted by his left-handedness—left-handers are forced to adapt to a world of right-handed utensils from an early age. Their lives are marked by improvisation in order to find a way of dealing with a world that never quite fits.

LEONARDO'S LEFTY TRAITS

VISUAL-SPATIAL SKILLS In his painting, anatomical drawings, sketches and designs, Leonardo exhibited some of the best hand-eye skills of anyone in history, which he then turned into a practical philosophy that exemplified his belief in the superiority of observable or empirical knowledge.

LATERAL THINKING One of the great lateral thinkers, Leonardo came up with designs for machines such as submarines, helicopters and armoured tanks hundreds of years before they were technologically possible.

ICONOCLASTIC Leonardo helped revolutionise the techniques of Italian painting, believed in the possibility of human flight and was a forerunner of the Age of Reason. He was also a vegetarian for ethical reasons, which made him very much a rarity in his society.

SELF-TAUGHT Leonardo lacked formal schooling and replaced it with self-education, based not on books but on the evidence nature presented to his powerful eye.

EXPERIMENTAL Leonardo often tested his inventions and was even rumoured to have built a prototype airplane, which he attempted to fly (unsuccessfully) from the top of a hill outside Florence.

OPPOSITE: PEN AND INK DRAWING, *VITRUVIAN MAN*, SHOWING THE PROPORTIONS OF THE HUMAN FIGURE, C.1492.

PAGES 58–59: ALL TOGETHER, LEONARDO'S NOTEBOOKS CONTAIN AROUND 13,000 PAGES OF SKETCHES AND NOTES ON ART, SCIENCE AND PHILOSOPHY.

Michelangelo

ALTHOUGH LEONARDO DA VINCI IS THE ARCHETYPAL LEFTY GENIUS, HE WAS not the only left-hander to dominate the art world of the Italian Renaissance. Michelangelo Buonarotti was born in 1475 when Leonardo was already 23 years old. By the time he died in 1564, at almost 90 years of age, Michelangelo was widely considered the great artistic genius of the Italian Renaissance, a brilliant sculptor, painter, architect and poet whose works, such as the ceiling of the Sistine Chapel, were unparalleled in their scale and achievement.

Michelangelo and Leonardo were conspicuous rivals. While they were both lefties, and possessed typical lefty talents—most obviously the enhanced visual-spatial skills often found in people with right-brain dominance— their personalities were very different. Leonardo was a self-educated polymath released from the burden of questing for social distinction by virtue of his illegitimacy. For Michelangelo the situation was rather different. To begin with he was the legitimate son of a family with claims to Tuscany's minor nobility. As such, Michelangelo was expected to follow his father, who was a magistrate, and seek employment that would be appropriate for the family's sense of social standing. However, Michelangelo had other ideas. As with Leonardo, his lefty genius for the visual arts was insuppressible.

AN INNATE ARTIST If Michelangelo's family were minor gentry, they were the impoverished kind and, with an increasing number of children, his father planned to apprentice his sons into relatively lucrative careers in the silk and wool guilds. To facilitate this, Michelangelo was placed in a school to learn the skills essential to becoming a merchant, such as grammar and math. However, he spent most of his time sketching, so much so that his father used to beat him for it. However, Michelangelo was stubborn. He became friendly with Francesco Granacci, who was apprenticed to the master painter Domenico Ghirlandajo. Granacci used to supply Michelangelo with copies of sketches and materials for the young artist to

work with. At the time, being an artist was a disreputable occupation for someone of noble birth and Michelangelo's father was appalled to see his son's strong predilection for an activity beneath his station. However, seeing the writing on the wall, he eventually capitulated to his son's wish to be allowed to express his enormous talent. At the age of 14, Michelangelo entered the studio of Ghirlandajo. Ironically, it turned out to be the best financial move the Buonarotti family ever made. While a brilliant artist, Michelangelo also proved himself, unlike Leonardo, to be an astute businessman and, throughout his long career, he bought a significant amount of property which added greatly to the family's prosperity and prestige.

AN ANGRY ARTIST The family resistance to Michelangelo's artistic aspirations had a definite effect on his psyche. Whereas Leonardo was known as a genial man, prone to procrastination and getting sidetracked, Michelangelo soon developed a reputation for a terrifying, obsessive perfectionism. His temper was legendary and he was unable to restrain his ire whether it was directed at a servant or a pope. The Florentines referred to his *terribilitas*, meaning 'fearsome willpower'. During his professional life, Michelangelo managed to escape getting into serious trouble for his temper by his awe-inspiring work and a personal devoutness, which he acquired from becoming a disciple of the fear-inducing fire and brimstone preacher Savonarola. In some ways, Michelangelo's temper resembled the existential fury that drove Alexander the Great. Both were men whose personalities were driven by the attempt to resolve powerful internal tension. Like the conqueror, Michelangelo's life was also played out in a competitive frenzy from which there was never any real chance of release.

TRADING LEFTS Michelangelo's relationships with other artists were notoriously thorny. Perhaps his most difficult relationship was with his fellow lefty Leonardo, whose genius Michelangelo felt he had to surmount in order to consolidate the recognition of his own. In many ways, he defined himself in opposition to Leonardo, a classic case of what the critic Harold Bloom has called the anxiety of influence, a kind of Oedipus complex of artistic inheritance. There's a case to be made that Michelangelo defined himself as an artist directly in opposition to Leonardo. Where Leonardo preferred painting, Michelangelo claimed sculpture to be the superior art form. Leonardo was noted for his commitment to nature, while Michelangelo viewed nature as an enemy that both art and culture had to overcome.

Following his painting apprenticeship, Michelangelo was effectively adopted into the humanities-saturated household of Florence's great ruler, Lorenzo 'The Magnificent' de Medici, where he was taught the mystic rationalism of Neo-platonism. As a consequence, Michelangelo's art saw a return to classicism, a terrain that the self-educated Leonardo seldom chose for his subject matter. The differences were personal too.

OPPOSITE: PORTRAIT OF MICHELANGELO. THE ARTIST WAS SO FAMOUS THAT HE WAS THE FIRST WESTERN ARTIST WHO HAD A BIOGRAPHY PUBLISHED WHILE HE WAS STILL LIVING.

PAGE 63: MICHELANGELO'S *DAVID* ILLUSTRATES THE IDEA OF 'DISEGNO', WHERE THE ARTIST'S INITIAL DESIGN OR 'CONCEPT' IS ALL-IMPORTANT.

MICHELANGELO'S LEFTY TRAITS

VISUAL-SPATIAL ABILITY Imagine standing in front of a block of marble and being able to hold an image in your head of how to achieve an almost perfect representation of the human form over thousands of hits with a chisel and hammer.

HOT-TEMPERED Michelangelo was one of the most famously grouchy artists of all time. Not even the Pope was immune from his rage. Most of all, however, it was directed inwardly.

SOLITARY Michelangelo's slovenly, dishevelled appearance was positively anti-social, especially for an Italian. A severe predilection for secrecy and paranoia compounded this. The tension between his devoutness and his homosexuality didn't help either. He never married, and his one great love was Tomasso dei Cavalieri, a 23-year-old youth who Michelangelo met when he was 54.

ICONOCLASTIC Michelangelo's work in the Sistine Chapel saw the fusion of classical and biblical imagery. Michelangelo's painting of naked figures was viewed by some people as sacrilegious. Although he was perhaps unaware of it, Michelangelo was iconoclastic in that his art was central to the way the Renaissance increased the importance of the human at the expense of the divine.

SELF-TAUGHT Michelangeo was apprenticed to an artist and studied under the Medicis, where he absorbed the lessons of the classics. However, when Michelangelo was commissioned to paint the ceiling of the Sistine Chapel he had to teach himself the art of painting frescoes.

OPPOSITE: THE DOME OF ST PETER'S BASILICA IN ROME, DESIGNED BY MICHELANGELO.

According to Paolo Giovio, a contemporary biographer writing around 1527, the two were chalk and cheese: Leonardo was elegant, Michelangelo slovenly; Leonardo well-mannered, Michelangelo anti-social; Leonardo famous for his generosity and grace, Michelangelo for his obsessive secrecy and terrible temper. Michelangelo also finished his commissions, something Leonardo often failed to do.

These two great left-handed artists probably didn't meet that frequently, but the sparks flew on at least one occasion when they did. Leonardo was walking by the seats at the Palazzo Spini, where a number of men were debating a passage in Dante's *Divine Comedy*. They called out to Leonardo hoping to ask him for his interpretation. At the same time, Michelangelo was approaching from another direction. Seeing him, Leonardo congenially told the gathering that Michelangelo would be able to explain it to them. Michelangelo, prone to paranoia, assumed Leonardo was mocking him and exploded, 'Explain it yourself, you who have made the design of a horse to be cast in bronze but was unable to and abandoned it in shame'. With this snarling reference to Leonardo's unfinished sculpture of the *Sforza Horse*, Michelangelo turned his back on the group and left, leaving the genial Leonardo red in the face. On the positive side, this tension between these egotistical and brilliant left-handers was at least partly responsible for generating some of the greatest art the world has ever seen.

MAKING DAVID If Michelangelo was openly contemptuous, Leonardo was privately dismissive of Michelangelo and his sculpture *David*. Although at times he worked in this medium, Leonardo was disdainful of sculpture per se. In his notebooks Leonardo wrote:

> The sculptor in creating his work does so by the strength of his arm by which he consumes the marble, or other obdurate material in which his subject is enclosed: and this is done by most mechanical exercise, often accompanied by great sweat which mixes with the marble dust and forms a kind of mud daubed all over his face. The marble dust flours him all over so that he looks like a baker; his back is covered with a snowstorm of chips, and his house is made filthy by the flakes and dust of stone.

It's easy to see how the elegant Leonardo might have found all this sweat and mess ungainly. Sculpture, however, was in sync with Michelangelo's temperament for several reasons. For one, the sheer physicality of it suited his angry temperament. Sculpting shapes out of marble blocks is ultimately a matter of creating beauty using controlled violence. The chisel has to be hammered into the stone thousands of times and, at each blow, there is the risk of making a mistake that cannot be undone.

Michelangelo's masterpiece, *David*, illustrates the immense effort that went into his work. The achievement of a man with remarkable willpower,

LEFTY LINKS

1. Michelangelo's paranoia and secrecy resemble that of left-handed scientist Isaac Newton. Both were solitary, hyper-competitive and hyper-sensitive to criticism. Both men held grudges, imagined rivals and magnified the antipathy of the rivals they actually had.

2. Being hyper-competitive is a personality trait often found in high achievers. The happiest people, however, seem to be those who achieve on their own terms, such as Leonardo. Many of the lefties in these pages were fiercely competitive. We can see this, for instance, in Nietzsche's attitude to his critics, or the angry antics of left-handed tennis players such as McEnroe and Navratilova, or in the lives of Alexander and Napoleon. It's even discernible in the guitar ambitions of Jimi Hendrix. Or take a look at the ruthless tactics of Microsoft under Bill Gates. While competitive relativity may be an aspect of many higher achievers keen to distinguish themselves from the herd, for the left-hander it's a little different, since they don't fully belong to the herd to begin with. In a sense, they are forced to compare themselves with the right-handed majority from the very beginning—which may explain, to some extent, why left-handers are more likely to be found at the upper and lower extremes of success.

3. A 2000 study by Canadian researchers found that homosexual men and women are more likely to be left-handed than their heterosexual counterparts. The reasons for this are unclear. However, it is possible that people who are different from the rest of the world are more likely to develop *more* differently as they reach maturity. The people surveyed in this book would tend to anecdotally support this theory. Michelangelo and Leonardo da Vinci were primarily homosexual, Alexander the Great was also known to sleep with men, computer scientist and code-breaker Alan Turing was gay, as is tennis star Martina Navratilova. Julius Caesar was also rumoured to have enjoyed homosexual affairs. That's way above the 10 per cent proportion of the population usually considered to be gay.

it took four years to carve the world's most famous sculpture. *David* was carved from a block of Carrara marble nicknamed 'the Giant', which had been lying unused for 25 years after its serious flaws had defeated the talents of two eminent Florentine sculptors—Agostino di Duccio and Antonio Rossellino. Using the Giant was an act of sculptural one-upmanship and, in doing so, Michelangelo conquered both the marble and his predecessors' reputations.

David was based on the artistic principle of *disegno*, in which the success of an artwork consists in its correspondence to the artist's original conception. Within this idea, it was believed that sculpture was the finest form of art because its three-dimensionality most closely mimicked the divine creation. To make a sculpture of the male body was the ultimate artistic challenge, since it corresponded to what Renaissance people believed was God's highest creative act. Because sculpture is three-dimensional, it utilises the superior visual and spatial abilities often associated with left-handedness even more than painting. Viewed from this perspective, Michelangelo's lefty genius is quite astonishing. When two anatomy professors from the University of Florence carried out the first anatomical survey of the statue during its cleaning in 2004, they found that, although *David* was not very well-endowed, the only physiological mistake Michelangelo had made was that there was a hollow instead of a muscle on the right side of the back, an error that the artist had acknowledged in correspondence of the time, where he said he hadn't had enough material to make the muscle.

Whereas Leonardo wanted to fly, at least part of Michelangelo had the dream of transcending his limitations and approaching God's capability by creating perfect artworks. There's more than a tinge of heresy in the immensity of Michelangelo's ambition. His ambition clashed with his devoutness (Michelangelo was no stranger to self-loathing) and this helped to generate the creative tension that kept him furiously brilliant for most of his life. As with Ancient World left-handed conquerors such as Alexander and Caesar, Michelangelo's kind of hyper-competitive over-reaching was insatiable, the product of an almost diabolical will. It can partly be attributed to the left-hander's insatiable desire to transform a world in which they never fully fit.

PAINTING THE SISTINE CHAPEL The ceiling of the Sistine
Chapel was very much the product of Michelangelo's outrageous will. Although he had a distinct preference for sculpture, he was unable to resist Pope Julius II's entreaties to paint a fresco on the ceiling of the Chapel. Rumour has it that the idea of Michelangelo painting the Sistine Chapel had been put into the Pope's mind by two of Michelangelo's artistic rivals, Bramante and Raphael, who were hoping that, distracted from his forté of sculpture, Michelangelo would either lose the Pope's favour by declining the commission, or simply fail. They were to be sorely disappointed, even if the task of finishing the ceiling to his own exacting standards would tax

Michelangelo immensely. 'After four tortured years, more than 400 over life-sized figures, I felt as old and as weary as Jeremiah. I was only 37, yet friends did not recognise the old man I had become', he said at its completion. He began painting towards the end of 1508 and, by the time he finished in 1512, he had painted those 400 life-size figures over an area of more than 465 square metres mainly single-handed. Not only did he achieve this but, because he was primarily a sculptor, he had to teach himself many of the techniques necessary for fresco painting.

When the third great left-handed artist of the Italian Renaissance, Raphael (who thought Michelangelo's grim personality resembled that of a 'solitary hangman'), saw the unfinished ceiling, it blew him away. He began to incorporate aspects of Michelangelo's style into the paintings he was making in the building next door. The secretive Michelangelo was angry that Pope Julius had allowed his two rivals, Bramante and Raphael, to see the work before it was finished. Such was Michelangelo's competitive pique that, in 1541, long after Raphael was dead, he was still complaining in letters that 'everything he knew about art he got from me'.

There are many notable features to the Sistine Chapel frescoes. To begin with, for a religious artwork, Michelangelo managed to incorporate a range of pre-Christian classical elements and portraits. There was also a lot of classically inspired nudity, which offended some in the Church but, fortunately not the Pope who had commissioned it, even if some years later another artist was employed to paint loincloths over the genitals. Another interesting feature is that Michelangelo concentrated on the Book of Genesis for his subject matter. Several of the central panels are representations of God creating the world. The whole fresco was, in this sense, a testament to the creation of God, but also to the creative power of the artist.

On the ceiling of the Sistine Chapel, Michelangelo displayed a brilliance that, had it been fully understood, may have seen him accused of heresy. Of all the panels, the most enduring is the *Creation of Adam* which has the image of Adam and God reaching out their hands towards each other. The hand Adam is using to touch God is his left. In medieval iconography it was frequently the devil whose left hand was outstretched. Perhaps Michelangelo's pride and drive to perfection were so powerful that he secretly believed them to be almost diabolical, so he was not merely glorifying, but competing with God in the stakes of creation. This might explain the great tension which pervaded his relationships with the world since, in other respects, he was extremely pious. The Renaissance was a time when the individual began to emerge from the shadow of God, a movement which would culminate in the combination of humanism and faith in science that fuelled the Enlightenment 200 years later. Michelangelo's iconography served as a preparation for these shifts in the belief system of European society. Perhaps he remained unaware he was doing this. Still, the one force in his life he was unable to deny was the powerful urge demanding to be expressed by the astonishing capabilities of his left hand.

'MANY YEARS AGO I WENT TO THE VATICAN AND LOOKED AT MICHELANGELO'S FRESCOS IN THE SISTINE CHAPEL. I WAS OVERWHELMED WITH THE FEELING THAT BEFORE MICHELANGELO NO ONE HAD EVER ARTICULATED AND DEPICTED HUMAN PATHOS AS HE DID IN THOSE PAINTINGS. SINCE THEN ALL OF US HAVE UNDERSTOOD OURSELVES JUST THAT LITTLE BIT DEEPER, AND FOR THIS REASON I TRULY FEEL HIS ACHIEVEMENTS ARE AS GREAT AS THE INVENTION OF AGRICULTURE.'

WERNER HERZOG, GERMAN FILMMAKER

PAGES 68–69: *THE CREATION OF ADAM*, A DETAIL FROM MICHELANGELO'S SISTINE CHAPEL CEILING, WHICH WAS COMPLETED BETWEEN 1508 AND 1512.

THE ITALIAN RENAISSANCE WAS A PINNACLE IN THE HISTORY OF Western civilisation that was reached largely with the left hand. Not only were the great artists Leonardo and Michelangelo lefties, but so was their successor, Raphael, who was inspired by them, came to rival Michelangelo and has joined them in the pantheon of Old Masters. This period in history was one of the great lefty peaks of all time and the Renaissance would have been a far lesser event if wasn't for the transformative aesthetics generated by the superior visual and spatial abilities of its southpaw stars.

While Leonardo was an illegitimate child who referred to nature as the ultimate arbiter in matters aesthetic, and lived a rich life of brilliant thought and often unfinished artworks, Michelangelo was a very different type of lefty; one who reacted against the right-handed strictures of parental expectation, and who lived his lefty dream with terrible passion and rage to conquer all the art forms he attempted. Raphael was a different case altogether, a sign of how harmonious left-handers can be if encouraged to develop their lefty abilities. In his short life—he died allegedly after an over-strenuous bout of sex with his mistress at the relatively tender age of 37—Raphael would paint some of the great masterpieces of the Renaissance. But he would also be renowned for his *grazias* (grace), as well as for his paintings and their ease of composition in evoking the Renaissance ideal of human grandeur.

A CONTENTED LEFTY CHILDHOOD Raphael was born
Raffaello Sanzio in Urbino, a small city state between Rome and Florence. His father was a court factotum who wrote poetry and painted, but was not particularly renowned for his talents in either of these arts. His greatest legacy was perhaps the sensible way he reared his lefty son. To begin with, he believed that children were better served if breastfed

by their natural mothers instead of wet nurses, as Michelangelo and Leonardo both were. Raphael's father also felt that his son should be allowed to grow into his own lefty nature rather than be forced into social hierarchies. The paradox was that this gave Raphael the ease and grace that made him such a brilliant social operator in his adult life. Raphael also benefited from the fact that his father was a painter. Unlike with Michelangelo, there was no struggle for Raphael to be able to pursue the natural gift of his enhanced visual-spatial abilities. He was introduced to art at a very early age, while helping his father out in his studio. His natural aptitude developed easily and in harmony with his family life. Raphael's father was also sufficiently astute to realise that his son possessed more talent than he had himself and, by the time of his death, when he left Raphael an orphan at the age of 11, he had introduced him to the master Perugino, with whom the boy would serve his apprenticeship.

AN EASEL FULL OF EASE Like his personality, Raphael's painting was renowned for its grace and ease. This was partly a result of what he learnt during his apprenticeship with Perugino, also famous for the gracefulness of his work. But this grace, it must be emphasised, was formed because Raphael's talent was permitted to develop untrammelled. By age 17, when he received his first important commission to paint a chapel altarpiece, Raphael was already being referred to as a master. His early style resembled Perugino in its gentle lyricism, yet outstripped his teacher's by virtue of its naturalism. Again here we are reminded of the right brain's preference for the concrete over the abstract, something the naturalism of the high Renaissance, with its trio of left-handed geniuses, was famous for. In fact, it's interesting to note that in the more abstract world of contemporary art, there don't seem to be as many great left-handed painters as there were in the heyday of realist art.

The highlight of Raphael's naturalism is perhaps his sensitivity towards his subjects. Whereas the faces in Perugino's paintings all tend to look the same, and the subjects are differentiated more by the clothes they wear, in Raphael's work we get the benefits of the lefty's intuition into other people's thoughts, as a result of him being a natural outsider. The people in Raphael's paintings exude a wonderful character and humanity that is conveyed with the kindness that was reflected in Raphael's easy disposition. His work displays a profound, emotionally literate naturalism and possesses a warmer atmosphere than the enigmatic portraits of Leonardo or the anatomically perfect chiselled fury of Michelangelo.

INFLUENCES Realising he had outgrown his master, Perugino, Raphael left Urbino in 1504 and moved to Florence. At the time, Leonardo was dazzling the world with his *Mona Lisa*. Raphael fell under the influence of Leonardo, his devotion to the cause of nature in particular, and his paintings came to be less inhabited by the kind of idealised sweetness

RAPHAEL'S LEFTY TRAITS

INTUITIVE More than Michelangelo or Leonardo, Raphael saw into the emotional lives of his subjects and was able to capture this in his work. His art is most of all remarkable for its human sensitivity, something not acquired by rational means.

EMPATHETIC One of the reasons for the particular beauty of Raphael's works is that they resonate with empathy towards the subjects painted. There is a generosity in his paintings, as if the artist seemed to care about the people he painted and understood the frailty of their humanity. His reputation for grace also equates with having an empathetic personality. In his social life he was famous for being able to put people at their ease.

VISUAL-SPATIAL ABILITY Raphael's astonishing skills with painting and draftsmanship, as well as his ability to engage with the three-dimensional concerns of architecture, are clear indications that this left-hander was powerfully developed in this area.

OPPOSITE: SELF-PORTRAIT BY RAPHAEL, C.1506.

PAGE 73: *THE TRIUMPH OF GALATEA*, FRESCO, 1512–14.

FOLLOWING PAGES: *THE SCHOOL OF ATHENS*, FRESCO, 1510–11.

seen in Perugino, in favour of the individualised portraits of humanity, where the gentleness lies in the painter's gaze upon his subjects.

Raphael's work has an aura of great tenderness. To achieve this effect he used Florentine depth composition, whereby figures are grouped but retain their individual characteristics, as well as the subtlety of Leonardo's sfumato (fine shading) technique in his colours and forms. Interestingly, Raphael's use of chiaroscuro, the light and shade technique developed by Leonardo, was sparing, as if it was inappropriate for the gentle atmosphere and effortlessness resonating in his works. Like all the great lefty creators, Raphael was an intuitive learner but he remained his own man.

Somewhat later in his career, when he was already one of the great painters of his time, Raphael fell under the spell of Michelangelo's work, particularly when his friend, the architect Bramante, sneaked him in to see the secretive Michelangelo's unfinished ceiling of the Sistine Chapel. From this period onward, Raphael's work acquired some of the grandeur that Michelangelo had invested in his classically ideal depictions of the body. As a result, Raphael's figures became more muscular, particularly in their torsos, though he would never master the human body to the same extent as Michelangelo. Still, his work was good enough to cause Michelangelo to develop the same kind of unfriendly rivalry with him as he had with Leonardo.

In his later career, Raphael also adopted techniques from the colourism practised by the Venetian painters, such as Titian. Unfortunately Raphael's life was cut short at the age of 37, according to his first biographer, Giorgio Vasari, after sexual over-exertion with his mistress.

Raphael's paintings, with their wonderfully resonant characters (his portraits of Pope Julius II and Pope Leo X are stunning examples), strongly reflect the emerging individualism of Renaissance thought. Of course, this is something the lefty, as a misfit in a right-handed world, is likely to have an affinity with. Surely, therefore, it can be no coincidence that the high Renaissance of Italian art should have three lefties as its undoubted titans, all of them idiosyncratic, all of them contributors to a movement which would plant the individual soul at the centre of the world, and all of them engaged in the dream of creating human perfection. These three megastars of the fifteenth and sixteenth centuries contributed hugely to the explosion of knowledge and culture over the last 500 years.

LEFTY LINKS

1. The Italian Renaissance was perhaps the pinnacle of achievement for left-handed artists. Other notable lefty artists in history include the great German Old Master Albrecht Dürer (1471–1528), and fellow German Hans Holbein the Younger (1497–1543) who painted at the court of England's Henry VIII. There is also inconclusive evidence that the great master Rembrandt (1606–69) was a left-hander. More recent left-handed visual artists include Swiss Expressionist Paul Klee (1879–1940) and Dutch painter of impossible realities, M. C. Escher (1898–1972).

2. The works of Leonardo, Raphael and Michelangelo were the epitome of *disegno*, the principle in art which emphasised the importance of the line in painting, as opposed to *colore*. Interestingly, all the left-handed artists mentioned above were also formidable draftsmen. Dürer was renowned for his drawing, as was Holbein, while the brilliance of Escher's visual-spatial imagination and ability to think through his drawings is clearly evident in his impossible staircases. Even Klee, whose Expressionism was heavily invested in colour, used to talk of his paintings as 'taking a line for a walk'.

3. After the death of his friend and mentor, Bramante, in 1514, Raphael was appointed the architect of St Peters, even though he was yet to design a building. Michelangelo, perhaps the greatest of the great lefty trio in terms of architecture, was appointed to the same position in 1546. Michelangelo's architectural brilliance is still on display today in buildings such as the Laurentian Library and Medici Chapel in Florence and the Palazzo Farnese in Rome. Leonardo was also interested in architecture and urban planning although, as with many of his paintings, the architectural drawings that clutter his notebooks were never realised. Interestingly, architecture is a profession known today for its large number of left-handed proponents.

OPPOSITE: RAPHAEL'S PAINTING OF POPE LEO X MEDICI, PICTURED WITH CARDINALS GIULIO DE MEDICI AND LUIGI DE ROSSI, 1517.

1643–1727 MORE THAN ANY OTHER PERSON, ISAAC NEWTON IS RESPONSIBLE for our understanding of the universe today. From inauspicious beginnings as the posthumous child of a Lincolnshire yeoman farmer in England, Newton became a Cambridge University mathematician then went on to become the most famous scientist in the world. His scientific discoveries and inventions include the universal law of gravity, the light spectrum and the reflecting telescope, while in mathematics he was the inventor of differential calculus. He achieved all this in a mass of mental activity—much of the heavy thinking was done in a short burst in his early twenties when he was sequestered at the family farm by the spread of the Black Plague—which effectively ended with a nervous breakdown in 1693 at the age of 50. Yet the price of this brilliance was the possession of a singularly unpleasant personality. Secretive and paranoid, Newton hid his discoveries from the world for 20 years. He had a bad and powerful temper and was also known for the length of time he was capable of holding a grudge.

YOUNG NEWTON From an early age Newton displayed a preference for solitude and independent thought. His left-handed mind was different from those around him and the circumstances of his childhood helped to consolidate this. His father died before he was born and when he was three years old his mother remarried an older man. One of the conditions of the marriage was that Isaac be left behind with his grandmother, who lived on a farm some kilometres outside of the town, where there was no one to play with, since social interaction with the local peasants was forbidden. It was a lonely, unhappy childhood and, in later life, Newton recorded how in a childhood rage he once threatened to burn down the house with his mother and stepfather in it. Abandoned by his mother, Newton's childhood was lived without the usual bonds of familial affection. When he was 10 his stepfather died and his mother returned

home with a half-brother and two half-sisters in tow. Two years later, however, Isaac was packed off again, to a high school in Grantham, a neighbouring town, where he boarded with the local apothecary.

This emotionally disconnected childhood allowed Newton's intellect to develop independently. It also meant that he was fuelled by rage against the world. If he hadn't had the capability for genius, it's possible Newton might have been a garden variety psychopath. His personality was circumscribed by a strange emotional-intellectual loop whereby rage at the outside world furthered his immersion in the solitary genius of the scientific musings he described as 'phantasie'. Mathematical thinking was probably an escape from having to deal with his emotions. Genius is often the product of imbalance and, in Newton's case, the left-handed (right-brain) fantasising, mainly in the language of mathematics—a language as far removed from the expression of emotion as possible—drew him further away from social interaction and reality. For much of his life, Newton was obsessed with alchemy as well as science. While he failed like everyone else in the transmutation of metals, he was far more successful in the transmutation of ordinary human emotions into an intellectual energy that produced some of the most scintillating insights into the construction of nature humans have ever had. It could be said that, unable to solve the problem of himself, he abandoned that exercise and proceeded to solve some of the most vital problems in science.

Many of the lefty geniuses in this book are conspicuous by either their lack of schooling or undisciplined attitude towards the schooling they received. At Grantham, Newton was no exception. In his first year he came 78th out of 80 students. The belief that writing should be carried out with the right hand renders school much more difficult and unnatural for the left-hander. In the case of left-handed geniuses it's also as if the pathways of their own thoughts and the innate knowledge of their differences from others are already too strong, their originality and intuitions too compelling to be reined in with concerns about the relative mediocrity of the received wisdom offered by formal learning. Formal education, however, is about teaching the paths of communication through which individuals come to participate in their cultures. Those who break the conventions can rarely truly belong, and the price for this, as in Newton's case, can be perpetuated isolation. Largely friendless, as a schoolboy Newton preferred to spend his spare time alone, engaged in pursuits such as designing and building working models of water clocks and wooden mills. In the attic of the Grantham apothecarist where he boarded while at school there, he was fond of engraving geometric shapes into the timber wall, a harbinger of where his solitary musings were to take him.

If Newton had already abandoned himself to 'phantasie', his mother completely failed to understand this. When he was 16 she hauled him out of school to run the family farm. He proved a complete failure. Already, his only interest in his surroundings were as fuel for his scientific

OPPOSITE: ENGRAVING (AFTER HOUSTON) OF ISAAC NEWTON INVESTIGATING THE PROPERTIES OF LIGHT.

PAGE 81: PORTRAIT OF THE YOUNG ISAAC NEWTON BY AN ANONYMOUS DUTCH ARTIST.

NEWTON'S LEFTY TRAITS

INTUITIVE Newton had the ability to intuit solutions to mathematical problems and provide step-by-step proof in order to check them.

VISUAL-SPATIAL ABILITY It took superb visual-spatial skills to work out that the universe was ordered according to the universal law of gravity. One of Newton's main areas of skill was geometry.

HOT-TEMPERED Newton was a suspicious man prone to fits of pique. When other scientists dared to disagree with him, he became livid and held grudges for excessively long periods of time.

SOLITARY Newton was not close to his family, he had very few friends and displayed an extraordinary lack of interest in sexual matters, which may have been a sign of autism. However, Newton didn't seem to need people and, when forced to interact with them, he could be ruthless. He was admired as the greatest scientist of his era, but this didn't mean he was popular.

SELF-TAUGHT Like many other left-handers, his initial school performance was unspectacular. However, he achieved enough for people to recognise his potential. Much of his education, even at Cambridge, was self-directed.

FANTASIST Newton used to refer to his mathematical and scientific musings as 'phantasie', suggesting that, from a very early age, it was a realm he entered at least partly as an escape from having to deal with the emotional deprivations of his familial world. It would become a pattern that remained with him for the rest of his life and ensured his brilliance was matched with an unbalanced personality. (After all, paranoia is a mode of fantasy too.)

speculations. He neglected his farm work, defied his mother and bullied his half-siblings. He built waterwheels in streams and gained a knowledge of fluid motion while his sheep ate the neighbour's crops. He hid out of sight of the house reading books and day-dreaming. He was fined for allowing his swine to trespass on other people's land. Recognising both the absurdity of this situation, and Newton's talent, his uncle and former schoolmaster managed to persuade his mother to let him leave Woolsthorpe and return to Grantham to prepare for entry to study at Cambridge. His mother grudgingly acceded and Newton, given this lifeline, became a more determined student and succeeded in gaining entry to Trinity College Cambridge where he enrolled in 1661. At Cambridge, he again proved a somewhat lax and lonely student, skipping lectures and only making one friend. However, his talent was noticed and he began to acquire intellectual acolytes including his professor, Isaac Barrow, who quickly realised his student was smarter than him and generously began to champion his mind.

PLAGUE AND PURPLE PATCH Ironically, much of the thinking for Newton's greatest discoveries were completed in the relative isolation of Woolsthorpe some five years later. In 1665 the Black Plague came to London killing one in six Londoners. It swept from village to village towards Cambridge. Students and professors alike abandoned the university for the countryside. Newton returned to Woolsthorpe. This time, however, he wasn't under pressure to become a farmer. As soon as he arrived he set about building himself bookshelves and setting up a study. He took a 1000-page notebook and set himself problems, gradually expanding his scientific knowledge. Mathematics suited Newton's solitary pursuit of truth, since it gave him the facility to check his intuitions with equations. His geometrical approach to maths was a conceptual manifestation of the enhanced visual-spatial abilities often found in left-handers.

During his 20-month sojourn, his family rarely saw Newton and, with the postal service drastically curtailed by the plague, he was operating almost incommunicado. So lost was Newton in his fantasy world of figures and penetrating the secrets of nature, that he didn't bother to sit down for meals and frequently completely forgot to eat until reminded. One day, he was sitting outside in the orchard garden of Woolsthorpe, when an apple fell to the ground. He stared at the apple, reliving its path through the air, his mind in a state of dreamy half-consciousness, puzzling over something still intangible. Then it hit him. The direction the apple fell, along with every other object on this round earth, was towards the earth's centre. It wasn't just that the apple fell, but that it tried to go to the earth's centre when it did. Now this might seem perfectly logical to us, but Newton's lefty genius saw this in terms of the moon. This was an example of the left-hander's superior capacity for transformational or

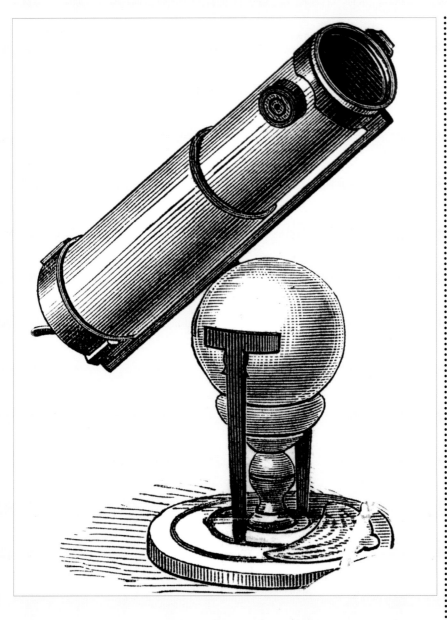

metaphorical thought—the ability to see one thing in terms of another. For some time Newton had been observing the moon and pondering why it remained in orbit around the earth, and indeed why the earth remained in orbit around the sun. With an intuitive flash, the apple falling in the orchard had given him an answer—gravity.

So what exactly did Newton's brilliant flash of lefty intuition with that apple mean? The observations of astronomers such as Galileo, Copernicus and Kepler had discredited the Aristotlean idea that earth was the centre of the universe, but none had been able to come up with a reason why, or for that matter how, the universe was stuck together. Galileo had made advances in the understanding of gravity by timing the descent of the objects of varying weight he dropped from the Leaning Tower of Pisa. Descartes argued that space was composed of invisible matter that rotated around the centre of the universe and maintained the relative position of the bodies in it. What Newton saw in the apple was that the earth, by some force, was drawing the apple to it. When he extended this to the moon, he decided that the moon remained in orbit around the earth for the same reason. From this he was able to extrapolate that every object in the universe draws every other object towards it, most likely in proportion to its mass. This theory became known as the universal law of gravity.

KEEPING SECRETS It's unlikely that Newton could have achieved this feat of thought if he wasn't a left-handed isolate. One of the most insightful commentaries on the peculiarity of his genius belongs to J. M. Keynes, the great twentieth-century economist, in a lecture he wrote called 'Newton the Man':

> I believe that the clue to his mind is to be found in his unusual powers of continuous concentrated introspection . . . His peculiar gift was the power of holding continuously in his mind a purely mental problem until he had seen straight through it. I fancy his pre-eminence is due to his muscles of intuition being the strongest and most enduring with which a man has ever been gifted. Anyone who has ever attempted pure scientific or philosophical thought knows how one can hold a problem momentarily in one's mind and apply all one's powers of concentration to piercing through it, and how it will dissolve and escape and you find that what you are surveying is a blank. I believe that Newton could hold a problem in his mind for hours and days and weeks until it surrendered to him its secret. Then being a supreme mathematical technician he could dress it up, how you will, for purposes of exposition, but it was his intuition which was pre-eminently extraordinary . . . The proofs, for what they are worth, were, as I have said, dressed up afterwards—they were not the instrument of discovery.

Keynes neatly captures the reason why, as a lefty solitary with immensely powerful muscles of intuition, Newton was able to formulate the universal law of gravity. Without the trajectory of removal from society which had its origins in his childhood, Newton would never have developed the capacity to close out the world in order to concentrate on his problems. What's also remarkable here is that his discoveries were intuition based. The mathematics which justified them was an afterthought, a way of checking, then ultimately of communicating, his discoveries to the larger community.

However, Newton showed considerable reluctance in sharing his discoveries. The first edition of the *Principia Mathematica* which contained the proofs for the universal law of gravity wasn't published until 1685, some 20 years after he had developed it. As Keynes astutely observed, Newton's:

deepest instincts were occult, esoteric, semantic—with profound shrinking from the world, a paralysing fear of exposing his thoughts, his beliefs, his discoveries in all nakedness to the inspection and criticism of the world . . . Until the second phase of his life, he was a wrapt, consecrated solitary, pursuing his studies by intense introspection with a mental endurance perhaps never equalled.

In its creative phase, Newton's mind was a thing of astonishing purity, whose lefty facility for difference, fuelled by isolation, was able to maintain the kind of concentration necessary to penetrate some of the deepest secrets of the universe. Yet the personality that came with it was a fairly twisted piece of work. He revelled in keeping his discoveries a secret, partly because he couldn't stand the thought of being criticised, but just as much because he enjoyed the magical thrill of being the only one to know the way the world truly worked. Newton was convinced of his lefty uniqueness and was prone to celebrating its superior difference as a mode of revenge against the world. When other scientists such as Robert Hooke disagreed with him, he held a grudge until either he was vindicated by their capitulation or they were dead. Newton was blessed and cursed by the fact that with the exception of minor errors he was almost always right.

Being a genius of Newton's order carries a bitter glory; a sentiment that can be found in many of the other great lefty isolates in the pages of this book. The lefty isolate, focused, touchy, paranoid but brilliant is a familiar pattern. Many of the greatest lefties have become addicted to solitude, their minds absorbed in lofty and lefty thoughts without having to make the compromises demanded by interaction with a right-handed world. Yet when they are forced to interact, as they inevitably are, their intuition can desert them. Their mindset is predominantly paranoid inhabiting an emotional field that includes paralysing insecurity, feelings of persecution and delusions of grandeur, where the fact of their brilliance and its reception by society are never quite at ease.

In 1693, Newton had a nervous breakdown which was roughly contemporaneous with the end of his creative thinking. Although he was still to publish great works such as his *Opticks*, which would reveal how white light was composed from the colour spectrum, they were the fruits of discoveries he had made in his solitary twenties and concealed from the world. Having stopped his creative thinking, Newton became more of a public man, holding the sinecure of Master of the Mint. Between 1703 and his death in 1727 he was the President of the Royal Society where at the same time as elevating it into the primary body of scientific opinion in Europe, he was also prone to unethical behaviour, stacking investigative committees against rivals such as Leibniz, with whom Newton competed for being credited with the discovery of differential calculus. The creativity might have gone but the rage, paranoia and solipsistic impulses, which had fuelled the great lefty leap of this Rolls Royce mind into the unknown, remained.

LEFTY LINKS

1. Newton's famous rage, obsessive solitude, competitiveness, secrecy concerning the sharing of his work and general paranoia are all character traits he shared with fellow left-hander, Renaissance artist Michelangelo, who behaved in a similar fashion with his concealment of the ceiling of the Sistine Chapel.

2. The list of left-handed scientists is a long, spectacular and somewhat contentious one. Scientists attributed as left-handers include Aristotle; Newton; Marie Curie; Benjamin Franklin; biologists Linus Pauling and James Watson, the discoverer of DNA; computer scientist Alan Turing; electricity pioneer Nikola Tesla; and physicists Niels Bohr and Richard Feynman. According to Chris McManus in his excellent *Right-Hand Left-Hand* neither Einstein nor Franklin was left-handed. However, educational pressures mean that people who write right-handed can still be left-handed. Einstein's history of poor performance at school followed by self-driven discovery is a pattern often found in left-handers and it has been suggested that if he was not a full lefty, he was at least mixed-handed.

3. When looking at Newton's character, it seems likely he had a form of autism, probably high-functioning Asberger's syndrome. This partly explains his mathematical ability in combination with his lack of emotional engagement with the world. Interestingly, scientific studies have shown that people with autism, if they display handedness, are 60 per cent more likely to be left-handed.

Napoleon Bonaparte

WITH A MILITARY RECORD UNEQUALLED BY ANYONE EXCEPT PERHAPS fellow lefty Alexander the Great, Napoleon Bonaparte is the greatest conqueror in modern history. From insalubrious Corsican beginnings, he climbed the dangerous hierarchies of Revolutionary France to become its leading general, before becoming First Consul and effective ruler of France in 1799. In 1804, he appointed himself hereditary Emperor of France and embarked on a series of military campaigns whose brilliant and surprising battle strategies led to the conquest of most of Europe. These invasions sounded the death knell for the feudal system in Europe. Wherever Napoleon went, he instituted the Napoleonic Code—systematic laws organised around the French Revolution's principles of liberty and equality. However, the cost of maintaining and supplying his massive armies, who remained in an almost constant state of warfare, was immense. His endless urge for battle, failure to translate military prowess into statesmanship, and the impatience that was part of his mercurial lefty temper, led to failed campaigns in Russia and Spain. Weakened by these, Napoleon was eventually defeated by the Sixth Coalition in the Battle of Dresden and exiled to Elba. Less than a year later, however, he escaped and raised an army to fight the Seventh Coalition. He lost the final battle of his career at Waterloo and was imprisoned on the remote Atlantic island, St Helena, where he died. Despite the series of losses which marked the end of his career, he nonetheless remains the most successful general in the modern world.

EARLY BONAPARTE Napoleon was born in 1769, the second son in a family of eight to impoverished Corsican nobility. His father was a lawyer allied with the independence movement, led by Pasquale Paoli, while his mother was a tough nut who never fully subscribed to the success of the child she had given birth to. As a boy, Napoleon was notable for a fiery lefty temper

🖐 LEFTY LINKS

1. One of the reforms Napoleon introduced throughout Europe was the practice of driving on the right-hand side of the road. In feudal times, most traffic had passed on the left. A reason for this was that right-handed horsemen could hold onto their reins with their left hands, while they shook hands with the oncoming traffic, or held their weapons with their right. The 'keep to the right' rule was introduced by the Jacobins in 1794. As he built new roads and conquered most of Europe, Napoleon maintained that traffic should pass on the right. It's often said that the reason behind his decision is that, being a left-hander, he wanted the superior defensive position for himself. By the end of the Napoleonic era most of Europe drove on the right. The exceptions were mainly members of the coalition against him: Britain, Russia, Finland, Sweden, Italy and the Austro-Hungarian Empire. Today all of them except for Britain drive on the right: Finland changed in 1858, Russia with the Bolshevik Revolution, Italy and Portugal in the 1920s, while the Austro-Hungarian states changed with their invasion by Hitler. The last state in continental Europe to change was Sweden in 1967.

2. Napoleon shared with Alexander and Caesar the quality of alternating between enlightened despotism and utter ruthlessness. The part of the world which is now Israel, Lebanon, Palestine and Syria seems to have borne the brunt of this across the millennia. At Jaffa, during his Middle Eastern campaign, Napoleon ordered the butchering of 2000 Turkish soldiers who were trying to surrender. His army then embarked on a massacre of the civilian inhabitants, which lasted for several days. Following this, Napoleon ordered the execution of a further 3000 Turkish prisoners. It was a display of cold-blooded ruthlessness, reminiscent of Alexander's mass crucifixion after the Siege of Tyre. Both acts were designed to strike fear into the hearts of the enemy.

that remained with him throughout his life. Although a year younger, and much smaller, he often beat up his brother Giuseppe. His nickname as a kid was *rabulione*, which meant the one who meddles in everything.

Unlike many of the left-handers in this book, Napoleon showed an excellent aptitude for formal education. He first went to school when he was five and was taught by the local nuns. Even at this young age, he showed a precocious talent for mathematics, a faculty in which left-handers often excel. At the age of eight he went to a local farmer's mill and spent the day calculating its production. He was exceedingly good at doing math in his head, a talent that would serve him well, especially when having to form strategies and move armies in the heat of the battle. As France had bought Corsica in 1768, Napoleon was eligible for a scholarship granted to impoverished children of the French nobility. It offered training for either the military or the priesthood. In 1778, Napoleon was enrolled in the military school while his brother Giuseppe was enrolled for the priesthood.

After a preparatory year, where he learnt French, Napoleon spent six years at the military school in Brienne, the only Corsican among boys from some of the wealthiest families in Europe. Like many lefties, this would only have confirmed his pre-existing sense of difference from the status quo. It undoubtedly spurred Napoleon's ambition. Following Brienne, he went to the elite Ecole Militare where he specialised in artillery and graduated in one year from a course that normally took several. At the age of 16, his formal education was complete and Napoleon became a second lieutenant in the French Army.

YOUNG AND BONEY One of the reasons Napoleon chose to join the artillery was because his mathematical skills were strong, and gave him an advantage in working out the angles, trajectories and ranges essential to accurate bombardment. Napoleon's mathematical ability was augmented by the left-handed, visual-spatial gift of being able to visualise terrain from the often erratic contents of maps. It gave him a major strategic advantage over other officers, in that he was able to accurately place his artillery. He could also calculate the time it would take to bring an army to a given place. He would use this knowledge time and time again to split the armies of the numerically superior coalition forces that fought against him.

After graduation from military school, Napoleon continued to educate himself in the affairs of the world through a course of self-determined reading. He also took leave from the French Army to go and fight with Paoli in Corsica. However, the two ended up falling out and the entire Bonaparte family had to leave Corsica in a hurry.

Napoleon achieved his first actual battle success at the siege of Toulon in 1793. Although only a captain, he devised a plan that eventually crushed the British and Royalist hold over the city. He used his strategic acumen to formulate a way of breaking the ring of British artillery around the city. In doing so, he surprised the enemy, who had boasted of their position's impregnability by calling it a 'Little Gibraltar'. Napoleon bombarded the British positions and was wounded in the thigh by a British bayonet in the ensuing battle, which ended in a naval evacuation by the British and Royalist forces. His brilliance at Toulon saw Napoleon promoted from Captain to Brigadier General in one hit. He became a marked favourite of the Jacobin leader, Robespierre, and returned to Paris where his political star also began to rise. It almost fell under the guillotine soon after with the denunciation and decapitation of Robespierre in 1794, but Napoleon was lucky. Although arrested as Robespierre's protégé, he was quietly released, perhaps out of recognition of his potential for assisting the nation with his prowess on the battlefield.

Napoleon further enhanced his military reputation through his tactics in battle against the Austrians at Dego, Italy, in 1794. He returned to Paris and began to agitate for greater responsibility. His third success after Toulon and Dego came when he successfully stood down a 30,000-person mob of malcontents by using grapeshot fired from his cannons in Paris. This battle is a good example of Napoleon's intuitive know-how. He believed that if you could inspire fear in the enemy, then the battle was more than half-way won. He used grapeshot because it would hit a lot of people, creating fear and bloodshed, yet with insufficient fatalities to turn it into an incident of mass martyrdom that might be used against him in the future for the purposes of revenge. As a consequence of this adroit handling of the situation, he found a new patron, Director Barras. When he applied to become commander of an army to invade Italy in 1796, he got the job. He also got Barras' former mistress, Josephine, another left-hander, as a wife.

Napoleon's reasons for pursuing the Italian command (other than his innately martial instincts) were largely based on his interpretation of the life of his fellow lefty Julius Caesar. Because of his Gallic campaign, Caesar had been able to build a power base independent of the swirling political allegiances of Rome. When he returned from Gaul with a triumphant army, it massively enhanced his popularity with the people, not least because of the riches that returned with him. Importantly, when Pompey militated against him, Caesar had a loyal army and a base outside of Rome that he could use to advance his cause.

With the political situation so volatile in Paris, this was a lesson Napoleon took heed of. When Napoleon took over his Italian army, it was a motley, ill-disciplined and poorly fed assemblage. But, like Caesar, he knew how to pull it into shape. Through conquering territory, the army was able to feed itself. Italy was also full of loot and Napoleon earnt the loyalty of his men by giving them a share of it, and setting up a system by which these gains could be remitted easily to their families. It was in this campaign where his men nicknamed him the 'Little Corporal', to indicate their affection for a leader who looked after their interests and behaved without the usual airs and graces of the mostly aristocratic military leaders. Napoleon also began to acquire the personal wealth that was necessary for

3. For intellectuals such as Beethoven, stuck in despotic regimes like the Austro-Hungarian Empire, Napoleon's rise and the reforms he instigated felt like a breath of fresh air. After the turmoil of the Terror, it appeared that he might be capable of rescuing the ideals of the French Revolution. For this reason, his military actions did not always arouse complete hostility in the countries at which they were directed. However, disillusionment set in when Napoleon crowned himself hereditary Emperor of France. Beethoven, who had planned to dedicate his Third Symphony to Napoleon, was so furious that he scratched the Frenchman's name out and wrote in the name of one of his aristocratic Austrian patrons instead.

4. One of the main reasons for Napoleon's ultimate defeat was that his brilliant strategical insights into battle were almost entirely restricted to land. As such, the British Navy were able to gain nautical superiority over the French and use this to interfere with troop movements and block supplies. The key battle was the 1805 Battle of Trafalgar, where the British were led by left-handed admiral, Horatio Nelson. Nelson was originally right-handed but, in 1797, while in command of four ships trying to attack French-allied Spanish assets in the Canary Islands, his right arm was hit by a cannonball and had to be amputated. Nelson prepared to retire from the navy, writing: 'A left-handed admiral will never again be considered as useful; therefore the sooner I get to a very humble cottage the better, and make room for a sounder man to serve the state'. Before this he had also lost the sight in his right eye. The British Admiralty, however, thought differently, and Nelson continued to harass the French Navy, until heading the decisive victory at Trafalgar during which he was killed.

PAGE 89: PORTRAIT OF NAPOLEON IN HIS STUDY, 1812, BY JACQUES LOUIS DAVID.

NAPOLEON'S LEFTY TRAITS

INTUITIVE Napoleon knew how to inspire fear in his enemies and was renowned for his amazing instincts about the right time to attack. He also had an excellent understanding of the needs of, and how to maintain the loyalty of, his men.

VISUAL-SPATIAL ABILITY Combined with his mathematical ability, this skill enabled Napoleon to visualise a battlefield from a map and to organise his artillery with great precision.

LATERAL THINKING Evidence of this trait can be found in Napoleon's battle stratagems, and also in the way that he constructed his own propaganda, such as the Egyptian scientific expedition.

HOT-TEMPERED Like many great left-handers, this was Napoleon's Achilles heel. His temper was legendary and was accompanied by an insatiable love of war, as well as the impatience that played a major part in his undoing.

ICONOCLASTIC Napoleon's Enlightenment-based reforms, including the Napoleonic Code, made a serious contribution to the end of feudalism in Europe.

FANTASIST In his early life Napoleon wrote fiction and history, but it is perhaps his dream of glory, and inability to see its limits, which mark him as a man with a fantastic streak to his imagination.

PREVIOUS PAGES: *NAPOLEON AT THE BATTLE OF IENA, PRUSSIA*, 1806, BY HORACE VERNET.

his own political ambition, enabling him, for instance, to start his own newspaper and talk himself up, while some of Italy's greatest artworks and cultural artefacts were shipped to Paris, where their display in museums such as the Louvre became a measure of national glory.

The Italian campaign is often considered Napoleon's greatest. He defeated both the Austrians and the army of the Papal States and took control of a huge swathe of Italy. His army captured 160,000 prisoners and 2000 cannons. Battles were won by surprise and deception. He was a pioneer in the field of military intelligence, deploying new technology such as the Chappe semaphore, a coded system of displayed rods at angles which dramatically increased the speed at which information could travel. Napoleon had the lateral gift of being able to instinctively apply his impressive book knowledge of military matters to the concrete situation of the battlefield and visualise the outcome. He rather arrogantly claimed, 'I have fought sixty battles and I have learnt nothing which I did not know at the beginning'. To a certain extent, this was true.

FIRST CONSUL TO SELF-CROWNING In 1798, Napoleon followed the trail of his left-handed military heroes, Alexander and Caesar, to Egypt, where he achieved massive propaganda success by incorporating a scientific expedition into his mission. The expedition discovered many Ancient Egyptian artefacts, including the Rosetta Stone, which enabled French scholars to translate the Egyptian hieroglyphs, without which the story of Ramses the Great would never have become known. The results of the Egyptian campaign were mixed. There were brilliant victories, but also defeats, mainly due to the prevalence of bubonic plague among his troops and British naval superiority. (Napoleon never really got his head around the importance of the navy, which is ultimately one of the reasons why he was defeated.)

In 1799, however, with Egypt left as unfinished business, Napoleon was summoned back to France, where the situation was precarious. There was a threat of invasion by the members of the Second Coalition, comprised of Britain, Austria, Russia and the Ottoman Empire. The Directory which was running France was incompetent and out of favour with the public. One of the directors, Sieyes, approached Napoleon for military support in a coup. On 9 November 1799, they seized control and Napoleon, like Caesar, became a member of a ruling triumvirate. His title was First Consul of France.

Napoleon's period as First Consul was relatively free from war and in this period he, as ever restlessly intelligent, instituted wide-ranging reforms to the law, education and banking systems, sewers and roads, which earnt him a reputation for spreading the values of the Enlightenment. The intelligentsia, who still lived under despotic rule throughout Europe, viewed him as a potential saviour and disseminator of the ideals of the French Revolution.

They were disappointed. In 1804, using an assassination plot against him to argue the need for dynastic inheritance to ensure political

stability, Napoleon declared himself hereditary Emperor of France and it wasn't long before the Napoleonic Wars had begun in earnest.

WAR WAR WAR In 1805, Britain, Austria and Russia united against Napoleon in the Third Coalition. At the Battle of Ulm, Napoleon used a brilliant and rapid wheeling manoeuvre to isolate the Austrian Army of General Mack. It was an example of how his visual-spatial intelligence, and ability to move his army at speed, proved superior to the opposing forces. On 2 December 1805, Napoleon enjoyed his greatest victory at Austerlitz. It was again a masterpiece of strategical thinking. With his supply lines stretched, Napoleon was hoping the Austrians and Russians, led by Tsar Alexander, would come to him and engage him in battle. In order to facilitate this, he deliberately weakened his army's right flank in order to create the illusion of vulnerability. He hoped the enemy would notice, and find it too tempting to resist. Once they were attacking the right flank, Napoleon then planned to mount an assault through the centre of the Allied Forces, which were thinned out due to the attack on his right flank. It was a fiercely fought battle which lasted for over nine hours before the French forces prevailed. As the Allied troops retreated over the ice, Napoleon displayed his brilliant ruthlessness and ability to surprise by ordering his cannons to fire at the ice and break it up so that the enemy would be drowned. Many did. The Allies lost 27,000 out of 75,000 men, while Napoleon only lost 9000 from a smaller army of 67,000. In three months, the French were in Vienna.

THE OVER-REACHER Like Alexander the Great, once Napoleon had a taste for conquest, it was impossible for him to stop. Perhaps there is something in the combination of obsessive singularity of purpose, combined with a fierce temper, which affects left-handed conquerors, making them blind to their own weakness while under the influence of the red mist. The Fourth Coalition, consisting of Prussia, Russia, Saxony, Sweden and Britain, went to war against Napoleon in 1806. After another brilliant military victory, this time over the Prussians at Jena, continental Europe was effectively split between the French and Russians. But soon afterward, cracks began to appear in Napoleon's seemingly invincible veneer. In 1807, he ordered Spain to invade Portugal, who had continued to trade with the British. The Spanish refused, so he decided to attack them as well. The ensuing revolt lasted until 1814 and was a significant drain on French resources.

Even more disastrous was Napoleon's invasion of Russia in 1812. Avoiding engagement, the Russian generals drew Napoleon deeper and deeper into Russia. As they marched through Russia, the peasants practised a scorched earth policy, denying the French Army food. With his own supply lines hopelessly stretched, Napoleon's army was vanquished by hunger and the Russian winter. Of the 650,000 French troops who entered Russia, only about 40,000 completed the retreat. For Napoleon, the writing was on the wall.

While he enjoyed a magnificent victory over the Allies of the Sixth Coalition at Dresden in 1813, following a bloody defeat at Leipzig later that year, his army was reduced to 100,000 against five times as many Allied troops. No amount of left-handed brilliance could undo such odds and, in March 1814, Paris was occupied and Napoleon was forced to abdicate and was replaced by Louis XVIII.

SWANSONG Napoleon was exiled to Elba, an island 19 kilometres off the coast of Italy. Knowing that the reign of Louis XVIII was incompetent and unpopular, and aware of rumours that he was about to be banished to an island in the South Atlantic, in February 1815, Napoleon escaped from Elba. Louis XVIII sent the Fifth Regiment of the Line under one of Napoleon's former off-siders, Marshall Ney, to detain him. When he met with the army Napoleon, never one to shrink in the face of danger, cried out, 'Soldiers of the Fifth, you recognise me. If any man would shoot his emperor, he may do so now.' After a brief and tense hesitation, the soldiers responded, *'Vive L'Emperor'*, and Napoleon was once again in command of an army and marching towards Paris. He took Paris, raised another 200,000 men and governed for 100 days until he was beaten by the Allied Forces, under the Duke of Wellington, at the Battle of Waterloo. This time there was no coming back. Trying to escape to the United States, Napoleon was intercepted by the British and sent to the remote island of St Helena, where he lived out the remainder of his days.

OPPOSITE: *NAPOLEON CROSSING THE ALPS AT THE ST BERNARD PASS, 1800,* BY JACQUES LOUIS DAVID.

PAGES 96–97: *THE CONSECRATION OF THE EMPEROR NAPOLEON AND THE CORONATION OF THE EMPRESS JOSEPHINE BY POPE PIUS VII, DECEMBER 1804,* BY JACQUES LOUIS DAVID (DETAIL).

Beethoven

1770–1827 WHEN WE SPEAK OF TORTURED GENIUS, THE NAME BEETHOVEN IS NEVER far from our lips. Some have argued that this German composer, who produced some of the world's most enduring musical works, despite suffering from increasing deafness from the age of 27, is the greatest mind humanity has ever known. While this may be open to debate, it nonetheless comes as no surprise to hear that Beethoven was a lefty. He revolutionised classical music through the introduction of Romanticism and organic structure, thereby making possible the careers of many of the great composers who followed him. With his unruly mane of silver hair, dishevelled dress, foul temper and conspicuous eccentricity, this left-handed iconoclast is one of the first images to appear in our minds when we think of the tempestuous lives of great artists.

YOUNG LUDWIG Ludwig van Beethoven was born in Bonn in West Germany in 1770. At the time, Bonn was the capital of the Electorate of Cologne, a principality significant for being a trading centre and also because its Elector was one of the princes responsible for electing the Holy Roman Emperor. Beethoven was a third-generation musician. His grandfather, also called Ludwig, was the master of the Court Chapel choir and enjoyed a reputation as a fine bass singer. Beethoven's father, Johann, who was an alcoholic, had been less successful, but was still a court musician who sang and played the violin and clavier.

Beethoven showed early signs of being a prodigy, but was hampered to some extent by his father's ambivalence towards his talent. There were times when Johann lauded his son's precocity, yet at other times he tended to resent it. On one occasion, according to an account by his childhood neighbours Gottfried and Cäcilia Fischer, Johann admonished his son for improvising—a classic case of mediocre talent repressing the lefty individuality of the great. Nonetheless, his father arranged Beethoven's

first performance at the age of seven, with the hope of inviting comparisons with the child prodigy of the previous generation, Mozart.

Like many of the great left-handers in these pages, Beethoven ceased his formal schooling while relatively young. He went to a Latin primary school until he was 10 but did not go on to the Gymnasium (German for high school). The originality of Beethoven's lefty mind perhaps profited from his lack of formal schooling. Certainly, by the time he went to Vienna aged 22 and studied with Haydn, he had strong opinions which made him resistant to Haydn's teachings. The fact that he was sufficiently strong and wilful to resist convention, even when being taught by a great composer, was a clear sign of his individuality and brilliance.

HEARING PROBLEMS

When he was about 27 years old and still fairly new in Vienna, Beethoven began to notice a constant ringing in his ears. At the time, he was already regarded as arguably the best and certainly the most daring concert pianist in Vienna, and his renown as a classical composer was growing. The ringing worsened and, in 1802, his doctor prescribed a sojourn in the rural quiet of Heiligenstadt, an hour by carriage from Vienna, to allow his hearing a chance to recover. Around this time, Beethoven had expressed dissatisfaction with the direction his music was taking. Previously his composition had been largely in the classical tradition, whose expression had reached a pinnacle with Mozart and Haydn. There were signs, however, that Beethoven wanted to leave this affiliation and create something new.

While he was recuperating at Heiligenstadt, Beethoven had an existential crisis. Although he was enjoying the peacefulness of the countryside, his hearing wasn't getting any better. In fact it got worse; a situation that provoked Beethoven into a serious contemplation of suicide as can be seen from the Heiligenstadt Testimony which he wrote to his brothers but never sent:

O ye men who think or say that I am malevolent, stubborn or misanthropic, how greatly do ye wrong me, you do not know the secret causes of my seeming, from childhood my heart and mind were disposed to the gentle feelings of good will, I was even ever eager to accomplish great deeds, but reflect now that for six years I have been a hopeless case, aggravated by senseless physicians, cheated year after year in the hope of improvement, finally compelled to face the prospect of a lasting malady (whose cure will take years or, perhaps, be impossible), born with an ardent and lively temperament, even susceptible to the diversions of society, I was compelled early to isolate myself, to live in loneliness, when I at times tried to forget all this, O how harshly was I repulsed by the doubly sad experience of my bad hearing, and yet it was impossible for me to say to men speak louder, shout, for I am deaf. Ah how could I possibly admit such an

LEFTY LINKS

1. Both Beethoven and Leonardo profited from the fact that their formal schooling ended when they were about 10. It affected their attitudes towards their art dramatically. Instead of looking to the masters who preceded them as the ultimate authority, they preferred to make nature their ultimate authority. Leonardo placed his priority on the primacy of the natural world as perceived by the eye. Beethoven appealed to nature through the Romantic belief that creativity was an organic process that intuitively penetrated the essence of nature.

2. The left-hander with perhaps the greatest influence on Beethoven's life was Napoleon Bonaparte, who he once thought the greatest man in Europe—only to change his mind when the Corsican betrayed the French Revolution by declaring himself Emperor of France.

3. Other great classical composers and musicians who were left-handed include Carl Philipp Emanuel Bach, Sergei Rachmaninoff and the brilliant, eccentric Canadian piano virtuoso Glenn Gould.

4. One area of the orchestra where you won't see much left-handed playing is in the string section. It's the musical equivalent of lefties and righties bumping each other at the dinner table. Perhaps this is the reason why Beethoven, who played both violin and piano, was reputed to be a mediocre violin player yet, until the onset of deafness, was one of the greatest piano virtuosos of his time.

OPPOSITE: PORTRAIT OF BEETHOVEN AFTER A PAINTING BY CHRISTIAN HORNEMAN, 1803.

PAGE 101: IN 2003 THE MANUSCRIPT FOR BEETHOVEN'S NINTH SYMPHONY WAS AUCTIONED AT SOTHEBY'S IN LONDON. IT SOLD FOR A RECORD US$3.5 MILLION.

BEETHOVEN'S LEFTY TRAITS

INTUITIVE As a Romantic composer, Beethoven introduced individual emotion to music which transcended the formalism of the classical music that preceded his.

HOT-TEMPERED Beethoven's temper made him difficult to deal with from an early age, as is evident from his failed relationship with Haydn. Undoubtedly his increasing deafness did nothing to improve this. As he lost the ability to participate in conversations, he was forced to rely on the direct expression of emotion and conversation books (blank notebooks in which people would write their questions).

SOLITARY Again, Beethoven's deafness caused him to become isolated from the world. This was also compounded by the fact that Beethoven never married. Throughout his life, Beethoven had the unfortunate habit of falling in love with socially unattainable women. Although the great age of Romantic genius was beginning to flower, in Beethoven's time musicians still had a low social standing. His love life was disastrous, which fed his fury at the poor deal his genius had been offered by life.

ICONOCLASTIC Forget rock music, Beethoven was perhaps the most iconoclastic musician who ever lived. He completely revolutionised orchestral music, turning it into a stunning vehicle for the expression of tumultuous individualistic emotion.

EXPERIMENTAL This can be seen in the way that Beethoven adapted the musical forms he worked within. His many successful experiments included the dramatic elongation of the symphonic form, the incorporation of literature into his music by the use of choral singing, and the use of unconventional juxtapositions between the emotional textures of a symphony's movements.

OPPOSITE: BEETHOVEN'S MUSIC SYMBOLISED THE TRANSITION BETWEEN EIGHTEENTH-CENTURY CLASSICISM AND NINETEENTH-CENTURY ROMANTICISM.

infirmity in the one sense which should have been more perfect in me than in others, a sense which I once possessed in highest perfection, a perfection such as few surely in my profession enjoy or have enjoyed ... Forced already in my 28th year to become a philosopher, O it is not easy, less easy for the artist than for anyone else—Divine One thou lookest into my inmost soul, thou knowest it, thou knowest that love of man and desire to do good live therein ...

THE THIRD SYMPHONY 'EROICA'

Following this crisis, Beethoven's music became more daring, as if he had faced his fears and no longer felt beholden to anyone but himself. Much of the emotion of his determination to persevere, despite the handicap of encroaching deafness, is captured in the Third Symphony, also known as the Heroic Symphony, or 'Eroica', which Beethoven mostly composed during 1803. There had been no symphony like it before and, when it was first performed in 1805, it seriously divided its audience between those who found much of it senseless and fragmented bombast, versus those who saw a new kind of holistic brilliance embedded in its massive and often disruptive momentum. Some even argued that it would take the listening public a generation to develop sufficiently to fully understand such a masterpiece. The importance of Beethoven as the first Romantic composer cannot be underestimated. The Romantics valued music extremely highly, believing that since music was immaterial (without physical form) it was the art form most capable of expressing the individual's soul.

So what was revolutionary about Symphony No. 3? To begin with, it was half as long again as any symphony that had gone before it. From the enormous first movement with its 691 bars, it becomes clear that Beethoven's Third is responsible for taking the symphonic poem to an all new epic scale. With its radical disjunctions in mood between the funeral march of the second movement and the jaunty scherzo of the third, it introduced a new emotional palate into music, which had previously been constrained by the pursuit of formal elegance. The disjunctions of mood within and between movements helped create a sense of elevated personal expression, as if the listener was in direct communication with the soul of the composer—an effect not discernible in predecessors such as Mozart and Haydn. The deployment of an extra horn in the orchestra helped build a romantic sense of grandeur, which presages the enormous orchestras employed by later composers such as Mahler and Wagner.

The Third's form showed a strong left-handed disregard for the conventions of received musical wisdom. At the time, one critic derided it as 'a colossal piling of ideas'. Yet much of the magnificent tension in the music is a result of how Beethoven was able to synthesise several powerful narratives—his own crisis, the rise of Napoleon Bonaparte and the Prometheus legend of Greek mythology—to drive the Third along. Such

attempts to seek synthesis were very much a part of the Romantic view of the world, which placed emphasis on the holistic and organic, in opposition to the piece-by-piece linearity of scientific thought. It is unsurprising that the instigation of these Romantic approaches came from a left-hander, since holistic thinking tends to be more of a right-brain activity, while step-by-step logic is more the domain of the left. Furthermore left-handers tend to have greater communication between the two hemispheres of their brains than do right-handers. This is particularly useful in music where the right hemisphere of the brain tends to be responsible for pitch and melody, while the left is responsible for complex rhythms.

Critics have long pondered the reason why the funeral march of the second movement is followed by a joyous scherzo and finale. An obvious reading is of Beethoven confronting his darkest fears at Heiligenstadt then feeling release once he has decided to keep going. Another possible interpretation is that the symphony is about Napoleon rescuing the ideals of the French Revolution. According to a number of contemporary sources, Beethoven originally intended the Third to be dedicated to his fellow left-hander, Napoleon Bonaparte. At the time Bonaparte, as First Consul of France, was widely considered to have rescued the French Revolution and its ideals of liberty, equality and fraternity from the excesses of the Terror, the indiscriminate bloodbath that came with the fanatical leadership of Robespierre. For Beethoven, living in the largely benign but retrograde political environment of the Austro-Hungarian empire, the values of the French Revolution were attractive, as they were to most artists and intellectuals of the period. Yet there was also disillusionment. When Beethoven heard that Napoleon had proclaimed himself Emperor of France he was outraged. He ripped up the title page with the dedication to Napoleon and the Third instead was dedicated to one of his patrons, Prince Lobkowitz. There was a sting in the tail as well. Along with dedication were the words 'composed to celebrate the memory of a great man'. Napoleon, of course, was still alive.

Other listeners to the Third have noticed thematic similarities with Beethoven's ballet *The Creatures of Prometheus*, Opus 43, first performed in 1801. In the Greek legend, Prometheus is punished by the gods for giving humans fire. He is chained to a rock and an eagle comes every day and eats his liver. At night the organ regenerates and the agony begins all over again. This tale of the rebel (perhaps Prometheus was a lefty too), who breaks the divine rules in order to bring about an improvement of the human condition, resonated strongly with the Romantics. In his ballet, Beethoven changed the story so Prometheus is executed for his transgression then later reborn. It's easy to imagine how Beethoven, having been in a suicidal state because of his deafness, only to emerge from it to write greater music than ever, could have identified with a myth in which a man is punished by the gods for his betterment of humankind.

OPPOSITE: A PORTRAIT OF BEETHOVEN FROM C.1800, WHEN HE WAS ABOUT 30 YEARS OF AGE.

WAS BEETHOVEN REALLY A LEFTY?

As with many figures in history, it is often difficult to tell whether people were lefties or righties. There are undoubtedly people who, for reasons of discrimination, preferred to be known as righties rather than lefties. It is also generally assumed that if there is no mention of a person's handedness then they are right-handed. With pre-photographic cases, such as Beethoven's, the territory is murky. While a number of portraits show him as being right-handed, this has to be balanced against the testimony of Beethoven's friend, companion and first biographer, the violinist Anton Schindler, who claimed that Beethoven was a lefty. As a biographer, Schindler was notoriously inventive—but mostly in the cause of protecting Beethoven's posterity. Therefore, it is unlikely that he would have invented Beethoven's left-handedness. It is more likely the portraits are a misrepresentation due to the fact that Beethoven was a reluctant sitter. One portrait of Beethoven with a pen in his right hand, painted by Joseph Karl Stieler in 1819–20, is often used as evidence for Beethoven's right-handedness. Stieler claimed he was the only painter Beethoven agreed to sit for, and the painting was understood to be a very good likeness. However, the hands had to be painted from memory, as Beethoven could not be persuaded to stay for the required number of sittings. Perhaps Stieler assumed that Beethoven was right-handed, or maybe he chose to portray Beethoven as right-handed because the cultural stigmatisation of left-handedness might undermine the grandeur of his subject.

THE NINTH, OR CHORAL, SYMPHONY Beethoven's Third marked a break with symphonic tradition. Yet Beethoven's most famous symphony, and his last, is probably the Ninth, or Choral, Symphony. This work was also powerfully iconoclastic. It is an immoveable brick in the symphonic canon that every composer post-Beethoven has in some way had to deal with. With its radical setting of Schiller's poem *Ode to Joy* in the final movement, the Ninth was the first symphony to use choral singing—and to stunning effect. The Ninth has been used for national anthems, and the *Ode to Joy* movement (with altered lyrics) is the official anthem of the European Union. It has even had an effect on recent technology. The CD was originally designed to hold 74 minutes of music, because this was the length of Beethoven's Ninth Symphony.

The Ninth's impact on other composers was immense, sending some such as Schubert and Mendelssohn in search of texts to use to structure their works. Others such as Mahler and Wagner were inspired by the sheer grandeur of the music and the sound of such a large orchestra augmented with voices. Wagner wrote in 1846 that, 'It is wonderful how the master makes the arrival of the human voice and tongue a positive necessity, by this awe-inspiring recitative of the bass strings; almost breaking the bounds of absolute music already, it stems the tumult of the other instruments with its eloquence, insisting on decision, and passes at last into a songlike theme whose simple stately flow bears with it, one by one, the other instruments, until it swells into a mighty flood'. The French composer Claude Debussy wrote, 'It [the Ninth] is the most triumphant example of the moulding of an idea to the preconceived form; at each leap forward there is a new delight, without either effort or appearance of repetition; the magical blossoming, so to speak, of a tree whose leaves burst forth simultaneously. Nothing is superfluous in this stupendous work.' Here we get the sense of the Ninth as a supremely Romantic achievement of organic creation, left-handed in its holistic approach to composition and its iconclastic form.

The Ninth is even more astonishing when you consider that when Beethoven composed it he was completely deaf. Although he introduced radical new elements to the symphony, he heard none of them, except in his head. The symphony's composition was based entirely upon Beethoven's memories of sound.

At its premiere in May 1824 in the Kärntnertortheater in Vienna. Beethoven joined the Kapellmeister and conductor Ignaz Umlauf on the stage. Because he was deaf, Beethoven was unable to hear the orchestra and for this reason Umlauf instructed the musicians not to pay any attention to the composer. As the orchestra played, Beethoven, nonetheless conducted with great emotion. So carried away was he with the music in his head that when the orchestra finished the piece, he continued to conduct. Eventually one of the singers turned him round to face a bemused audience who had already begun to applaud. He looked like a

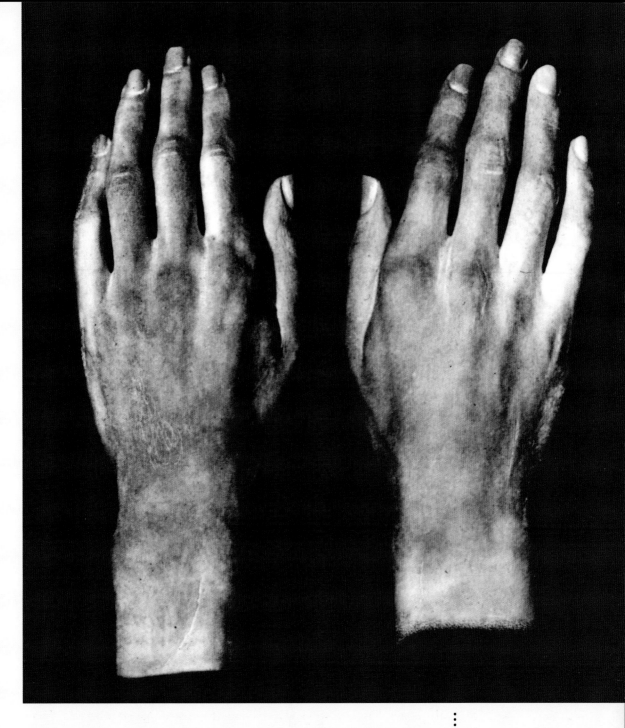

madman, and the applause was polite until it dawned on them that he had written the work without being able to hear. In sympathy and wonder at the achievement, the first round of applause became a second, then a third, fourth and fifth. In order that Beethoven could comprehend this they waved their handkerchiefs up and down. The maestro was profoundly moved. Three rounds of applause were generally reserved only for the Imperial Family, and after the fifth, the chief of police stood up and told the audience to desist from any further praise. Nonetheless it was a fitting tribute to an iconoclastic left-handed genius, who quite literally spent most of his life marching to the beat of his own drum.

PLASTER CASTS OF BEETHOVEN'S HANDS, PROBABLY MADE WHILE THE COMPOSER WAS STILL ALIVE.

WHEN QUEEN VICTORIA INHERITED THE THRONE OF BRITAIN AGED 18, it was in a fairly dire state. Following the long reign of mad King George III, the crown had passed to two of his sons, the high-living George IV, and William IV, whose reign saw considerable dimunition in the powers of the monarch. Aided by her left-handed abilities of intuition, empathy and the capacity to be at ease in times of great transformation, Victoria took control of her destiny and turned a monarchy that was losing popularity with the people into one of Europe's most beloved, while showing a political acumen and tact that helped guide Britain through the tumultuous changes of the nineteenth century. Her rule coincided with the apex of the British Empire and, by the time of her death in 1901, her dominion covered over a quarter of the habitable area of the world and her subjects numbered 400 million. Queen for 63 years, Victoria was the longest-reigning monarch in British history. Even today, the word 'Victorian' connotes a particular cultural flavour—sentimentality, an obsession with death and excessive mourning, a moral rigidity (at least in outward appearances), and the illusion of solidity in a world of constant flux. This emanated from Victoria herself, but also represented the values and beliefs of Britain's burgeoning middle class, who had grown wealthy on the profits of the Empire and relative peace, whose tastes the Queen shared and represented.

PRINCESS VICTORIA Victoria was the only daughter of Edward, Duke of Kent (the third son of George III) and the widowed Princess Regent of Leinigen, Victoire. As with many of the royal family, her father was rather broke and, as a consequence, was forced to live on the European continent where the cost of living was cheaper. However, the sons of George were making a poor show of producing legitimate heirs and when the 50-year-old Edward found out his young wife was pregnant, he insisted the baby be born in England.

Edward died some eight months later and Victoria's mother was left saddled with her husband's debts in a country where she couldn't speak the language and wasn't completely sure whether she was welcome. George IV reluctantly provided rooms for mother and child in Kensington Palace where Victoria grew up speaking only German until the age of three. Her childhood was not that of a typical princess. Due to her poor financial status, she was forced to share a room with her mother and to eat the cheapest cuts of meat, such as mutton.

Victoria's childhood was also fairly isolated. She mainly lived among the German ladies her mother kept as her retinue and, with the exception of the children of her mother's adviser, John Conroy, she had no one to play with. In some ways her childhood resembles that of fellow lefty Isaac Newton, who also suffered from the social isolation of being from a higher class, and therefore distant, to those around him. She didn't have fond memories of her childhood. In 1858, she wrote to her eldest daughter:

> I had led a very unhappy life as a child—had no scope for my very violent feelings of affection—had no brothers or sisters to live with—never had a father—from my unfortunate circumstances was not on a comfortable or at all intimate or confidential feeling with my mother …

Like Newton, Victoria found solace from her unhappy childhood in intellectual pursuits, though she didn't share his incommunicative tendencies. The princess was lucky enough to have two good tutors and a facility for languages, which would serve her in good stead since her children and grandchildren later populated most of the thrones of Europe. At the age of five, Victoria acquired a governess, Fräulein Lehzen, who initially was appalled by the outbursts of temper from the little princess, yet observed that she always told the truth and therefore was fond of her. Lehzen declared that she had never seen such a passionate and naughty child. This, combined with Victoria's instinct for truthfulness, is a sure sign of the instinctive left-handed rage which can emerge from the feeling of injustice that comes from being out of kilter with the world. It was a rage that, once she was monarch, she was able to rein in through a combination of self-awareness and powerful self-discipline. Under the stewardship of her governess, Victoria went from a recalcitrant student to an excellent one. As she got older, she acquired a tutor, the Reverend George Davies, who taught her subjects considered more fit for a prince than a princess, such as law, history and other real world matters, such as the technology of the Industrial Revolution which was driving Britain's prosperity. Novels, considered decadent, were banned, though she was allowed to read poetry. By the time she inherited the throne, Victoria could almost be considered a tomboy of the mind.

QUEEN VICTORIA Victoria was only 18 when she became Queen upon the death of William IV in 1837, just old enough to rule on her own without her mother being installed as regent. Physically she was far from

OPPOSITE: COLOURED LITHOGRAPH BY S. P. DENNING, OF PRINCESS VICTORIA AT FOUR YEARS OLD.

PAGE 111: QUEEN VICTORIA AT HER WRITING DESK, C.1878. SPEAKING ONLY GERMAN UNTIL THE AGE OF THREE, VICTORIA LATER BECAME CONVERSANT IN ENGLISH, CHINESE, GREEK, ITALIAN AND FRENCH.

FOLLOWING PAGES: AN ILLUSTRATION FROM 1887, DURING VICTORIA'S GOLDEN JUBILEE, PICTURING HER AT THE START OF HER REIGN IN 1837 AND AS SHE APPEARED 50 YEARS LATER.

E. GRIVAZ

VICTORIA'S LEFTY TRAITS

INTUITIVE Victoria performed best in one-on-one situations and had a talent for finding wise counsel and cultivating passionate friendships which belied the severe countenance of her public face post-Albert. She also proved to be an astute match-maker when it came to marrying her children and grandchildren into the Royal families of Europe.

EMPATHETIC Her ability to understand others proved a great asset in the popularity of Victoria's monarchy, especially in the overseas sections of the British Empire and abroad.

HOT-TEMPERED As a child the princess was famous for her stubbornness and temper and, although as an adult she achieved self-control, signs of this aspect of her character can be found throughout her long life. Some of her hot-headedness manifested itself in her passion for war.

ICONOCLASTIC While the idea of an iconoclastic monarch is perhaps paradoxical, in many ways Victoria broke the mould. Her liberality and tolerance were ideal for an age where the middle class were usurping the aristocracy as the driving force of the nation, and where many of her subjects inhabited foreign lands. The strength of her passion and mourning for Albert was also somewhat iconoclastic given that most royal marriages were made for dynastic rather than romantic reasons. The persistence of her mourning can almost be construed as rebellion against the rules of life.

FANTASIST Victoria was possessed of romantic and sentimental streaks which showed themselves most dramatically in the mourning for her husband Albert.

prepossessing as a monarch. She was just under 1.52 metres tall and on the way to becoming rather stout. Still, she immediately made her mark on the monarchy by asserting her independence from her power-hungry mother and her ambitious adviser John Conroy. Whereas William IV had attempted to remove Lord Melbourne as Prime Minister, Victoria made him her political intimate. Like Joan of Arc, Victoria had an instinctive ability to bend powerful men into believing in her although, unlike Joan, she did have the advantage of her crown. Her masculine education gave her a base from which she could engage with Melbourne, a Liberal whose politics were tolerant and slightly world weary. A widower who knew society and whose wife had had an affair with the poet Byron, Melbourne was enchanted by the enthusiasm Victoria showed for her new job and spent a great deal of time educating her. He wasn't just her Prime Minister but also functioned as an informal private secretary, dinner and after-dinner companion. Victoria had chosen her mentor wisely and his tolerance would inform the rest of her reign.

Melbourne's centrality in Victoria's life was displaced by the Queen's marriage to Albert, son of the Duke of Saxe-Coburg-Gotha, in 1840. On Melbourne's encouragement, Victoria had proposed to Albert as his inferior rank prevented him from doing so. Victoria and Albert proved a good match, a happy and mostly harmonious combination of left-handed female and right-handed male. In addition to having nine children, they effectively ruled (constitutionally, of course) as a team, although Parliament resisted granting Albert any actual titles for a long time. Whereas Queen Victoria was passionate, stubborn and prone to losing her temper, yet tolerant, Albert was more reserved, a scholarly minded man who was a stickler for morals. He really was her right-hand man, a perfect bureaucrat who enjoyed spending his hours writing ministerial minutes. The couple spent their days working side by side at their respective desks. Albert also ran the royal household and for the first time in decades managed to put the finances into the black. Perhaps the highlight of his career, however, was the Great Exhibition of 1851, held in Crystal Palace in Hyde Park, that he conceived to show off the achievements of Britain.

THE GRIEVING WIDOW

Unfortunately Albert also put Victoria into the black on 14 December 1861 when he died. Her grief was powerful and obsessive. It also showed her left-handed proclivity for fantasy. Victoria's fantasy was a sentimental one, and it became one of the dominant flavours of the Victorian era, to be found in the poetry, for instance, of Alfred, Lord Tennyson, but more than anything else embodied in the life of the Queen herself.

Following Albert's death she ordered the preservation of his rooms in the royal homes at Balmoral Castle, Osborne on the Isle of Wight and Windsor. Every evening, Albert's clothes were laid out on his bed and a pitcher of hot water and clean towels were brought in. The routine would

be maintained for the next 40 years and every night she went to her lonely bed with one of his nightshirts and a plaster cast of his arm, while a portrait of Albert hung above his side of the royal bed. Victoria herself adopted the widow's uniform of dressing in black which she would continue to wear for the remaining half of her life. When her daughter Alice was married the year after Albert's death, Victoria told her elder daughter, 'it felt more like a funeral than a wedding' and that it was like 'a dagger is plunged in my bleeding, desolate heart'.

In the years subsequent to Albert's death Victoria engaged in a bout of serious memorialising, composing an *Album Inconsolatium* which contained condolence letters as well as poems and literary musings on the nature of life after death. She commissioned a biographer to write the story of Albert's life. For Theodore Martin, this task would take five volumes and 14 years of his life. An elaborately decorated mausoleum was built in the grounds of Windsor Castle to house Albert's body, and Victoria intended hers to join him there. A national Albert Memorial was commissioned for Hyde Park, to be paid for by the government. Ten years after his death, the Royal Albert Hall was completed. At its opening, Queen Victoria was too overcome to make her speech and her son the Prince of Wales had to step in. In cities all around the British Empire, statues, roads, schools, parks and libraries appeared to immortalise the Prince Consort. It comes as no surprise to learn that Queen Victoria employed mediums to try and make contact with Albert in the afterlife.

This grieving ultimately had a damaging effect on her monarchy. Having been a conspicuous and popular monarch up until that time, as the monuments to Albert multiplied Victoria became more and more reclusive. The initial sympathy of her subjects cooled with the feeling as the

QUEEN VICTORIA AND HER CONSORT, PRINCE ALBERT, PICTURED WITH THEIR NINE CHILDREN IN 1857.

FOLLOWING PAGES: VICTORIA WRITING LETTERS AT A TABLE PILED HIGH WITH DESPATCH BOXES, WITH HER INDIAN SERVANT STANDING BY, 1893.

excessive grieving went on, that their Queen had abandoned them. To some extent she had. Her grieving was fantastic in that it constituted a refusal of reality. As a child, Victoria was known for her tremendous stubbornness, and her extended mourning was evidence of this trait. Like many of the great left-handers in this book, she was prepared to go against the world in order to express her sense of singularity.

WIDOW TO WIDOW Although it could be argued that Victoria had abandoned her public, in private she continued with the work of her monarchy, approving the decisions of Cabinet, following shifts in power in Europe while placing her children into beneficial marriages. For much of the time, Victoria was an interested participant in Britain's affairs of state, though she no longer had the power to exercise her will independently of Parliament. While her forceful character and keen intelligence enabled her to influence political decisions, she was rarely able to make them.

On one occasion, however, she intuitively used her grief to further the harmony between Britain and the United States. On hearing that Abraham Lincoln had been assassinated Victoria, who had already been the subject of several assassination attempts herself, wrote his wife Mary a touching letter:

> Dear Madam, though I am a stranger to you, I cannot remain silent when so terrible a calamity has fallen upon you and your country, and must express personally my deep and heartfelt sympathy with you under the shocking circumstances of your present misfortune. No one can appreciate better than I can, who am myself utterly broken-hearted by the loss of my own beloved husband, who was the light of my life, my stay, my all, what your sufferings must be; and I earnestly pray that you be supported by Him to Whom alone the sorely stricken can look for comfort in this hour of heavy affliction! With the renewed expression of true sympathy, I remain, dear Madam, your sincere friend, Victoria R.

Although the letter seems a bit over the top in a contemporary context, it was a heartfelt condolence and Mary Lincoln was very grateful. The public release of the letter also improved the reputation of Britain in its former colonies. Although Britain had initially seemed to favour the South, Victoria had declared neutrality in the Civil War. Her ability to empathise, from her own experience, with Mary Lincoln did much to erase any residual antipathy left over between the two former enemy states.

LIBERAL QUEEN Victoria's ability to empathise with those who were different from her was a hallmark of her reign, and a trait that left-handers often possess. It helps explain her capacity for friendship with a much older man such as Lord Melbourne. She also enjoyed a profound relationship with another prime minister, Benjamin Disraeli. Disraeli

LEFTY LINKS

1. Victoria's grieving for Albert was both excessive and obsessive. Obsessiveness is a trait many of the people in this book seem to share, although it's hard to know whether it might be related to handedness or is simply that people who achieve great things are likely to have obsessive personalities. Alexander the Great was certainly obsessive in his need to conquer, while Michelangelo's attempts to conquer nature through art displays a similar pathology and Ramses the Great's monument-building program showed a fanatical self-regard. Joan of Arc's adherence to her vision evidences an excessive streak in her character while Newton became so obsessed with a mathematical problem that he forgot to eat. Nietzsche was a philosophical obsessive, while Hendrix invested his obsessiveness in the guitar to the extent that he would rather starve than get a day job.

2. Although Victoria ruled over a period in British history known as the 99-year peace, she was something of a warrior queen during the small wars and skirmishes that punctuated the peace. The major military engagements were the Crimean and Boer wars, while there were a number of rebellions in Britain's colonies that necessitated military intervention. During these times, Victoria was prone to badgering her ministers to distraction. Lord Panmure, Secretary for War during the Crimean campaign, referred to Victoria's thirst for news of the war to a parched traveller in the desert's longing for water. Of course as a nineteenth-century constitutional monarch, Victoria was unable to instigate military action, but one wonders how she might have compared to other lefty conquerors such as Ramses, Alexander, Julius Caesar and Napoleon, with whom at least she shared the distinction of presiding over some of the world's greatest empires.

3. Left-handedness runs in Victoria's family. Contemporary members of the British Royal Family who are left-handed include Prince Charles and Prince William, while King George II and King George VI were also left-handed.

was the first person of Jewish descent to become Britain's Prime Minister (and the last). As a left-handed woman whose first language was German, Victoria knew what it was like to be an outsider. As the ruler of an empire which was composed of disparate peoples, this capacity to empathise with the strange came in handy, most notably when she took on the title of the Empress of India in 1877. Victoria was in many ways a proto-multiculturalist. She didn't believe all the subjects under her dominion needed to be Christian. When she met with subjects from India she enjoyed the exoticism of their native dress. She elevated one of her waiters, Abdul Karim, an Indian Muslim, into the role of one of her most intimate servants and spent many hours learning Hindi from him. He brought his family with him and they established a Muslim enclave at her court. On the other hand, she saw no reason why an educated black man couldn't become an Anglican archbishop.

JUST DON'T CALL ME QUEEN One prime minister who Victoria never got on with was the reformer William Gladstone. This was due to a clash of personality styles as much as disagreement over policies, such as Gladstone's fervent belief in Irish Home Rule and pacificism in matters of foreign policy. Whereas Melbourne and Disraeli appealed to the passionate spirit of Victoria and were romanticised as a consequence, she famously complained that Gladstone 'speaks to me as if I were a public meeting'. As an early biographer Lytton Strachey put it:

> She had no objection to being considered as an institution; she was one and she knew it. But she was a woman too, and to be considered only as an institution—that was unbearable. And thus all Mr Gladstone's zeal and devotion, his ceremonious phrases, his low bows, his punctilious correctitudes, were utterly wasted.

Here we get a sense that Victoria never completely lost the anti-authoritarian streak often found in left-handers. Even though she was the Queen, she preferred people who treated her as a person. Further evidence of this trait can be found from her choice of intimates in the second outwardly gloomy stage of her life: John Brown the high-spirited Scottish highlander who was frequently drunk and treated Victoria without any regal respect at all and the Munshi, Abdul Karim, whose role at court vexed many of her traditionalist aides.

CODA The Victorian era came to an end in 1901 when Victoria died at the home in the Isle of Wight that she and Albert had bought for themselves, and where she often went to escape the formal pressures of the monarchy. The period through which she reigned was the height of British greatness and although the dominant image of her in history is as a stern widow, Victoria was much more than this. A smart operator with an intuitive grasp of politics and family, her left-handed qualities made her a leader whose personality came to characterise an entire period of history.

1832–98

FEW BOOKS OCCUPY SUCH A BELOVED PLACE IN THE COLLECTIVE imagination as Lewis Carroll's *Alice's Adventures in Wonderland* and *Through the Looking Glass*. Tales of a young girl and her adventures in a nonsense world, they have fascinated adults and children alike for more than a century and are as fresh on the page today as the day they were published. The reputation of their creator is rather different. He was a shy and stammering Oxford mathematics don and Anglican clergyman, a conservative with a dull social persona who only came truly alive when writing or in the company of young girls. In this day and age, it's doubtful whether his pursuit of relationships with young girls, which included photographing them naked, would be tolerated. Even in his own era, he was clearly a square peg in a round hole, a classic case of a left-hander whose uniqueness never formed an easy fit with society. Despite being a gifted mathematician and pioneer in the field of photography, he ultimately preferred the transformational logics of his fantasy worlds, which were an imaginative and left-handed revolt against the repressive strictures of his boffinish bachelor existence. His writing has been a major influence, not just on children's literature, but on emerging literary genres, such as fantasy, as well as twentieth-century artistic movements, such as Surrealism and Absurdism.

YOUNG LEWIS Lewis Carroll was born Charles Dodgson in 1832 (Lewis Carroll was only ever his pen name). He was the third child and first boy in a family of 11 children, all of whom would survive until adulthood. His father was a gifted mathematician who had abandoned a promising academic career by becoming a country parson. As a child, Carroll was a comfortable and charismatic presence within his family, yet an awkward stammering child outside. It's possible that this trait may have been linked to his left-handedness, or to the attempt to make him

write with his right, though it is true that stammering (as well as a calling for the clergy and mathematical talent) seemed to run in the Dodgson family. Eight of the 11 Dodgson children stuttered, including six of the girls which, since women seldom stutter, was a conspicuous rarity. Since stuttering most often occurs in people with right-brain hemisphere dominance, this unusual statistic points to a strong predisposition towards right-brain dominance, and thus left-handedness, in the Dodgson family.

Unlike many famous left-handers, Carroll showed academic aptitude from a young age. Taught at home until he was 12, by the age of seven he was reading books such as Bunyan's *Pilgrim's Progress*. At 12 he was sent to a small boarding school, not far from his family rectory, in the Yorkshire spa town of Croft. The real shock to his system came, however, in 1846 when he was sent to the brutal English public school of Rugby, immortalised in Thomas Hughes' novel *Tom Brown's School Days*. The relatively delicate Carroll was not suited to such a haven of bullying and sport, and his left-handed tendency to isolate himself was exacerbated, often for good reason, since it seems he was tormented and possibly even sexually abused by older boys. The only compensation was his continued academic excellence. Carroll won prizes in maths and classics and was rated by his math master, R. B. Mayer, as the best student he had ever taught.

It was only logical perhaps, given his abilities and his family's long line of Anglican clerics, that Carroll would follow his father's footsteps to Christ Church Oxford as a preparatory movement towards a career in the church. (However, although he took holy orders, Carroll remained at Christ Church for more than 47 years without ever being away for a period of more than three months.) As an undergraduate, Carroll continued to win prizes in mathematics. Yet he pursued his subject unevenly due to his capacity to be distracted, often by writing humour. His mind had the left-handed propensity to follow its own avenues of interest, often at the expense of achievable and beneficial goals. He ascribed his failure to win a coveted mathematics scholarship to sheer laziness, but was still good enough to gain a prized Christ Church lectureship in mathematics that would guarantee him an income for the rest of his life.

WORK AND PLEASURE

By all accounts, Carroll found lecturing boring, and his students were bored with his lectures. Although he was passionate about mathematics, his self-consciousness with public speaking, exacerbated by his speech impediment, made him a wooden speaker. Perhaps if he hadn't been forced to write with his right hand, things might have been different, and his undeniable talents would have been realised in terms of equations rather than words. Carroll's father had outlined a career path that involved lecturing at Oxford for a decade or so, before marrying and finding a clerical posting in the church, since Christ Church fellows of the time weren't allowed to be married. However, partly again because of his discomfort with public speaking,

A BOAT BENEATH A SUNNY SKY

This following poetic reminiscence of Carroll's boat trips with the Liddell girls is afflicted with the wistfulness of someone who was never quite at ease with reality:

A boat beneath a sunny sky,
Lingering onward dreamily
In an evening of July–
Children three that nestle near,
Eager eye and willing ear,
Pleased a simple tale to hear–
Long has paled that sunny sky:
Echoes fade and memories die:
Autumn frosts have slain July.
Still she haunts me, phantomwise,
Alice moving under skies
Never seen by waking eyes.
Children yet, the tale to hear,
Eager eye and willing ear,
Lovingly shall nestle near.
In a Wonderland they lie,
Dreaming as the days go by,
Dreaming as the summers die:
Ever drifting down the stream–
Lingering in the golden dream–
Life, what is it but a dream?

OPPOSITE: AN 1865 ILLUSTRATION OF ALICE IN COURT BY JOHN TENNIEL, FROM THE ORIGINAL EDITION OF *ALICE'S ADVENTURES IN WONDERLAND*.

PAGE 125: CHARLES DODGSON (LEWIS CARROLL) POSES IN A 19TH-CENTURY PHOTOGRAPH FROM THE ARCHIVES OF CHRIST CHURCH COLLEGE, OXFORD, WHERE HE LECTURED FOR OVER 47 YEARS.

LEWIS CARROLL'S LEFTY TRAITS

EMPATHETIC Carroll was able to understand how children thought and invent stories and jokes which delighted them.

LATERAL THINKING A master of transformational thinking, Carroll converted logic into nonsense, parodied people and society and generated sufficient absurdity to create entire fantasy worlds, whose whimsy continues to enchant adults and children alike.

SOLITARY Carroll is another famous left-hander whose romantic life was non-existent. He was close to his brothers and sisters, and very fond of a long line of little girls, but his emotional life never seemed to make it into the real world.

ICONOCLASTIC Although in life Carroll was deeply conservative, his imagination was paradoxically anarchic and afflicted with a kind of comic nihilism.

EXPERIMENTAL Carroll pretty much created a whole new genre of comic writing whose influence stretches from the nonsense verse of Edward Lear to the shenanigans of Britain's Monty Python and the Goons, to Douglas Adams' *Hitchhiker's Guide to the Galaxy*. Carroll also demonstrated his experimental side as a pioneer of the photographic arts.

FANTASIST Carroll has written what is arguably the most famous literary fantasy of all time.

OPPOSITE: PHOTOGRAPH BY LEWIS CARROLL OF ALICE LIDDELL, AGED 10, WHO WAS THE INSPIRATION FOR THE CHARACTER ALICE IN HIS BOOKS.

Carroll was deeply ambivalent about the idea of becoming a full-time clergyman. He viewed his academic job as a stepping stone and means of financial support for his real ambitions which were primarily literary. By the end of his first full year of teaching, Carroll wrote in his diary:

> I am weary of lecturing and discouraged. It is thankless, uphill work, goading unwilling men to learning they have no taste for, to the inevitable neglect of others who really want to get on.

Still, he would remain a math lecturer for another 25 years.

Carroll had been writing creatively since a very young age. It was something of a family hobby that Carroll shared with his brothers and sisters, who swapped and competed against each other with poems whose contents were filled with the surreal violence that children love. One can almost imagine the close siblings also getting great satisfaction out of their kind of 'violence' to the words—which caused them so much bother in public due to the stammering—by turning them into nonsense. The rectory in Croft was a hive of creativity with Carroll at the helm, writing and acting out plays, showing off to his sisters with conjuring tricks, perplexing them with riddles, and entreating them to contribute to editions of the family's in-house magazine. The satisfaction Carroll obtained from this period determined the way he would achieve posterity, and the unparalleled happiness he experienced with his young sisters, may be the reason he would enjoy the company of little girls for the remainder of his life.

ALICE During his university years, Carroll contributed to national humour magazines such as *The Comic Times* and *Train*, as well as more local publications such as *The Whitby Gazette*. He was constantly thinking of ways in which he could earn money by writing. The impetus for his great success, however, would come not from the conventional pursuit of a literary career, but from hanging out with the daughters of his effective boss, the Dean of Christ Church, Henry Liddell.

Carroll inveigled his way into friendship with the Liddell children through photography. Like many left-handers, Carroll had an experimental streak and was a pioneer photographer who bought his first camera in 1857. One day that year, he and a friend entered the Deanery garden with the intention of taking photos of Christ Church Cathedral, and ended up taking photos of the Liddell children, Harry, Lorina, Alice and Edith, instead. After this, Carroll became a frequent visitor to the Liddells, often behind Mrs Liddell's back, though it is unclear as to whether snobbery or maternal instincts were the reason for her uneven resistance to Carroll's increasing presence.

Carroll seems to have won over Mrs Liddell's confidence, however, since she allowed her children to go on boating excursions with him over several summers. During these excursions Carroll would make up stories to

entertain his young charges. On one journey in 1862, Carroll made up a story about a girl called Alice who was bored on a picnic with her big sister, went searching for adventure, fell down a rabbit hole and found herself in an alternative universe. Alice was so delighted by this story that she begged Carroll to write it down so it wouldn't be forgotten. Carroll duly did and three years later, after expanding the original 18,000 word story into 35,000, *Alice's Adventures in Wonderland* received its first outing in book form.

The book is a fantastic tale that remains delightful reading today. In the 150 years since its publication, there has been a mass of literature designed to try and explain its symbolism. For its original audience, however, it was primarily a brilliant and witty transformation of a world and people they actually knew. One of the skills for which left-handers are renowned is their ability to transform things. It makes sense. The left-hander, living in a right-handed world, is a natural adapter from a very early age. Moreover, this natural propensity for adaptation and transformation can escape the original context of handedness and replicate itself in any number of activities that the left-hander might choose to engage in. Therefore, we find Lewis Carroll writing nonsense, Jimi Hendrix expanding the sonic palette of the guitar, while Leonardo was obsessing with the adaptations necessary for humans to be able to fly.

Lewis Carroll was an adult who preferred the world of children, since his childhood was where he himself had spent his happiest days. Of course, to return to childhood was impossible. Yet it was possible to create a world that delighted children and earnt their friendship. It was a vicarious return to childhood, yet simultaneously one that dabbled with impossibility. In many ways Carroll's obsessive left-handed temperament was mounting a protest against the inevitable trajectories of his own life.

We can see this in *Alice's Adventures in Wonderland*, from the very outset when Alice falls down the rabbit hole. Faced with a door too small, Alice drinks from a bottle that says 'DRINK ME' which makes her 10 inches tall, only to find that she has left the key for the little door on a table she can no longer reach. After chastising herself, she finds a piece of cake that advises her to 'EAT ME' and grows to nine feet tall, until her head hits the roof. Having obtained the key, after tears and some consternation, Alice then manages to shrink herself to the right size by putting on one of the White Rabbit's gloves. Having done this she is able to go through the door and into the garden. It's a classic example of how Carroll sets up a fictional world where the impossible transformations, such as the reversal of growth, that he desires, are able to occur. In the sequel, *Through the Looking Glass and What Alice Found There* (first published in 1871), Alice encounters a flustered White Queen who lives backwards, something Carroll would have liked to have been able to do himself. Humpty Dumpty is also on hand to advise Alice that, with help, she could have done the superior thing and stopped getting older when she was still seven instead of seven and a half.

Alice's Adventures in Wonderland and *Through the Looking Glass* are fantastic stories based around anarchic transformations of people, things and processes. For instance, the poem that Alice recites, *How doth the little crocodile*, is a parody of Isaac Watts' moralistic nursery rhyme, *Against Idleness and Mischief*, which begins, 'How doth the little busy bee'. Similarly, many of the characters in Alice are bizarre transpositions. The characters who feature in Chapter Three are the original members of the boating expedition: Lory (Lorina), Alice (Alice), the Eaglet (Edith) and Duck (Carroll's friend, the Reverend Robinson Duckworth). Carroll himself features as the Dodo, a self-deprecating joke on his tendency, because of his stutter, to introduce himself as Do-Do-Dodgson.

These books are masterpieces of transformation for transformation's sake. Moral poems become absurd poems, characters are lampooned and violence resounds with the Red Queen's continual cry of 'Off with their Heads'. Logic itself is rendered absurd by the bizarre axioms set out in the book. The characters argue ludicrous points, whose wit consists precisely in the fact that they are both absurd and logical. The left-handed capacity for transformation breeds like bunny rabbits in these works.

THROUGH THE LOOKING GLASS

A particularly interesting aspect in the sequel to *Alice's Adventures in Wonderland* is the way that Alice enters the alternate reality. She is sitting in a chair talking to her kitten, when she begins to imagine what the world is like through the mirror on the mantel. Without really knowing why she is doing it, she climbs up there to look closer, only to find the mirror dissolving before her and allowing her to cross into its alternate realm. The idea of a mirror world is, of course, one where left becomes right. As a left-hander and pioneer photographer, Carroll was fascinated by these inversions. Soon after Alice enters the looking glass world, she is confronted by the poem *Jabberwocky*. Initially, she can't read it. Then she realises that it's in mirror writing—the kind of writing sometimes used by left-handers, most notably Leonardo da Vinci. Unsurprisingly, she soon adapts and is able to read the poem. Yet, it is far from the first adaptation that Alice, in this adventure, will have to make.

It's as if Alice were entering a world that is both a left-handed and a mirror world, a bizarre chessboard where the subversive logic of Lewis Carroll is allowed to roam free. Like her adventure down the rabbit hole, the left-handed mirror world Alice enters belongs to the impossible. While not a Utopia—Alice spends much of her sojourn there either confused or in tears—it is a world of wit and energy that offers escape, if not respite, from the rules and repressive social codes of Victorian England. It's the left-handed capacity for transformation taken to the extreme by a man who, despite his external conservatism, never fully fitted into the adult world.

LEFTY LINKS

1. Carroll was a naturally gifted mathematician. Although he tended more to the verbal or symbolic aspects of mathematics, rather than the visual-spatial aspects such as geometry, his mathematical ability is connected to his left-handedness. Mathematics is a field known for its surfeit of left-handers. Other brilliant lefty mathematicians include Isaac Newton, Leonardo da Vinci, Alan Turing, Bill Gates and Marie Curie.

2. According to research, right-brain-dominant children are more likely to develop speech impediments as children. Alan Turing was another left-handed mathematician with a stammer. The guitarist Jimi Hendrix, whose father tried to force him to use his right hand, also stammered, as did the left-handed English King George VI. When George VI was a child, his father, George V, ordered that a long string be attached to his left hand and that he should be encouraged to use his right hand by having the string on his left hand pulled violently whenever he tried to use it. Such incidences support a theory based on the fact that stammers are caused by early childhood trauma.

1835–1910

Mark Twain is one of America's greatest authors, and the first to write books in American colloquial English. Twain was a man who cultivated experience. His restless spirit saw him lead a varied life and, in addition to being a novelist, he was also a lecturer, journalist, travel writer, miner, printer, Mississippi steamboat pilot and failed inventor. In this he was the classic left-hander, a divergent thinker and dabbler whose many experiences found value through their deployment in the subject matter of his books. The popularity of his books and his quick-witted, peppery personality endeared him to the world and, along with authors such as Charles Dickens, he was at the pinnacle of a late-nineteenth century vogue for celebrity novelists. For some time, Twain carried the reputation of being the funniest man in the world. Yet in his view, laughter was only ever a kind of compensation for its sufferings. His personal life was marred by the death of his wife and three of his four children and led to the bleak and aphoristic conclusion that 'there is no laughter in heaven'. However, his humour, in books such as *The Adventures of Tom Sawyer* and *The Adventures of Huckleberry Finn*, struck powerful blows for racial equality and the commonsense of the everyman against the pretensions of 'society'. The iconoclastic intention of his humour was an embodiment of both the left-hander as rebel and the ethos of life in the American West. The vivid worlds he re-created in his books surge with human energy and have delighted millions of readers and continue to do so today.

SAMUEL CLEMENS Samuel Langhorne Clemens was born in Florida, Missouri, but he moved to Hannibal, Missouri on the western banks of the Mississippi as a small child. His father was a socially respectable, but financially disastrous, judge and Clemens' childhood was one of genteel poverty, exacerbated by his father's death, which saw

Clemens forced to leave school at the tender age of 11 to begin an apprenticeship as a journeyman printer.

It was in the printery, rather than in the constricted confines of the classroom, where Clemens' love affair with the English language flourished. He read everything he could get his hands on and soaked up the earthy masculine speech of his seniors. As a left-hander, the young Clemens would have suffered in the classroom. In the nineteenth century, and for much of the twentieth century, picking up a pen with your left hand in an American school was likely to end up with a rap over the knuckles or cuff to the ears. Persistent lefties often had their left hand tied to the desk or behind their backs. As a printer's apprentice, Clemens was able to do typesetting, a process where metal letters are placed on the press, then inked, before the paper passes through. Unlike in the classroom, in the business environment of the printery, it didn't matter whether typesetting—or writing for that matter—was done with the left or right hand, as long as it got done.

Clemens' school experiences left a definite mark on him. We can see this by the way he draws upon them in *The Adventures of Tom Sawyer*. Like many lefties who have suffered stigmatisation for their natural inclinations, Clemens developed a rebellious and independent streak that was harnessed to a ethic of fairness, whose frame of reference lay beyond the conspicuous hypocrisy of authority figures. It was a natural position to adopt for an intuitive person who realised that the world didn't quite fit, and was thus compelled to find, by trial and error, his own set of values.

In Clemens' case, this rebelliousness manifested itself in a preference for natural humanity over the formal strictures of society. Like Tom Sawyer, the young Clemens was known for his unruly behaviour and for only turning up to school in bad weather. If the sun was shining, he was to be found outside, playing with his friends, including the socially disreputable son of the town drunk, Tom Blankenship. Together they explored the islands in the Mississippi River near their town, or the massive cave network just out of Hannibal. At other times they went hunting and fishing. These experiences seemed far more valuable to the young lefty author than the dry abstractions being taught in the classroom or at Sunday school. If Clemens was a kid today, like some of the other lefties in this book, he would probably be diagnosed with attention-deficit hyperactivity disorder and be on Ritalin.

TOM SAWYER Twain's value system is strongly apparent in his fictional boyhood alter ego, the hero of *The Adventures of Tom Sawyer*, which chronicles a series of events in a town rather similar to the one where Clemens grew up. The book begins with Tom in trouble. He has played truant and gone swimming, yet is lying to his aunt, who is subtly figuring him out, unaware that Tom has already cottoned on to her strategy. She surreptitiously checks his shirt which is dry, then Tom sidesteps the question of his hair still being wet by telling her how he put it under a faucet to cool down. Instantly suspicious, his aunt then checks the collar of his shirt to see if it is still sewn on. It is and Tom has almost gotten away with it, except Sid, his young, goody two-shoes half-brother, squeals on him by pointing out the fact that the thread has changed colour from white to black since Aunt Polly sewed it on. Tom is a naturally good but rebellious boy, who thinks laterally, if not always successfully, to avoid getting into trouble.

The episode concludes with the observation that Tom, 'was not the Model Boy of the village. He knew the model boy very well though—and loathed him.' To be a model boy is to conform to the entire set of right-handed values and achieve social propriety well before one's time. For Tom and Twain, the ideal is to be found in the opposite direction. In *The Adventures of Tom Sawyer* we also meet Huck Finn, who Twain argued was based on his friend Tom Blankenship:

> In Huckleberry Finn I have drawn Tom Blankenship exactly as he was. He was ignorant, unwashed, insufficiently fed; but he had as good a heart as ever any boy had. His liberties were totally unrestricted. He was the only really independent person—boy or man—in the community, and by consequence he was tranquilly and continuously happy and envied by the rest of us. And as his society was forbidden us by our parents the prohibition trebled and quadrupled its value, and therefore we sought and got more of his society than any other boy's.

This statement eloquently summarises Twain's left-handed value system. The abstract world of school is less interesting than the tangible realities of nature. Rules are to be disregarded if they are stupid, while the ultimate arbiter of values is the natural feeling of the heart—the right hemisphere of the brain is, after all, also primarily responsible for emotional processing. Independence from society is also valued: a person being able to live in his or her natural condition is the happiest, something lefties also learn when they begin to be socialised by school. Of course it's possible for right-handers to share these feelings but, because the social world is in so many ways a right-handed world, the lefty is likely to feel this situation more keenly.

EXPERIENCE After working in the Hannibal printery, Clemens left Missouri to work in Philadelphia and New York before returning to St Louis, Missouri, in 1857 where he became an apprentice Mississippi steamboat pilot, earning his licence a year later. His job was to read the shifting waters of the great river for depth, snags, reefs and mudbanks as the steamboats paddled their way between St Louis and New Orleans. In his memoir of this time, *Life on the Mississippi* (1883), he wrote:

LEFTY LINKS

1. When Huck says 'All right, then, I'll GO to hell', when he decides to help the runaway slave Jim, he really is taking a left-handed path. The term 'left-handed path' is often used to describe religions which place themselves in opposition to the mainstream, often with links to occult practices. Originating from a dangerous form of tantrism that embraced the breach of Hindu taboos, the term was adopted by European occultists such as Madame Blavatsky and the Satanist Aleister Crowley. In recent times, the left-handed path has come to mean a more general individualistic, anti-conventional approach to spiritual/ethical living on the roads less travelled.

2. Twain's greatest hero was fellow lefty Joan of Arc. Although the critics begged to differ, Twain thought his novel *The Personal Recollections of Joan of Arc* (1895) was the best he ever wrote. He also thought that Joan was the most amazing person to have lived. In his essay, 'Saint Joan of Arc', Twain wrote, 'In the history of the human intellect, untrained, inexperienced, and using only its birthright equipment of untried capacities, there is nothing which approaches this. Joan of Arc stands alone, and must continue to stand alone, by reason of the unfellowed fact that in the things wherein she was great she was so without shade or suggestion of help from preparatory teaching, practice, environment, or experience. There is no one to compare her with, none to measure her by; for all others among the illustrious grew towards their high place in an atmosphere and surroundings which discovered their gift to them and nourished it and promoted it, intentionally or unconsciously . . . Taking into account, as I have suggested before, all the circumstances—her origin, youth, sex, illiteracy, early environment, and the obstructing conditions under which she exploited her high gifts and made her conquests in the field and before the courts that tried her for her life—she is easily and by far the most extraordinary person the human race has ever produced.'

Be good + you will be lonesome.

The face of the water, in time, became a wonderful book—a book that was a dead language to the uneducated passenger, but which told its mind to me without reserve, delivering its most cherished secrets as clearly as if it uttered them with a voice. And it was not a book to be read once and thrown aside, for it had a new story to tell every day.

This job of 'reading the river', which involved acute observation honed by experience and intuition, was ideally suited to Clemens' lefty temperament. He relished the aura of being a river sage and, if the Civil War hadn't intervened to close down much of the river traffic, and his younger brother, Henry, hadn't been killed in an explosion while working on a steamboat, Clemens may well have remained on the river for the rest of his life. Being a riverboat pilot certainly helped Clemens hone his observational skills, of both people and his natural surroundings. Like Leonardo da Vinci's belief in the importance of basing one's art directly on nature, Clemens believed in the priority of the senses, of the value of interpreting the real world, writing about the people he knew in the language they spoke. Clemens also derived his more famous nom de plume from this period of his life. 'Mark Twain' was the call the pilots used to indicate the depth of two fathoms (3.7 metres), meaning the boat was safe from running aground.

After a brief interlude as a member of Confederate militia, Clemens escaped the Civil War by heading west with his older brother, Orion, who had been appointed Secretary for the Nevada Territories. He embraced the possibilities of frontier experience, including a period living in a miners' camp, in an unsuccessful attempt to find his fortune in gold at California's Jackass Hill.

Having failed as a miner, Clemens reverted to journalism and increasingly made his living by transforming his experiences into humorous pieces signed 'Mark Twain', which were published in newspapers and magazines across America. His rising popularity as a humorist led to a tour to Europe, which he popularised in his second book, *Innocents Abroad*, which remains the number one selling American travel book. By this stage, those who didn't already know Samuel Clemens never would. To the world, Clemens had effectively become Mark Twain and it was Mark Twain who would mine the experiences of his former self.

So how is all this related to the fact that Twain was left-handed? One thing left-handers have been proven to be good at is adapting or transforming objects for new uses. This is not surprising, given that everyday objects and tasks, such as scissors, or writing in a notebook, can demand some form of adaptation. On a more profound level, there is also evidence to suggest that the right hemisphere of the brain is more responsible for new associations such as finding new uses for things, or navigating new places, while the left hemisphere is more involved in the maintenance of everyday associations. This might partly explain the restless hunger for

'ALL MODERN AMERICAN LITERATURE COMES FROM ONE BOOK BY MARK TWAIN CALLED *HUCKLEBERRY FINN*. AMERICAN WRITING COMES FROM THAT. THERE IS NOTHING BEFORE. THERE HAS BEEN NOTHING AS GOOD SINCE.'

ERNEST HEMINGWAY

OPPOSITE: MARK TWAIN ON THE DECK OF A STEAMBOAT, 1901. IN 1857, CLEMENS BECAME AN APPRENTICE MISSISSIPPI STEAMBOAT PILOT. HIS NOM DE PLUME, 'MARK TWAIN', WAS A TERM USED BY RIVERBOAT PILOTS TO MEAN 'TWO FATHOMS'.

MARK TWAIN'S LEFTY TRAITS

INTUITIVE Twain was a powerful believer in the primacy of the naturally good heart as a way for finding one's way in the world. In his own life he followed his impulses, even if it did lead to mistakes.

EMPATHETIC As a writer, one of Twain's strengths was his ability to see the action from the perspective of his characters. This is one reason why *Huckleberry Finn* is a far better book about anti-slavery than other works, such as Harriet Beecher Stowe's *Uncle Tom's Cabin*, which viewed the issue as a matter of Christian morality, without letting go of racial distance. It is Huck's actual friendship with Jim that determines his moral choices.

LATERAL THINKING In his early life, Twain had many careers. Even when he became a wealthy author he invested in a number of madcap business schemes which eventually cost him his fortune, forcing him to embark on an around-the-world lecture tour in 1895, to rescue himself from bankruptcy. His humour is also based on surprising combinations and ironies, again an example of lateral thinking.

HOT-TEMPERED Twain's dry and sardonic sense of humour could be biting and his quotes and aphorisms have a decidedly peppery flavour. However, he was also prone to losing it completely for stupid reasons. For example, a visitor turned up to Twain's Hartford Connecticut house to find him throwing all of his extensive shirt collection out of a second floor window. The reason—because he had found ONE shirt where a missing button hadn't been sewn on.

ICONOCLASTIC Twain changed the whole direction of American literature by writing in the colloquial voice.

SELF-TAUGHT Twain learnt by experience and throughout his life preferred this form of learning over the dry abstractions of learning in the classroom.

EXPERIMENTAL Twain liked to try new things. Many of his experiments in life, business and art were unsuccessful, yet this very openness was a crucial part of the way he became one of the first great American authors.

new experience in Clemens' character which is evidenced by his many careers, his travels and the multitude of places he chose to live in. It's also interesting in terms of the way that Clemens became Mark Twain. One of the striking things about most lists of famous left-handers is how many left-handed actors there are. While actors rarely change the world (hence their relatively small representation in this book), they are particularly good at changing themselves. Actors earn their living by finding new uses for themselves through their transformation into different characters. In both his non-fiction books like *Life on the Mississippi* and his novels such as *The Adventures of Tom Sawyer*, as well as his renowned performances on the lecture circuit, Twain showed a similar ability to transform himself and his experiences into richly humorous situations that were based on events from his actual life.

HUCKLEBERRY FINN By the time Twain wrote his masterpiece, *The Adventures of Huckleberry Finn*, in 1884, he was wealthy and living in Hartford, Connecticut. He had escaped from his boisterous frontier days to marry a frail, deeply religious and socially superior woman named Olivia Langdon. Together they had four children of whom only one, Clara, would survive her father. For the unruly boy turned riverboat pilot, turned miner, turned western humorist, it was another work of self-transformation, which included the adopting of the white suit as his everyday dress. Yet, this life change was also about setting himself up in a world where he could feel iconoclastic, as he settled down to write the majority of his books that were based on the comparatively rude joys of his former life.

Huckleberry Finn was a powerfully iconoclastic book. The language used in the dialogue between Huck and the runaway slave, Jim—the protagonists of *Huckleberry Finn*—is not the kind of English Twain would have learnt at school. Nor is it the language he would have been likely to use in the genteel environs of his Connecticut home. It is the kind of language Twain knew from his childhood and youth. Until he wrote *Huckleberry Finn* it wasn't the kind of language you'd be able to find in a book. Unsurprisingly, the book was banned from many libraries. The Concord Library in Massachusetts, home to some of America's early literary culture, banned it because it was 'trashy and vicious', while the Brooklyn Public Library banned it in 1902 because it used 'scratched' as well as 'itched', and 'sweat' instead of 'perspiration'. Here we can see the division between the earthy language favoured by Twain and the more abstract preferences of America's literary elite, which mirrors the distinction between experiential versus schooled knowledge, seen in both *The Adventures of Tom Sawyer* and *Huckleberry Finn*. Many agreed with him. Twain wrote to his publisher that the Concord ban should sell them another 20,000 copies of the book.

Of course it's not just the language which is iconoclastic in *Huckleberry Finn*. One of the most radical things about the book is the fact that Huck,

the barely schooled son of the local drunk, is the book's narrator. While such characters often appeared in books, it was extremely rare to find them telling the story directly. Throughout his book, Huck Finn has the moral dilemma of whether to turn Jim in so he is sent back to his owner, Miss Watson, or to help Jim's quest for freedom. Again, Huck is faced with a choice between the concrete and the abstract, between natural goodness versus social codes, between Jim—whom he grows to recognise as a human being—or the antebellum moral code, which the Christian religion used to justify slavery. After being puzzled by this dilemma for most of the book, Huck eventually takes the left-handed path and commits to helping Jim with the exclamation, 'All right, then, I'll GO to hell'. As always, Twain comes down in favour of the unorthodox informed by the natural goodness of the heart.

Huckleberry Finn ends with Huck saying, 'But I reckon I got to light out for the Territory ahead of the rest, because Aunt Sally she's going to adopt me and civilise me, and I can't stand it. I been there before.'

Friedrich Nietzsche

1844–1900

ALTHOUGH LARGELY UNHERALDED IN HIS LIFETIME, NIETZSCHE HAS become one of the foremost figures in the Western philosophical tradition. He wrote his philosophy in a witty, iconoclastic style and, like a true left-handed rebel, refused the logical convenience of a philosophical system. He is primarily remembered for his notion of the 'Ubermensch', or 'Superman', and his philosophy of extreme individualism and self-overcoming was particularly influential in the emergence of Existentialism. His idea of the 'Will to Power', which he developed from his engagement with the work of the German philosopher Arthur Schopenhauer, was misappropriated by the Nazis (Nietzsche had contempt for anti-Semitism) and was also crucial in the thinking of the French post-structuralist movement, which is the dominant philosophical fashion of today.

Nietzsche was a man with appalling health, but immense intellectual vanity—and the genius to justify it. He lived the latter part of his life on the hop, stopping at various destinations in Germany, France, Switzerland and Italy, lodging in cheap boarding houses, where he worked far beyond the limitations of his delicate health. The close circle of friends who remained devoted to him, despite his increasingly erratic behaviour, were prone to talk of him in awe and pity as a man who had left society behind. Freud would describe him having 'more penetrating knowledge of himself than any man who ever lived or was likely to live'.

The stories of great lefties in this book are often those of people going against the tide, using their lefty uniqueness to resist the crushing forces of convention in order that their innate genius may flower. The tragic tale of Nietzsche is one of the most powerful examples. Despite an outer life that, at times, seems hardly a life at all, his philosophical texts broke radically new ground in the field and continue to be vital to our conception of the world today. His writing style, with its use of pithy aphorisms and

lively fragments, was equally revolutionary and influential, as were concepts such as the 'Eternal Recurrence', the 'Will to Power' and 'Superman'. He proselytised an ambition of the self overcoming itself, and could almost be considered the patron philosopher of the lefty.

EARLY NIETZSCHE

Nietzsche's father was the last in a line of Lutheran pastors, and died when Nietzsche was only five. The following year his younger brother, Ludwig, also died. Much of Nietzsche's childhood was spent at his paternal grandmother's house in Naumburg, at the time part of Prussia in eastern Germany. He lived there with his mother, sister, grandmother and two unmarried aunts, the only male in the house.

In contrast to many of the left-handers featured in these pages, the signs of brilliance in Nietzsche were present from an early age. His academic performance in school was conspicuously excellent and earnt him entry to Schulpforta, one of the most prestigious boarding schools in Prussia.

After graduating from Pforta, in 1864 Nietzsche began to study theology at the University of Bonn. After one semester, he arrived at his first great iconoclastic moment: he lost faith in God and abandoned theology (as well as a family tradition) to study philology. His mother was horrified. He followed his philology Professor, Friedrich Ritschl, to the University of Leipzig the next year, where he also discovered the work of Arthur Schopenhauer in a second-hand book store.

With Ritschl's support, Nietzsche was appointed Professorship of Philology at the University of Basel (Switzerland) at the almost unheard of age of 24. At the time, he had neither completed his doctorate nor teaching certificate, usually the prerequisites for such a position. Nonetheless, Nietzsche proved a popular teacher and more than competent at his job, although he was somewhat frustrated by the narrow constraints of philology as an academic field. His early writings while he taught at Basel showed the persistence of his iconoclastic streak. *The Birth of Tragedy* (1872) caused controversy because it attacked the conventional wisdoms on how Ancient Greek culture operated. *Untimely Meditations* (1876) attacked German cultural philistinism. *Human, All Too Human* (1878) saw the origin of Nietzsche's epigrammatic style, a groundbreaking approach to the writing of philosophy, which was normally written with dry (often dull) rigour.

After 10 years at Basel, bedevilled by bad health and the inability to fit into the strictures of a normal life, Nietzsche quit his professorship. He became a wandering philosopher, moving from place to place around continental Europe, staying only a few months at a time in each location, surviving on meagre rations. It was during this phase of his life that he wrote most of his famous works. Nietzsche abandoned his German citizenship and became a stateless person, unbound by belonging to any institution. His solitary existence is almost the ultimate expression of the kind of lefty who is unable to conform to the dictates of society. Elements

EXTRACT FROM *THUS SPAKE ZARATHUSTRA*

Zarathustra, however, looked at the people and wondered. Then he spake thus: Man is a rope stretched between the animal and the Superman—a rope over an abyss. A dangerous crossing, a dangerous wayfaring, a dangerous looking-back, a dangerous trembling and halting. What is great in man is that he is a bridge and not a goal: what is lovable in man is that he is an over-going and a down-going. I love those that know not how to live except as down-goers, for they are the over-goers. I love the great despisers, because they are the great adorers, and arrows of longing for the other shore. I love those who do not first seek a reason beyond the stars for going down and being sacrifices, but sacrifice themselves to the earth, that the earth of the Superman may hereafter arrive. I love him who liveth in order to know, and seeketh to know in order that the Superman may hereafter live. Thus seeketh he his own down-going. I love him whose soul is deep even in the wounding, and may succumb through a small matter: thus goeth he willingly over the bridge. I love him whose soul is so overfull that he forgetteth himself, and all things are in him: thus all things become his down-going. I love him who is of a free spirit and a free heart: thus is his head only the bowels of his heart; his heart, however, causeth his down-going. I love all who are like heavy drops falling one by one out of the dark cloud that lowereth over man: they herald the coming of the lightning, and succumb as heralds. Lo, I am a herald of the lightning, and a heavy drop out of the cloud: the lightning, however, is the Superman.

OPPOSITE: UNLIKE OTHER FAMOUS LEFT-HANDERS, NIETZSCHE SHOWED HIMSELF TO BE A BRILLIANT STUDENT FROM A YOUNG AGE.

PAGE 141: NIETZSCHE BECAME A UNIVERSITY PROFESSOR AT THE AGE OF 24.

NIETZSCHE'S LEFTY TRAITS

INTUITIVE Nietzsche worked without a philosophical system and Sigmund Freud credited him with having more knowledge of himself than anyone, something that can only be achieved through intuition rather than logic.

HOT-TEMPERED Nietzsche was scathing of his enemies and prone to being over-demanding of his friends and family. However most of his rage was distilled and delivered in the brilliant iconoclasm of his work which embodied the Dionysian principle. As Zarathustra said, 'I love the great despisers, because they are the great adorers'.

SOLITARY Nietzsche considered marriage, but the only time he proposed he was rebuffed. He spent huge amounts of time by himself, something that was amplified by the fact that he rarely stayed in the same place for more than a couple of months.

ICONOCLASTIC One of the great iconoclasts of all time, Nietzsche once wrote, '[I am] a man who wishes nothing more than daily to lose some reassuring belief, who seeks and finds his happiness in this daily greater liberation of the mind. It may be that I want to be even more of a freethinker than I can be.'

EXPERIMENTAL The aphoristic style of philosophy that Nietzsche evolved was a revolutionary new way of writing philosophical texts. To a large extent he was also the guinea pig of his own philosophy.

of it are noticeable in lefty geniuses as diverse as Michelangelo, Beethoven and Joan of Arc, but none seems to have been possessed by the drive for individuality as strongly as Nietzsche. For this reason he has been an inspiration to legions of social rebels since, including Jean Paul Sartre, rock star Jim Morrison, author Henry Miller and Beatnik writer Jack Kerouac.

THE BIRTH OF TRAGEDY (1872) One of the key lefty moments in Nietzsche's philosophy was in his first book, *The Birth of Tragedy*, when he offered a radical and romantic reinterpretation of Ancient Greek and European Culture. At the time, the prevailing view in Europe was that Ancient Greece was the highlight of civilisation, a society predicated upon the complementary values of rationality and serenity. Nietzsche turned this on its head by arguing that this 'Apollonian' (the ancient Greek sun god) rationality, whose most conspicuous proselytisers were post-Socratic philosophers, such as Plato and Aristotle, had been preceded by a darker creative energy which Nietzsche characterised as Dionysian—after Dionysus, the ancient Greek god of wine and intoxication, also the patron of the stage. For Nietzsche, the Dionysian was an instinct-driven, wild, chaotic, amoral and natural energy that was the well-spring not just of creativity but of life itself. Against this he contrasted the Apollonian forces of rational order, peace and maintaining the status quo.

The Dionysian is the energy of the rebel, the individualist and the artist. It also speaks to the left-hander, whereas the Apollonian, with its social order and rational harmony, speaks to the right. Nietzsche was a fan of this Dionysian energy and he thought Ancient Greek civilisation started to decline as soon as the Apollonian energies of order came to dominate it.

Nietzsche's interpretation of the Dionysian is classic left-handed philosophy. We can see the Dionysian principle in Beethoven, for instance, who initiated the shift from the neatness of classical music to the craggy, creative grandeur of the Romantic era. It can also be found in the angry touch-play of John McEnroe and the nomadic wine, dine and conquer lifestyle of Alexander the Great. As Dionysus was also the Greek god of the stage, it is perhaps no surprise that so many actors are left-handed. Left-handers are often to be found at the epicentre of change. Because the world never completely fits their nature, they have less investment in the status quo to begin with. Because they are used to adapting and transforming to cope with a right-handed world, left-handers have a instinctive affinity with the forces that anticipate, instigate and facilitate change. And they often also seem to have an affinity with the creative rage that is also part of the Dionysian spirit.

SUPERMAN Nietzsche's masterpiece, *Thus Spake Zarathustra, A Book for All and None* (1883–85), was written once he had retired from Basel and begun his life as a wanderer. It was a remarkable work illustrating

Nietzsche's left-handed brilliance at synthesising characters, stories, imagery and philosophical style from a range of thought traditions including the Bible, pre-socratic philosophy, Zoroastrianism and Romanticism, to create a radically new philosophical movement. It is written from the perspective of Zarathustra (Zoroaster), a Persian prophet who lived in Persia about 1000 years before the birth of Christ. Like Nietzsche, Zarathustra had trouble gaining acceptance for his philosophy and spent much of his life as a wandering thinker in self-imposed exile. The religion he founded is notable for its lack of hierarchy and the emphasis it places on individual free will. (It is not known whether Zarathustra was left- or right-handed.)

The most famous idea of *Thus Spake Zarathustra* was the concept of the Ubermensch, literally meaning 'Over-man', but usually translated into English as 'Superman'. Nietzsche believed that human life was dominated by what he characterised as the Will to Power. Yet those who succeeded in this quest were not so much the politicians, conquerors and despots who achieved power over others, but those who managed to achieve power over themselves. Only these people, thought Nietzsche—and there was no doubt that he considered himself among them—were able to rise beyond their humanity. Zarathustra, as the unpopular prophet who eschews society to do battle with himself in the wilderness, is the epitome of the Nietzschean superman.

Arguably, Nietzsche's formulation of the Superman is a particularly lefty notion of greatness. Because the order of society is traditionally stacked against lefties, they often prefer to do battle with themselves, relishing the challenge of the Nietzschean overcoming of the self. Beethoven's deaf composing is a powerful example of self-overcoming, as were the not always successful, on-court antics of John McEnroe—a manifestation of a struggle that was not so much about the opponent, but of conquering one's own inner demons. The perfectionism of Leonardo and Michelangelo is another instance of the Superman mode of struggle. At a certain level of greatness, lefty geniuses become their only competitor. In his maturity, Beethoven knew no artistic equal, just as Alexander had no rival. However, the struggle to become a Superman is more likely to generate intensity than to end in success, something Nietzsche eventually discovered to his cost.

THE TRAGEDY OF MADNESS We talk today of extreme sports. Nietzsche was a man who practised extreme thinking. A solo explorer of the mind, his philosophy was radical and is widely considered to have marked a conceptual break between the nineteenth and twentieth century. He remains one of the most vital influences in modern philosophy today. However, like many who base-jump from buildings or climb the world's highest mountains, his extremism would eventually cost him his health and sanity. Lefties seem to stand a better chance of being geniuses than righties, but they also seem to have a greater chance of being insane, particularly in terms of schizophrenia. Nietzsche combined both of these statistical likeli-hoods. After a writing career of yet-to-be acknowledged brilliance, one day, while he was in Turin in Italy in 1889, he threw his arms around the neck of a horse being whipped by its coachman and collapsed. When he was revived, he wrote a series of missives to his friends and the political leaders of Europe signed by two of the characters in his philosophical texts, Dionysius and The Crucified—clearly schizoid behaviour. One of the great ironies was that Nietzsche's breakdown came just at the point when his work was begin-ning to gain acceptance. He would live for another 10 years, first in an asylum, then under the care of his mother, then sister, while gradually deteriorating into catatonia. He spent virtually all of the last years of his life mute and lying in bed.

Along with Isaac Newton and John McEnroe, Nietzsche also had an aggressively paranoid streak. Another famous paranoid left-hander is former Sex Pistols lead singer John Lydon, who coined the very Nietzschean mantra 'Anger is an Energy'.

SCHIZOTYPE THINKING, CREATIVITY AND THE LEFTY

Nietzsche may well have been what we call a schizotypal person. These are people who have tendencies towards the schizophrenic condition, but don't spend most of their lives afflicted by schizophrenia. According to research conducted by psychologists Brad Folley and Sohee Park at Vanderbilt University in Nashville, Tennese, while the thoughts of schizo-phrenic people are usually too disorganised to think creatively in a productive fashion, schizotype people prove to be better creative thinkers than either schizophrenics or the normal control subjects. This result was based on a test that measured people's ability to invent new uses for familiar kitchen objects. While the schizophrenics (medicated) and normal control subjects exhibited roughly the same degree of inventive-ness, they were outstripped by the schizotype thinkers. When the neural activity involved in this process was measured, the researchers discov-ered that the schizoptypes had a much stronger concentration of activity in the right hemispheres of their brains. It is also proven that left-handers are more likely to be schizophrenic. Further research has shown that schizotype people are more likely to be either left-handed or mixed-handed. In other words, this is more scientific evidence for the link between creativity and leftiness. The re-use of familiar objects is also a classic mark of the adaptability and flexibility frequently found in the thinking of great left-handers, from the unorthodox battle tactics of Alexander, the ability of Isaac Newton to translate an apple falling to the ground beside him into the theory of gravity, or Bill Gates to see the potential for Windows in the binary code of DOS.

One of the reasons for Nietzsche's poor reception as a philosopher for many years was the perception that he had no philosophical system. This was an extremely right-handed criticism, dependent upon the criteria of

1885

NIETZSCHE PHOTOGRAPHED IN 1895, THE YEAR HE COMPLETED *THUS SPAKE ZARATHUSTRA*.

order and step-by-step rational thinking. Nietzsche deliberately chose not to have such a system, partly because of his preference for the Dionysian principle, but because he believed such systems tended to be delusional. Perhaps because of the penchant for system building that pervades philosophy, relatively few philosophers seem to be left-handed. A case has been made for the left-handedness of Aristotle, while the medieval philosopher, Thomas Aquinas, who translated much of Aristotle, was left-handed.

Nietzsche's Dionysian principle had its creative side, but was also destructive. In many ways Nietzsche destroyed himself in creating his works. Despite poor health, he worked incessantly, unable to relax and unable to see that his work was aggravating his illness. This ultimately led to his mental collapse. More conspicuous acts of self-destruction are to be found in left-handed rock stars such as Jimi Hendrix or Kurt Cobain. Although, self-destruction is far from being an exclusive lefty pastime, it's possible that left-handers, with their greater predilection for both substance abuse and genius, and their natural outsiderdom, are more prone to this kind of behaviour.

Henry Ford

1863–1947 IN 1888, WHEN HENRY FORD LEFT THE FAMILY FARM IN DEARBORN FOR the factories of Detroit with a head full of mechanical dreams, the ratio of America's urban to rural population was 1:4. By the time he died in 1947, it was 4:1. One of the main causes of this was that the car he invented, the Model T Ford, had extended the range of people's daily lives, making possible the kinds of cities with roads and suburbs we know today. In its years of manufacture between 1908 and 1927, the Model T, also known as the Tin Lizzie or Flivver, sold over 15 million units. It was the biggest-selling car of its time by far. At one stage during its production, more than 90 per cent of the world's cars were Fords. Henry Ford is widely credited as the man who 'put America on wheels'. In doing so he revolutionised manufacturing by pioneering the assembly line. By 1947, one in seven American workers were employed in the automotive and related industries. Ford's novel thinking in terms of staff salaries was also a crucial factor in the expansion of the middle classes that was necessary to create a mass consumer society. Sadly, the latter part of Ford's life was a classic case of left-handed brilliance gone awry. He became a crank, and an advocate of causes such as anti-Semitism. Unable to move past his perfect moment of the Model T, Ford also resisted further innovation at his motor company. By the time he died, his paranoid, erratic and autocratic management had brought the Ford Motor Company to the brink of collapse.

PUTTING THE CAR ON THE ROAD Like many great lefties, Ford was a man whose thoughts were not bent into shape by too many years of formal education. As the eldest son, he was expected to take over the family farm but, like Isaac Newton, he had no interest in farm work at all. Ford saw his first self-propelled machine at the age of 10 when a steam-powered engine that was used for threshing and powering saws

GENTLEMEM OUR COUNTRY

HENRY FORD AND HIS FIRST CAR.

was attached to a set of wheels by a drive train. The experience, said Ford, 'showed me that I was by instinct an engineer'. By the time he was 15, Ford had become known in the neighbourhood as a watch repairman. In 1879, he left for Detroit to work as an apprentice machinist. While he returned at times to work on the farm, his heart was never in it and he was always looking for a way to escape. In 1891, Ford became an engineer with the Edison Illuminating Company, a position whose salary allowed him the luxury of funding his own inventions. His garage tinkering culminated in 1896 with his first self-propelled vehicle, a quadricycle.

Ford's subsequent attempts to start an automobile company reveal his stubbornness in pursuit of his vision, and capacity for bucking against received wisdom. While not a lefty solitary in the true sense, since he was very close to his wife, Clara, and a fond, if flawed, father to his son, Edsel, Ford was an extremely singular character. Before he gained sole control of Ford, he was involved in a number of car companies, which failed due to his singular vision and inability to share power. His first car company, the Detroit Automobile Company, went broke because Ford spent too much time in improving the design of his auto and not enough selling it. He

resigned from the subsequent Henry Ford Company when they brought in Henry M. Leland to run production (the company later became Cadillac). Finally, he started the Ford Motor Company in 1903, whose history is full of power struggles involving its founder. Perhaps most notable was his overbearing treatment of his only son, Edsel, the stress of which helped bring about Edsel's premature death. In his dotage, Ford completely lost his bearings and the negative consequences of his singularity affected the Ford company dramatically. Grown inflexible and viewing necessary changes as a challenge to his authority, he behaved like a classic paranoid despot, playing favourites and employing an evil henchman—former navy boxer, Harry Bennett—to run a capitalist version of the secret police within the corporation.

THE MODEL T Without doubt, Henry Ford's greatest achievement was the Model T Ford. The genius of Ford and the reason behind the Model T's success was a classic example of left-handed lateral thinking. Whereas other car manufacturers at the beginning of the automobile age saw things in pieces, Henry Ford's vision for the Model T was complete. His holistic vision saw that the design, production and market for the vehicle were intricately related, in a way that no one else had imagined.

The first Model T was built in 1908 and sold for the sum of US$850, about one third of the price of other cars on the market at the time. Eleven thousand were sold until Ford opened a new factory in Highland Park in 1910, the first major manufacturing plant to implement the assembly line process that would revolutionise the industrial world. At his old factory it had taken 12 hours to assemble a Model T. With the new process a car could be constructed in 93 minutes.

The assembly line was the result of a change in perspective about the making of cars. The traditional approach focused on the car. Each car would occupy a space in the factory and various workers would come and work on the car in that same place until it was finished and driven away. Ford had the vision to see the bigger picture of the factory as a quasi-organic entity, through which the car passed in its various stages of production, kind of like the way blood passes through the various organs of the body. In Highland Park, the car came to the workers. An elevator took materials up to the fourth floor, where the body of the car was assembled and the upholstery fitted, before it passed down to the third floor to have its wheels and tires put on and be painted. Parts were distributed via conveyor belts, with each worker assigned a particular job. On the second floor the cars were fully assembled, then driven down a ramp past the offices on the first floor. This holistic mode of production made it eight times quicker to produce a Model T. By 1920, the factory was turning out a car a minute, and one out of every two cars in the world was a Model T.

MAKING THE MARKET In the early days, Henry Ford was an extremely idealistic kind of capitalist. He was a hands-on enthusiast who often expressed his loathing for the dispassionate kind of business thinking that was practised from a distance by eastern states banks and financiers such as the Rockefellers. In Ford's mind, his factories were a direct extension of himself. When the new assembly line at Highland Park was built, with its 15,000 machines over four floors, Ford, who had a powerful lefty distaste for the bureaucratic processes of administration, spent most of his time on the factory floor where he watched and encouraged his employees as they operated the machines. Workers on the Model T were used to seeing their boss on the floor, full of energy and enigma. He would punch them playfully in the shoulder and tell them folksy and funny anecdotes while they laboured under the increasing demand. When he saw a new employee struggling with his machine, he would step in and show him how to use it properly, advising him to let the machine do the work for him so he would have enough energy to go home and enjoy his family at the end of the working day. Ford workers of this era are frequently on record as saying they would have done anything for Henry Ford.

Because he was hands-on, he was in touch with the people who made and bought his automobiles. As such, he was in the position to take the approach that the success of the Model T would be massively enhanced if the kind of man making the Model T was also able to buy one. Until the Model T, owning a car was a rare and expensive business, restricted largely to the wealthy. The manufacturers were committed to the idea of the automobile as a luxury product. In the early days of the Ford Motor Company, for instance, Ford had to fight with his fellow directors in order to build the Model T in preference to larger and more exclusive vehicles.

Ford believed, as he explained to his attorney of the time, that, 'The way to make automobiles is to make one automobile like another automobile, to make them all alike, to make them come through the factory just alike, just as one pin is like another pin when it comes from a pin factory'. Because the Model T was a uniform product, made using the assembly line process, it was far cheaper to build. With the assembly line, the original price of US$850 was reduced to US$300. This increased its availability and popularity greatly. The profits came in a flood. Ford and the other shareholders were earning more money than they knew what to do with.

At the same time as he was raking in all this money, Ford, whose unspectacular background and hands-on attitude to his factory made him capable of empathising with his workers, noticed discontentment on the factory floor. The workers were paid US$2.36 a day, which was barely enough to keep a family going. The assembly line meant that individual skills were no longer as necessary, and the faster worker had to wait for the slower ones to catch up. By 1913, for every 100 permanent worker slots, the company had to employ 1000, as the turnover was so great. The training alone was costing over US$3 million a year. One day, as he was walked through the

☞ LEFTY LINKS

3. Along with Isaac Newton, Ford defied his family's expectations that he would take over the family farm. While neither of these lefties had an interest in farming, they did benefit from a quiet rural background, which gave their minds space to think freely. Ford's later residence was a virtual wilderness retreat and he deliberately kept away from high society. Other lefties to have enjoyed the thinking space of rustic quiet include Leonardo, Beethoven and Nietzsche.

4. Ford's antipathy towards bureaucracy was typical of the intuitive lefty thinker. Once, while passing the office of a clerk and seeing his desk stacked high with paperwork, on impulse Ford picked up all the paper and stuffed it in the trash can, then told the clerk that he now had a free day. However, while intuitive and holistic approaches are great for creativity and managing small enterprises, they cause problems when organisations become so big that they need an effective administrative chain of command. Perhaps because he saw the company as an almost organic extension of himself, Ford was appalling in terms of relinquishing control. One of the problems with a lefty base of intuitive, holistic thinking is that if you lose perspective, there is no rational system to fall back on. The consequences of this are often paranoia and poor decision making. In some ways, the Model T was such a complete vision that Ford was never really able to move on from it. Despite his brilliance, after the Model T his autocratic personality, bad temper and deteriorating decision-making capacity caused a massive decline in the fortunes of the Ford Motor Company. Its survival was finally contingent upon Ford being shunted sideways by his grandson.

FOLLOWING PAGE: HENRY FORD GIVING AN ADDRESS ON NBC RADIO, C.1940. DURING WORLD WAR II FORD BECAME QUITE OUTSPOKEN ON THE SUBJECT OF ANTI-SEMITISM.

assembly line at Highland Park with his son, Edsel, a worker lifted a hammer and feigned smashing the machine he was working on. Ford saw that the factory, which he thought of as an extension of himself, was not doing too well, and he instinctively knew he needed a solution.

Henry Ford decided to more than double the wage to US$5. It proved to be an iconoclastic stroke of left-handed genius. To begin with, the raise was qualified as profit-sharing, which insulated it from downturns in business. Following the announcement, 12,000 people turned up at Highland Park, lining up for a job. In business circles the decision was met with alarm. America was at the end of the robber baron era, whose traditional business model was all about screwing down labour costs as much as possible and charging as high a price as the market could afford. Ford's fellow automobile makers described him as a class traitor, while the *Wall Street Journal* described the move as 'blatantly immoral, a misapplication of biblical principles where they don't belong and an economic crime'. With typical lefty disregard for the status quo, Ford responded to his critics that it was a decision made for business not humanitarian reasons, and he was right. The rate of absenteeism dropped from 1 in 10 to 1 in 200 and to work for Ford became a matter of pride and status. Workers would even wear their Ford uniforms on the weekends. Productivity increased dramatically.

Most importantly, Ford's workers were able to buy the products they worked on. Not only this, but Ford's move to up wages changed the entire employment market. As a consequence, other companies were also forced to raise their wages, with the result that their workers were suddenly also able to afford a Model T. Furthermore, by instigating the US$5 a day wage, Ford had made himself a national icon. It was the best publicity the Model T could hope for. As an entire new class of people began to be able to afford an automobile, they were more likely to buy one from the man who had made it possible, especially since the Model T was such a durable and easy-to-run car.

It's doubtful whether Ford had this fully mapped out in his head when he made these decisions. Like many lefties, Ford was famous for his intuitive flashes rather than the step-by-step behaviour of systemic logic. What is clear from the story of the Model T is that these intuitive flashes made connections which crossed over business domains that were normally sectioned off from each other. The consequences of Ford's lefty thinking are everywhere around us today. We see them spatially, in the way our cities are designed around the automobile. Even more important, perhaps, was how Ford was the first of the major industrialists to make the nexus between the worker and consumer. By helping the working class to become middle class, Henry Ford was a pioneer of the kind of mass consumption that is the driving force behind the prosperity that most citizens of the developed world enjoy today.

HENRY FORD'S LEFTY TRAITS

INTUITIVE When Ford was designing the Model T, he would mentally leap six or seven steps at a time, leaving his offsiders to work out the logistics. Also, there is no way that his sense for producing and creating the market for the Model T could ever have been achieved by step-by-step logical thinking.

EMPATHETIC In his early days, Ford showed great empathy for his workers, and inspired their loyalty. His desire to see their standard of living raised was crucial to the establishment of the Model T as the first genuinely mass market automobile. However, in his later life he lost his empathy, becoming cranky and paranoid.

VISUAL-SPATIAL ABILITY Ford's ability to design cars and also to see the automobile factory as an entirety shows he was gifted with this left-handed trait.

LATERAL THINKING Ford had this in spades. You can see it in his decision to raise wages so the worker could buy his car and his innovative use of materials such as soybeans.

HOT-TEMPERED Always impatient, by the end of his career Ford had become an irascible crank, a left-hander out of step with the world.

ICONOCLASTIC Ford's decision to more than double the wages of his workers had him branded as a class traitor. Ford had no respect for tradition and an even greater contempt for the pretensions of the social classes.

SELF-TAUGHT Ford lacked formal education and was unhindered by schooled grooves of thought. His mechanical knowledge came from tinkering and working jobs.

EXPERIMENTAL Ford radically changed the automobile and its methods of manufacture.

FANTASIST Ford's inventions were grounded in reality but his political thoughts were always on the crazy fringe. Most notable was his rabid anti-Semitism. Just as fantastic, however, was his vision of a peace ship full of American luminaries, which he sent to Europe in 1915 in the hope of bringing about the cessation of World War I.

1867–1934

AGAINST ALL THE ODDS, THIS BRILLIANT LEFT-HANDED POLISH WOMAN remains the only person ever to win Nobel prizes in two different scientific fields. Her prizes in Physics (1903), which she shared with her husband, Pierre, and Chemistry (1911), which she won after his death, were both related to the discovery of the radioactive element radium. In addition to a wide range of medical applications, radium was crucial for developing our understanding of how the atom is composed. This scientific under-standing of the atom made possible the development of nuclear energy and weapons. Throughout her life, Marie Curie showed a powerful determina-tion and singular focus. Unafraid to be different, she managed to break new ground in both science and society. Along with her discoveries and prizes, she was also the first female university professor in France.

EARLY MARIE From her early life, Marie's left-handedness was just one of the attributes which set her apart from the norm. The fact that she became a scientist at all was a victory of single-minded determination, and willingness to be different, against some serious obstacles. As a left-hander, knowing she was already different must have helped her to stick to her guns, despite the fierce social and financial obstacles that were often leveraged against her.

Marie Curie was born Maria Sklodowska, the youngest of five children in Warsaw in 1867. Her parents were of aristocratic origins but were not wealthy and struggled to make their living as teachers. At the time, Poland was split into three sections, ruled by the Russians, Prussians and Austrians respectively. Warsaw was controlled by the Russians and, following an attempted uprising in 1863, there had been a clampdown on Polish culture. Schools, for instance, were compelled to teach in Russian and, for some school children, even speaking Polish in the playground was banned. Marie's parents, patriotically Polish, rebelled against such

MARIE CURIE'S LEFTY TRAITS

LATERAL THINKING Marie was innovative in her refusal to apply for patents to her discoveries and in the way she managed relations with the mining businesses who supplied her with materials. Her invention of the X-ray car, the engine of which powered the X-ray machine, is another example of her lateral problem solving.

HOT-TEMPERED Marie wore her heart on her sleeve and was prone to exploding. Her students described her as terrifying, and she never avoided a fight when she perceived an injustice was at work.

SOLITARY Marie sacrificed friendships for the long hours of study, and fought with her brother-in-law because he talked to her too much. In the end she found her match in a man equally fond of his solitude, who would support her single-minded devotion to science.

ICONOCLASTIC Marie consistently broke barriers in the quest for education. When the Nobel Prize committee urged her to refuse the Nobel Prize due to her affair with Paul Langevin, she wrote back to them to say that her scientific achievements had nothing to do with her private life.

EXPERIMENTAL Marie conducted experiments, then developed theories, rather than the usual scientific method of using experiments to test a pre-existing theory. She also experimented in other areas of life, such as creating among her colleagues a communal form of home schooling for their children. Her X-ray trucks are another example of the practical bent of her experimental mind.

strictures and surreptitiously helped to maintain their nation's cultural identity. At one stage her father was demoted by the Russians and the family was forced to take in student boarders in order to keep food on the table. The family's difficulties were compounded when one of these boarders brought typhoid into the house, which killed Marie's eldest sister, Zosia, in 1876. Marie's mother already had tuberculosis and, devastated by her daughter's death, she weakened and died in 1878.

Both of Marie's parents were understandably passionate about education and, unlike many left-handers, Curie was an excellent student at school. Just a few months after her mother's death, her father sent her to the Russian Gymnasium (the German name for high school), where she wasn't supposed to speak Polish at all. Despite this oppressive regime, four years later she graduated Dux in a language she didn't really like.

Once she graduated from high school, her gender made it difficult for her to continue her studies. Polish universities of the time did not admit female students and there was insufficient money in the family to fund her education in Paris. Her studies were restricted to classes taken at the illegal Flying University until she and her sister Bronia struck a deal. Marie was to work as a governess in Poland and help out her sister financially, while she studied medicine in Paris. Then when her sister had graduated, she would help support her.

After three years as a governess in the countryside, Marie returned to Warsaw and resumed classes at the Flying University while looking after her father. It was there, aged 22, that she encountered her first scientific laboratory. Until then she had been toying over whether to study literature or science but, after spending time in the laboratory, when she left for Paris a year later it was with the fixed intention of studying science.

LIFE ON THE LEFT BANK
When Marie signed up to study science at the Sorbonne, she was one of only 23 women in a Faculty of Science that had over 1800 students. Compared to Poland there was at least the opportunity of going to university. In Poland, however, the school of Polish Positivism, which advocated nationalism by education, was in favour of women's rights, as was shown by underground institutions such as the Flying University. In some ways sexism in France was stronger than in Poland. Most of the female students at French universities were foreign, which is not surprising given the sentiments of writers such as Octave Mirbeau, whose views that, 'Woman is not a brain, she is a sex, and that is much better', were widely held.

Standing apart from the crowd was something that nurtured rather than crushed Marie. Just by being left-handed, she knew she was innately different from the vast proportion of the world. Why then should it be a problem to be Polish in France, or a woman in a world unready to acknowledge the possibility of female scientific genius? As her studies progressed, Curie became more absorbed in them. One of the consequences was a developing urge for solitude, often found in left-handed geniuses, in which she could engage with her own thoughts. First, she moved out of her sister's house, partly because her brother-in-law was too noisy. In a letter home, she wrote:

> I am working a thousand times as hard as at the beginning of my stay: in the rue d'Allemagne my little brother-in-law had the habit of disturbing me endlessly. He absolutely could not endure having me do anything but engage in agreeable chatter with him when I was home. I had to declare war on him on this subject.

It was unusual in the extreme for a female student to live by herself. Until she got married, Marie lived in a succession of small, spartan student apartments, often up five or six flights of stairs, where the water in the sink would freeze in winter. For the first year or so of study she hung out with a group of fellow Polish ex-patriot students, but again the companionship was distracting. She later remembered, 'I was forced to give up these relationships, for I found that all of my energy had to be concentrated on my studies . . .'.

For many people, studying in a cold apartment with little in the way of companionship would be lonely and miserable, but such was the singularity of Marie's personality and her inner compulsion that she would later remember this period of intense learning as 'one of the best memories of my life, that period of solitary years exclusively devoted to the studies finally within my reach, for which I had waited so long'.

The hard work was rewarded. In 1893, she took first place in the licence examination for the physical sciences at the Sorbonne, roughly the equivalent of a masters degree. In July 1894, she managed second in the Sorbonne's licence examination for mathematics.

PIERRE Marie's self-imposed solitude was interrupted, however, when she met Pierre Curie, a scientist, who was also possibly left-handed, and even more of a natural outsider than Marie. While he was already a considerable scientist he was an appalling networker who, from a combination of stubbornness and shyness, showed no inclination for playing the game. For a French male academic at the time, the career path was fairly well delin-eated: high school at one of the grandes écoles, passage to the Sorbonne or another university, a PhD, then a career as a professor at one of France's universities. Pierre, however, had been tutored at home, hadn't bothered to take a PhD—even though he had conducted enough original research for several—and was teaching at an unfashionable school which offered him limited laboratory facilities. He lacked the superficial charm and small talk to prosper in the greasy world of academic politics. Yet his major research projects, first into the electric properties of crystals, then into magnetism, were ground-breaking.

Like Marie, Pierre craved solitude. But not completely. Within a year, the tall, dreamy-eyed 34-year-old had proposed to Marie. She in turn was

PAGE 157: MARIE CURIE WORKING IN HER LABORATORY AT THE UNIVERSITY OF PARIS, 1925.

FOLLOWING PAGES: MARIE CURIE GIVING A LECTURE TO AN AUDIENCE OF MEN AND WOMEN AT THE CONSERVATORY OF ARTS AND CRAFTS, PARIS, 1925.

powerfully drawn to this ponderous man who viewed the world with detachment, as if lost to the intense computations happening inside his head. Unlike many outsiders who dream of marrying into society, Marie felt that marrying a fellow outsider was the best way of maintaining her own autonomy. At one stage Pierre even proposed that they live in the same apartment, but in separate rooms. Torn between returning to Poland and looking after her father, and remaining in Paris and marrying, the 26-year-old Marie dithered, before finally accepting Pierre's proposal. They were married in July 1895, then set off on a bicycle tour of northern France.

SHACKED UP AND GLOWING

While Pierre got round to organizing his papers so he could get the salary raise that came with possession of a PhD, Marie researched the magnetic properties of steel, ran the household, studied for a licence to teach science at a girls' high school (she came first again) and became pregnant. On 12 September 1897, their first daughter, Irene, was born. Not long after giving birth, Marie began casting around for a topic for her own PhD.

In 1895, Wilhelm Röntgen had discovered X-rays while conducting experiments with the cathode ray tube. This launched a wave of experiments in order to ascertain the nature and application of a variety of energy rays. When Henri Becquerel, a physics professor at Paris' prestigious École Polytechnique, placed uranium salts on top of photographic plates wrapped in black paper, and put them out in the sun, he was hoping that the energy of the sun might cause the salts to emit X-rays, which would then show up on the photographic plates. The first results were positive, and he decided to repeat the experiment, adding a copper cross between the black paper and the salts, hoping its pattern would appear on the plates. This time the sun refused to shine. After some days Becquerel became impatient and developed the plates anyway. He was amazed to find they clearly showed the outline of the salts. He put the result down to a kind of invisible phosphorescence. In other words, the salts seemed to be emitting their own energetic rays.

Becquerel presented his results, but they were far less sexy than X-rays, and no one paid much attention. Except for Marie Curie. She found that the theories based around cathode ray tubes were inadequate to account for this phenomenon, and determined to discover the source of the mysterious phosphorescence that had appeared on Becquerel's plates. She begged and borrowed mineral samples from whoever would give them to her, and set up her lab in a dark, dusty shed provided by Pierre's boss. Using a small, coal-powered stove to refine the samples, and a piezoelectric quartz electrometer (invented by Pierre during his work on crystals) to measure their electric output, Marie began the quest which would lead to the discovery of radium.

OPPOSITE: MARIE AND HER HUSBAND, PIERRE, C.1904. TOGETHER THE COUPLE WOULD DISCOVER TWO NEW ELEMENTS: RADIUM AND POLONIUM.

Like many left-handers, who are known to prefer the concrete to the abstract, Marie took a practical approach to her work. She was always more an

experimental, rather than a theoretical, scientist. As such, she was a perfectionist in the laboratory. As one of her research associates later described her:

> The series of operations involved in opening the apparatus, pushing down the chronometer, lifting the weight, etc. as the piezoelectric method requires, is accomplished by Madame Curie with a discipline and perfect harmony of movements. No pianist could accomplish with greater virtuosity what the hands of Madame Curie accomplish in this special kind of work. It is a perfect technique which tends to reduce the coefficient of personal error to zero.

The raw material Marie mainly used was a mineral called pitchblende, known to contain uranium. Using the piezoelectric method, she determined that pitchblende made the air around it more conductive than pure uranium. The chances were that another radioactive element was at work. Pierre put aside his work on magnetism and began to help Marie with her research. On 20 July 1898, Marie announced the discovery of a new element called polonium, named after her homeland. By December 1898, their research revealed another element, which they called radium, since initial reckoning showed it to be 900 times more radioactive than uranium. Eventually they would demonstrate that it was 1 million times as radioactive.

Not only had Marie hit the chemist's Holy Grail of discovering not one, but two, new elements, her research had shown that radioactivity was the property of the atom. It was a crucial step in the transition from the stable matter of the Newtonian universe to the unstable atomic world of quantum mechanics.

As an experimental and hands-on scientist, Marie didn't put her energy into pursuing these changes to the theory of the universe. Both polonium and radium existed only as trace elements in pitchblende and Marie spent most of the next three years perfecting her technique for distilling tiny quantities of these elements from the raw material, while wondering what radium would look like when enough of it was accumulated to give it physical presence.

NUCLEAR FISSION In 1903, Marie and Pierre were given half of the Nobel Prize for Physics, shared with Henri Becquerel. Yet the discrimination because she was a woman remained. Despite the fact it was Marie who had made the actual discovery, the prize would have been given to Pierre only if wasn't for his insistence that she share in it. When Pierre was appointed Professor at the Sorbonne the year after, social convention usurped their scientific equality and Marie was appointed as his assistant. Still, the chance to leave the shed for a spec-built laboratory and be paid to work together overcame any irritation at the discrimination. The year 1904 also saw the birth of their second daughter, Eve.

Tragedy struck in 1906 when the absent-minded Pierre was crushed to death by a carriage loaded with six tons of goods. Marie was devastated and retreated into her laboratory. Ironically Pierre's death was good for her career. Marie was appointed Assistant Professor at the Sorbonne, the first female professor in France.

One person Marie became close to was the physicist Paul Langevin, who had been good friends with Pierre. He was in an unhappy marriage and the two of them became intimate. By 1907, this intimacy had developed into a full-blooded affair. In 1911, just as the Swedish Academy was deciding to give Marie her second Nobel Prize (for Chemistry), the scandal of their affair became public. From being considered a French heroine, Marie was then perceived as a Pole whose scientific abilities paled before her theft of the husband of a French woman. The situation worsened when extracts from their love letters were leaked and published in the press.

Spooked by the publicity, the Nobel Prize Committee wrote to ask Marie to refuse the prize until the true accusations of her adultery had been proven false. Again, Marie showed a left-hander's capacity to stand up to social convention, writing back to them, 'The action which you appear to advise would be a grave error on my part. In fact the prize has been awarded for the discovery of Radium and Polonium. I believe there is no connection between my scientific work and the facts of private life.' Deciding to accept her second Nobel Prize means that, even today, Marie Curie is the only person in its history to win Nobel prizes in separate disciplines. She is also one of only four women to win the prize in the hard sciences. Of the other three, one is her left-handed daughter, Irene Joliot-Curie, who won the Chemistry prize in 1935, together with her husband Frederic, for their work on the synthesis of radioactive elements.

LATER LIFE Most of Marie's breakthroughs were achieved while Pierre was still alive. The rest of her career was primarily devoted to accumulating radium and creating the scientific infrastructure to explore its usefulness. Her other achievements include the foundation of the Radium Institute. During World War I, she observed the need for X-ray facilities at the front. Although horses still outnumbered vehicles, she realised that X-ray machines could be powered by motor vehicle engines, so she established a fleet of X-ray trucks to go out to the military hospitals. They carried out over a million wartime examinations with the result that many limbs and lives were saved. Similarly, she mounted two campaigns in America to raise money to buy grams of radium: one to further the Radium Institute's research, the second to set up Poland's first nuclear medicine facility. She was also appointed to the League of Nations Committee on International Co-operation.

Marie's experiments with radium weakened her health over a long period of time, and her latter years were marked by illness. In the end she died of aplastic anaemia brought about by exposure to radiation. Yet through her left-handed capacity to be different and stay different, she was able to overcome myriad social and economic hurdles to become one the greatest scientists the world has known.

LEFTY LINKS

1. Not only was Marie Curie left-handed, but photographic evidence suggests it is likely that both Pierre and daughter Irene were also left-handed. This is particularly interesting since Irene also went on to win a Nobel Prize for her work with her husband, Frederic Joliot-Curie who, judging by the way he holds his cigarette in photos, may also have been left-handed.

2. Something Curie shared in common with her fellow left-handed scientist Isaac Newton, was a tendency to get so absorbed in her work that she frequently forgot to eat. At one stage she became so weak that she fainted and was forced to confess to her brother-in-law, Kazimierz, that she had only eaten radishes and cherries in the preceding 24 hours.

3. Marie Curie like many left-handers, demonstrated a preference for the experimental over the theoretical; the concrete over the abstract. This inclination is also found in the writing of Mark Twain, in Leonardo's belief in the primacy of the eye and nature, and even in Nietzsche's aversion to philosophical systems.

ONE OF THE GREAT FIGURES OF THE TWENTIETH CENTURY, GANDHI emerged from an unspectacular childhood to become an icon for oppressed people the world over. His doctrine of *satyagraha*, which advocated non-violent resistance to tyranny, was possibly the crucial factor in the unravelling of the British Empire in India. A shrewd strategist, his 'battle' tactics in South Africa, and later India, were as ingenious as those of any military commander. He had a brilliant intuitive grasp of how to maximise the symbolic value of his actions, and his armoury of non-violent marches, demonstrations, hunger strikes and deliberate mass breaching of absurd and inequitable laws became the basis for activists the world over. The Civil Rights movement in America led by Martin Luther King, the anti-Vietnam war protests, the campaign of jailed IRA member Bobby Sands, and environmentalists who chain themselves to trees in forests, all owe a concep-tual debt to Gandhi. Gandhi's vision for India as a nation of self-sufficient villages growing their own crops and spinning their own cloth, with the caste hierarchy removed, never really came to fruition. Yet his influence remains in the struggle to reconfigure Indian society on a more equitable basis and can be found in the social activism and anti-globalisation of activists such as Arundhati Roy. Indeed, the image of a small, thin, bald man in a loincloth, who changed the course of history, is one of the twentieth century's most enduring.

YOUNG GANDHI Mohandas Gandhi was born in Porbander, a small principality on the Arabian Sea in western India which is now in the state of Gujarat. Although Gandhi's family belonged to the merchant class (the name Gandhi meant grocer), his father was Prime Minister there. His devout mother belonged to a Hindu sect, the Pranamis, who merged Hindu and Muslim texts and believed in harmony between religions. Like many in Gujarat, the Gandhis were also influenced by the ascetic religion of the Jains, who advocate non-violence to all living beings. In its most extreme

🖐 GANDHI'S LEFTY TRAITS

INTUITIVE Gandhi was a great intuitive thinker who not only had ingenious and unexpected answers to political problems, but a powerful grasp of political timing to maximise the impact of his actions.

EMPATHETIC Although Gandhi could be a tyrant in his ascetic demands on his followers, he was revered as *bapu* (father) to India's people. His empathy was fuelled by his Jainist philosophy of non-violence to living things.

LATERAL THINKING Gandhi was quite brilliant in this arena. How many people could turn a long walk in search of a pinch of salt into a fully fledged independence movement?

HOT-TEMPERED As a child Gandhi was known for his temper, which followed him into his youth. As an adult, however, he sought to control this with spiritual discipline.

SOLITARY Gandhi was not really solitary, but he was celibate. He also tried to keep every Monday as a day of silence and meditation, during which, if forced to communicate, he did so in writing.

ICONOCLASTIC Gandhi used the British tradition against itself and, while remaining a devout Hindu, did much to break down some of its traditional inequalities.

SELF-TAUGHT Gandhi read few books and gained his wisdom from action and having the humility to learn from his mistakes.

EXPERIMENTAL Gandhi described his life as a series of 'Experiments with Truth'. Rather than scientific experiments, Gandhi conducted tests on how to live and how to get one's way against powerful opposition when one had moral right.

FANTASIST Gandhi believed in a rustic India that was never really possible, but his dream was beautiful and inspiring nonetheless.

form this involves wearing a face mask to protect bugs from death by inhalation and the refusal to eat root vegetables because it means killing the whole plant. The powerful influence of his mother's beliefs meant that, throughout his life, Gandhi was a non-drinking vegetarian who fasted for spiritual benefit, and believed in asceticism and the energy to be gained from the sublimation of sensual urges. Gandhi's father died when he was 16. At the precise moment of his death, Gandhi had been having sex with his wife, Kasturbai—whom he had married when he was 13—and the coincidence germinated an abhorrence for the sexual act. In his adult life, he would prove his powers of lateral thinking by incorporating these spiritual influences of his childhood into a mode of political action.

The young Gandhi, however, showed little sign of his impending greatness. He was a poor student and one of the reasons may well have been because he was forced to write with his right hand. Left-handedness was strongly stigmatised in India. One reason for this was that Indians traditionally eat with their hands. As such, the right hand is used for food, the left for ablutions. While left-handers can swap hands, it is often viewed with suspicion. Furthermore, in some Hindu religious practices, the right hand is sacrosanct and the left hand banned. Taboos exist, for instance, against the use of the left hand for *pooja* (worship ritual) and *prasad* (holy food). In some areas (especially rural), a marriage can be rejected if the bride or, less commonly, the groom, is left-handed. This can lead to harassment since wives are not allowed to use the left hand for cooking or serving. To ensure this, the hand can be branded, burnt or hit to discourage its use. Children are also dissuaded and prevented from using their left hands for writing, eating and many daily activities. Upon showing a preference, their left hands might also be hit or have chilli powder rubbed into them, be tied behind their backs or put in a bag. Some photos show Gandhi writing with his right hand and this is probably why. Interestingly, he never developed a love of reading or of writing, despite becoming a lawyer.

When he finished school his parents sent him to England. It was an act of desperation. He had only just graduated from high school in India and his grades weren't good enough to guarantee entry into an Indian university, let alone pass once he got there. On the other hand, the exams to join the bar at London's Inner Temple, as much a guild as an educational establishment, were reputed to be so easy that even a dunderhead son like Gandhi should be able to pass.

ENGLISH LESSONS Gandhi arrived in England in 1888 at the age of 18. Somewhat comically, he tried to use his lefty facility for adaptation to turn himself into the complete Englishman. He bought a morning suit, a top hat and a silver-headed cane. He purchased a violin and embarked on a range of 'civilising' classes—violin, elocution, dancing and French. He learnt the hit songs of the time and accompanied young women to dances without informing them that he was already married.

All this aping of the English ended, however, when Gandhi ran out of money. Unable to eat the mutton dishes served up by his landlady, he was extremely happy when he came across a vegetarian restaurant while walking around London. Inside the restaurant was a book by the anarchistic thinker H. S. Salt titled *A Plea for Vegetarianism*. As he read this book a bell went off in his brain. It provided reasons, through rational argument, for what had been dictated to him by custom, myth and religion. With his frivolous pursuits behind him, Gandhi was inspired. He joined the Vegetarian Society. More importantly, he began a series of dietary exercises based on Salt's book, which became the first of what he called his 'Experiments with Truth', whereby he would measure the effect of adopting a discipline on his spiritual well-being.

Some of the Vegetarian Society members also belonged to the Theosophy movement, which believed that every religion contained a portion of the absolute truth, a belief compatible with Gandhi's Pranami heritage. As Gandhi moved in these circles, he was introduced to a variety of literature. Importantly, he began to become acquainted with Indian culture via British scholarship. Although he knew Hinduism intimately from direct experience, the first time he read its holy text, the *Bhagavad Gita*, was in English translated by Edwin Arnold from the ancient Sanskrit. Through his access to these ancient texts, Gandhi came to form a picture of his ideal India; one that was spiritual yet different from the image perpetuated by the Brahmins, who had arrogated knowledge of the Hindu scriptures into a self-serving system of hereditary caste. Gandhi learnt about the Buddha through Arnold's long poem, *The Light of Asia*, read the Bible and was deeply influenced by the New Testament—while abhorring the Old. He also learnt about Mahomet via English writers such as Thomas Carlyle. It was the most significant reading period of Gandhi's life. In later life, preferring reality to theory, he was never a big reader and these texts, with the addition of works by Tolstoy and Ruskin, were the bedrock of his literary influence.

At the same time that he was absorbing these books, Gandhi was also learning the practical tradition of the English Common Law with its organic system of precedent, whereby judgments in former cases came to constitute the law. Having abandoned his attempts to emulate the English, and probably without really knowing it, he was intuitively positioning himself to become a hybrid of traditional Indian and progressive English liberal values, perfectly placed to take on the British, on their own terms, while simultaneously appealing to his fellow Indians.

BOERISH SOCIETY When Gandhi completed his studies in 1891, he returned to India. It wasn't a happy time. His mother had died and the family's influence at the court in Porbander had waned. He tried to set up as a barrister in Bombay, but made a laughing stock of himself when he was struck dumb with stage fright when presenting his first case. In 1885, a Muslim trading house in Porbander asked him to travel to

PAGE 167: MOHANDAS KARAMCHAND GANDHI WAS GIVEN THE NAME *MAHATMA*, MEANING 'GREAT SOUL', BY NOBEL PRIZE-WINNING BENGALI POET, TAGORE, FOLLOWING HIS TRIUMPH OVER THE BRITISH AT CHAMPARAN.

South Africa to oversee some legal issues they were having there and, in 1895, Gandhi sailed for Durban.

In their own land, Indians were a majority, discriminated against by the British, while in South Africa they were a discriminated-against minority—roughly 80,000, or three per cent of the population. After the civility of his treatment in England, South Africa came as a shock to Gandhi. On a business trip, he purchased a first-class ticket from Durban to Pretoria. He was sitting in the first-class compartment when a white person boarded in Pietermaritzburg and came into Gandhi's compartment. He took one look at Gandhi, then turned around and left. Minutes later, he returned with a conductor who ordered Gandhi out of the first-class compartment and into the luggage van. When Gandhi protested, showing them his ticket, he was ejected from the train and had to spend the night freezing in the station's waiting room. The next day he had to catch a stagecoach for part of his journey. The guard of the stagecoach initially refused to let him sit inside, then forced him to sit at the driver's feet. When Gandhi protested, the guard beat him until the other passengers intervened.

Gandhi saw this journey as a major turning point in his life. Even though he had the necessary paperwork to justify his presence in first class, he was thrown out on the basis of utterly irrational discrimination, something the sensitive left-hander develops an instinctive aversion to from a very early age. With the Boer War just concluded, the Indian population was in a precarious position. In addition to the kinds of daily discrimination, as experienced by Gandhi, Indians were faced with the threat of deportation and removal of their right to vote. It was the proposed legislation by the Natal government to remove Indians from the franchise that led Gandhi to stay on as an activist after his contract had finished.

As a lawyer, Gandhi's initial belief was that discrimination could be progressively eradicated through legal action. Yet the worsening predicament of the Indian population in South Africa eventually dispelled this. In 1906, after the Transvaal government passed a law compelling the registration and fingerprinting of the colony's Indian population, Gandhi first deployed *satyagraha* (a Gujarati compound word meaning 'truth-force') as a tactic in the battle against discrimination. He called on his fellow Indians to defy the law and accept the punishment, instead of using violent resistance. The result was a seven-year struggle, in which thousands of Indians (including Gandhi) were jailed, beaten or even shot for non-violent acts such as striking, refusing to register, or burning their registration cards.

Gandhi's strategy was based upon brilliant intuition into the way the dominant class in society perceived themselves. By advocating non-violent resistance, he undermined white South Africa's sense of its own moral superiority. The harsh tactics the Smuts government used to repress the Indians came to appear more and more unreasonable in the

LEFTY LINKS

1. One of the lesser known aspects of Gandhi's character is his wit. When once asked what he thought of Western civilisation, he gave the celebrated reply, 'I think it would be a great idea'. On a trip to Britain, he visited London's East End, whose residents saw him as an Indian version of their hometown boy Charlie Chaplin, a tramp-like eccentric who stood up for the little man.

2. Another great left-handed advocate of non-violence was Alsatian musician, doctor and philosopher Albert Schweitzer (1875–1965). According to some reports he taught himself to write with both hands because his cat used to like sleeping on his left arm and he didn't want to wake her up. In addition to being nice to his cat, Schweitzer ran a hospital in Africa, wrote about Gandhi, and won the Nobel Prize for Peace.

3. Gandhi was one of the great sexually sublimated lefties, joined by Beethoven, Joan of Arc, Nietzsche, Newton, Michelangelo, Lewis Caroll and Queen Victoria—a reason perhaps why lefties have remained only 10 per cent of the population.

4. Gandhi joins Joan of Arc as one of the holy characters in this book. One of Gandhi's favourite people was Jesus, whose philosophy of 'turn the other cheek', Gandhi improvised on. Unfortunately, it is not known whether Jesus was left- or right-handed.

OPPOSITE: PHOTOGRAPH TAKEN OF GANDHI C.1900, AGED AROUND 31, WHILE HE WAS IN SOUTH AFRICA.

face of the Indian's non-violent resistance. This caused a public outcry against the government by the white people it was pertaining to represent. Gandhi believed that it was important to the possibility of peace that people be able to relinquish their positions without losing face. Smuts was eventually forced to negotiate with Gandhi and a compromise was reached, even if its conditions would be eroded after Gandhi had returned to India.

HOME RULE When Gandhi returned to India in 1915, he set up an ashram devoted to truth, non-violence (*ahimsa*), celibacy, vegetarianism, non-materialism and serving the Indian people. It was a strict and ascetic outfit, over which Gandhi ruled somewhat tyrannically.

It wasn't long, however, before he became involved with India's Congress Party and with campaigns that used *satyagraha* to fight injustice. Gandhi's first success came while advocating the interests of the indigo farmers of Champaran near the border of Nepal. The price of indigo had collapsed due to the invention of aniline dyes. As a result, the mainly British landowners began charging their tenant farmers cash on top of the indigo they supplied, reducing the farmers to a state of desperate poverty. The farmers had been protesting this through local lawyers, who claimed their fee, but had thus far failed to deliver a result. Gandhi entered the region of dispute and convinced the lawyers to become his assistants. Soon after, the police ordered him to leave because his presence was considered a danger to public peace. He refused and was brought before the courts, where he pleaded guilty. Instead of being sent to prison, the charges were dropped. An enquiry ensued which resulted in the landowners being forced to compensate the farmers.

At Champaran, Gandhi had stood up to the British and won. For this he was given the title *mahatma* (meaning 'Great Soul') by Nobel Prize-winning Bengali poet, Tagore. It also made him a hero across India. His next campaign was within the Indian community: leading a strike against a mill-owner over wages. After two weeks of strike, the boss wasn't budging and, faced with hungry families, the workers began to weaken. Seeing this, Gandhi had an intuitive brainwave. He announced that he would go on a hunger strike if the strikers relinquished their claim. It was the first time he had used this strategy and it worked. Not only did the strikers keep going, but faced with this new resolve the mill-owner gave in.

Following the 1919 Amritsar massacre, in which British troops fired on an unarmed Indian crowd, killing at least 400 with thousands more casualties, Gandhi's attitude began to harden towards the English, while still opposing the violence advocated by other members of the Indian resistance. His policy of non-cooperation encouraged people to boycott British products and wear *khadi*, an Indian cloth which everyone could make at home. He also urged that people should resign from government employment and boycott British institutions—schools, universities, the law courts and the system of honours. The catchword was *swaraj*, meaning full independence, not just political but spiritual and individual too.

OPPOSITE: GANDHI SEATED NEXT TO JAWAHARLAL 'PANDIT' NEHRU AT THE AICC GENERAL SESSION, 1942.

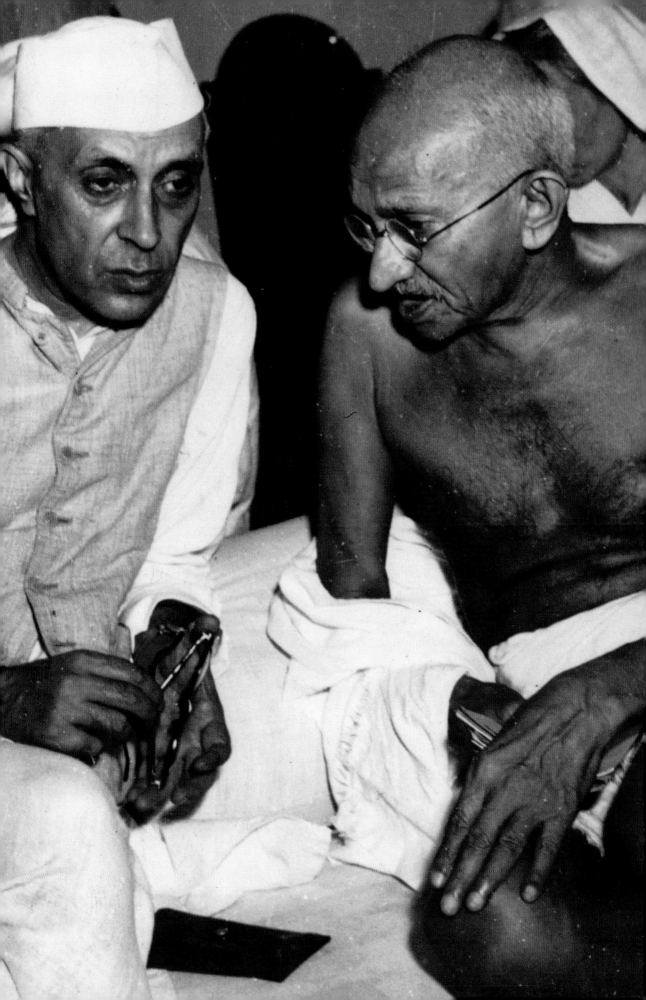

The first blossoming of *swaraj* lasted two years until police used gunfire to disperse a crowd picketing a liquor store in Uttar Pradesh. The angry crowd responded by burning down the police station with 22 policemen inside. As a result, Gandhi called the movement off. A month later, in March 1922, Gandhi was arrested for sedition and sentenced to six years' jail. Although he was released in 1924 for medical reasons, he stayed out of politics for most of the decade.

In 1930, after calls to negotiate independence had been ignored by the British, the Indian National Congress declared independence. To mark the occasion, Gandhi delivered another inspired moment of *satyagraha*. This time his target was the British tax on salt. Over four weeks, Gandhi marched 388 kilometres from Ahmedabad to the Gujarat coast. He set off with 79 volunteers and was joined by thousands more. Villagers laid down green leaves for the marchers to walk on as they passed through. When Gandhi reached the sea, after ceremonially bathing, he picked up a fragment of salt.

It was a magnificently successful symbolic gesture. All through India, people began to make their own salt. The movement spread—2500 people attempted a non-violent invasion of a government salt factory and were brutally beaten back by police. Gandhi and his fellow Congress leaders were arrested, as were an astonishing 100,000 people. By the end of the campaign, the British were forced to negotiate. However, independence remained off the table and Gandhi spent more time in jail during the 1930s.

One of his major focuses during this period was transforming the status of India's untouchables who he renamed *harijans*, meaning children of God. Again he used tactics such as hunger striking to advocate their cause.

A consequence of this were three assassination attempts against him by Hindu extremists in 1934 alone. The activism on behalf of the untouchables was all part of Gandhi's program of social reconstruction, based on the unit of the village. He was very much a practical thinker who, while brilliant at utilising the symbolic moment, also concentrated his experiments upon improving the daily amenities of Indian life. All over India his army of volunteers, called *satyagrahis*, concentrated on village reform, dismantling discrimination against caste and also against women, through traditions such as *purdah* and child brides. Working as healers, teachers, agricultural advisers and latrine superintendents, the *satyagrahis* improved the sanitation, health and economic conditions of many Indian villages.

During World War II, Gandhi initially proposed the non-violent support of the British war effort. However, he then decided that it was impossible to support the protection of a nation's democratic freedoms when it refused to ratify your own. He was the effective leader of the Quit India movement and, as such, he was imprisoned again for two years, during which time his wife died. Gandhi was released after a bad attack of malaria, because the British were frightened of the backlash if he died while in custody. Despite its draconian repression at the time—another 100,000 Indians became political prisoners—by the end of the war, with Britain exhausted, an agreement was reached to grant India its independence.

CODA From this point, while Gandhi remained a spiritual leader of the nation, his influence dwindled. The independence period was marked by Hindu–Muslim violence, and the partition of the subcontinent into Pakistan and India ruined Gandhi's dream of unity. On the actual day of Independence, while the Congress Party celebrated, Gandhi was mourning the partition. For the last two years he had expended a great deal of energy in trying to heal the schism between the two new nations. These efforts resulted in his assassination by a Hindu extremist, Nathuram Godse, on 30 January 1948, on the way to a prayer meeting. The execution of Godse after his trial is something Gandhi wouldn't have approved of. However, much of his idealism had already been hijacked and the India that emerged after independence, with its political corruption and perpetuated inequities, would probably have disappointed him deeply.

Charlie Chaplin

1889–1977

CHARLIE CHAPLIN'S LITTLE TRAMP IS ONE OF THE MOST ENDURING characters in cinema. Dapper and indigent, the 'eternal non-conformist', as one critic described him, is a classic left-hander at odds with a right-handed world which always seems to be putting its dangers in front of him.

For his creator, this downtrodden everyman brought enormous power and wealth, granting Chaplin the means to try and erase the scars of an unhappy childhood and rise to the pinnacle of society. From a childhood in the slums of London, with a mentally troubled single mother forced to prostitute herself to make ends meet, at the height of his fame Chaplin was probably the most famous man in the world. Like many of his friends, he was able to build himself a fantasy life, remote from the social conventions that most of his audience lived by. The impoverished protagonist of his wonderful silent films made possible an improbable lifestyle of mansions, swimming pools, tennis courts and liaisons with a vast array of stunningly beautiful women. In many ways, Chaplin's life was a kind of human alchemy, perhaps one of the most resonant examples of the left-hander's facility for transformation.

UPBRINGING Chaplin was the second son of music hall entertainers, who separated when he was three. His father was a ballad singer, while his mother, who had gypsy heritage, sang and played the piano. Charlie Chaplin Snr was a committed alcoholic who rarely saw his son, except for a brief period when Charlie and his half-brother Sydney lived with him and his mistress. He died from alcohol-related cirrhosis of the liver when Charlie was only 12. Life for Charlie and Sydney was tough, living with their mother, who lost her singing voice, and whose straight acting skills weren't sufficient to provide a living. They all lived in unsalubrious lodgings, ate sparingly and, like many in the theatre, Hannah Chaplin turned at times to prostitution to make ends meet when roles were not

forthcoming. She had the added problem of schizophrenia, a fear of which Chaplin would have for most of his life. As a consequence of her disintegrating mental health, Hannah was in and out of the mental asylum. In between stays with their mother, Charlie and Sydney were shunted between orphanages, workhouses and schools for the children of the poor.

From an early age Charlie learnt the power of the stage as a means to transform reality. According to one story, he made his debut at the age of five. In order to cover for his mother, who had lost her voice, Chaplin went on stage and sang a popular song. The audience apparently threw a stack of coins on stage (Chaplin's reminiscences are not particularly reliable) and his career in showbiz was born.

Chaplin's first tour was at age eight, in a musical called *The Eight Lancashire Lads*. He and his brother worked in a number of shows until they both joined Fred Karno's Fun Factory vaudeville troupe. It wasn't long before Charlie, with his brilliant mimicry and exquisite comic timing, had become the star of the troupe which also included Stan Laurel. In 1913, while on his second American tour with Karno, he was hired by Mack Sennett's Keystone Film Company and acted in his first films.

Like many of the great lefties, aided by solitary tendencies and the need for emotional compensation against the injustices of the world, Chaplin's work ethic was extraordinary. His first movie, *Making a Living*, premiered in 1914, a year in which Chaplin made 35 films, often working from seven in the morning and staying on set long after most of the cast had gone home.

THE LITTLE TRAMP The folk at Keystone were less than impressed with *Making a Living*, and Mack Sennett was unsure whether his signing of Chaplin was a dud. Chaplin's second film, *Kid Auto Races at Venice* (1914), however, introduced the Little Tramp, and confirmed his talent. To make the outfit, he borrowed from his fellow actors. The Little Tramp wore baggy pants borrowed from Fatty Arbuckle, size 14 shoes belonging to Chester Conklin, a tiny jacket, a Derby hat and a piece of black crepe cut to form a moustache. The Little Tramp was an instant hit and would appear in about 70 movies, shorts and features, over a period of 22 years.

Chaplin wrote about this seminal moment in his autobiography: 'I had no idea of the character. But the moment I was dressed, the clothes and the makeup made me feel the person he was. I began to know him, and by the time I walked on stage he was fully born.' By the end of this year he had refined the character and his presentation. In many ways the Little Tramp was a study in contrasts. Although shabbily dressed, Chaplin drew laughs from the audience through the delicacy of his gestures and his amazing sense of his own body—which was at least partly a by-product of the way left-handers are instinctively aware of their bodies due to their difference, and the necessity of learning to adapt to a right-handed world. By comparison, many of the other actors working for Keystone at the time were heavy-handed in their pursuit of the audience's mirth. While Chaplin

CHAPLIN'S LEFTY TRAITS

INTUITIVE Several of Chaplin's female friends and co-stars also remarked on his feminine qualities. Actress and co-founder of United Artists, Mary Pickford, said, 'one would never say he was effeminate, but I would consider that he is at least 60 per cent feminine. You can see it in his work; he has feminine intuition.'

EMPATHETIC Chaplin's ability to mime demanded strong powers of observation and the ability to get under the skin of others. Many people also described Chaplin as a great listener, a charm quality shared with fellow left-hander Bill Clinton.

VISUAL-SPATIAL ABILITY The way Chaplin used his body in films showed an incredible spatial awareness. This also translated into his directing methods where, rather than writing a script, he filmed until happy with the results.

LATERAL THINKING A master of transformations both in his life and art, Chaplin's skewed perspective had the left-handed gift of seeing one thing in terms of another.

HOT-TEMPERED A complete control freak, Chaplin was famous for his bad temper on set, but even more so in the conduct of his personal relationships.

SOLITARY Chaplin only liked to mix with his friends and family when he was in the mood. Most of the time he preferred the solitude of his work.

ICONOCLASTIC Chaplin managed to get himself effectively booted out of the USA during the McCarthy era for Moral Turpitude and the suspicion of being a Communist.

SELF-TAUGHT Chaplin never went to school and always had a troubled relationship with authority figures, preferring to work everything out for himself.

EXPERIMENTAL Although Chaplin's cinematographic methods weren't always the most innovative, he was a pioneer of the cinema.

FANTASIST Chaplin was a short, funny, left-handed guy from the London slums who, through the mass fantasy mechanisms of the cinema, built a fantasy Hollywood life for himself.

operated with delicacy and impeccable timing, the effect of the humour was earthy and sometimes cruel, in some ways reminiscent of the earthy and spiky anti-Puritan, anti-authoritarian satire of fellow left-hander Mark Twain.

THE MOGUL Because Hollywood and movie-making techniques were in their pioneering days, there was considerable latitude for those with the talent to exercise it. Chaplin worked this to his advantage and, when he left Keystone a year later, not only was he its top actor, he was also directing his own films. Being a left-hander in a world designed for the right can amplify the urge to control your immediate environment. Given Chaplin's appallingly unstable childhood, where he moved around at the whim of his mother's mental health, and was effectively supporting himself by the age of eight, it's no surprise that this tendency was magnified in Chaplin's personality. Becoming a movie director was the perfect opportunity for him to exert this need to control. While the character of the Little Tramp, who made Chaplin wealthy and famous, was a figure of anarchy and decency, in real life Chaplin frequently adopted the role of the petty tyrant, intent upon controlling every miniscule aspect of both his work and personal circumstances.

From Keystone Chaplin moved to Essanay, who had studios in Chicago and Northern California, where he made over ten movies, including *The Tramp*. Preferring Hollywood, and increasingly able to name his terms as his fame increased, Chaplin only lasted a year with them before signing up with the Mutual Film Corporation, who not only gave him creative control over his pictures, but promised to build a studio in Hollywood for him. The salary, a whopping US$670,000 a year, was five times as large as the combined salaries of the nine justices of US Supreme Court, and a harbinger of the financial stratosphere associated with Hollywood stardom. In the space of two years, Chaplin had become the hottest property in Hollywood. He made 12 movies over an 18-month period for Mutual, including *Easy Street* and *The Immigrant*, before the lure of independence and control saw Chaplin change again. In signing with First National, Chaplin made the first million-dollar deal in Hollywood history. Not only this but the deal to provide eight pictures established him as an independent. Chaplin built his own studio on Sunset Boulevard. The time it took to make a movie became longer since he now had the means and authority to indulge his perfectionism. Having made 35 films for Keystone in a year, for First National he made eight in five years including silent classics such as *A Dog's Life*, *The Kid* and *Pay Day*.

In 1919, Chaplin made a further move towards autonomy when he set up United Artists with fellow stars, Douglas Fairbanks, Mary Pickford and director, D. W. Griffith. Having been desperately poor throughout his childhood, Chaplin had an acute sense of finance. United Artists was primarily a way of guaranteeing that the spoils of the actors' stardom went into their own pockets. It also offered even more artistic freedom and, with no one to answer to, or for that matter consult with, Chaplin's dictatorial

personality went into full swing, producing the greatest of his silent films such as *Gold Rush*, *City Lights* and *Modern Times*. In this last film, made in 1936, Chaplin retired the Little Tramp. It also marked his cross-over from silent films to sound, a medium he never fully mastered. Among the more notable of his talkies, however, were *The Great Dictator*, *Monsieur Verdoux* and *Limelight*.

A TRAMP AMONG THE TRAMPS

It's interesting to note that few of the great left-handers chronicled in this book are womanisers. In a milieu of gays, asexual solitaries and monogamous men and women, Chaplin, Hendrix, Bill Clinton and Babe Ruth are the only men with a reputation for womanising. Many great lefties seem to enjoy the solitude of their own minds or the company of a tight circle of familiars. Chaplin, however, was married four times, usually to women in their teens, and took full advantage of the fabled Hollywood casting couch in between. His conquests were a veritable who's who of the silent screen and included Hetty Kelly, Edna Purviance, Rebecca West, Mildred Harris, Pola Negri, Lita Grey, May Reeves and Paulette Goddard. His taste for young women was a sexualised version of Lewis Carroll's love of young girls. His marriages to Mildred Harris and Lita Grey were both shotgun marriages, concluded only because of the potential for scandal and criminal charges if it became public knowledge that Chaplin had impregnated a minor. While his creative juices were in their prime, he needed to revitalise himself through new sexual and emotional connections. It's a pattern that bears some similarity to Martina Navratilova's partner swapping (both tennis and bed) at turning points in her career. Chaplin's womanising, however, was imbued with a strong sense

ABOVE: CHAPLIN AS THE DICTATOR OF TOMANIA, IN THE FILM *THE GREAT DICTATOR*, A SEND-UP OF HITLER AND NAZI GERMANY, 1940.

FOLLOWING PAGE: CHAPLIN DANCING WITH HIS WIFE, ACTRESS PAULETTE GODDARD, 1940.

of compensation: for the insecurity of his childhood and the, not always, happy creativity that ruled his temperament.

The waning of Chaplin's creative powers saw him enter the final great relationship of his life. At the age of 54 he married 18-year-old Oona O'Neill, daughter of American playwright Eugene O'Neill (who never spoke to his daughter again after her marriage). It proved an enduring and loving, if not entirely happy, marriage, and they had eight children together.

LATER LIFE All through his career, Chaplin showed a studied indifference for social conventions and got away with it. He put risqué material into his comedy that contraverted the ill-policed Hollywood code of conduct, and he slept with innumerable teenage starlets. While he was one of the wealthiest figures in Hollywood, he also became known as a communist sympathiser, and began associating conspicuously with the cream of the artistic and intellectual left. As someone whose life trajectory had proven so preposterously against the odds, he continued to ride them, carefully managing his cinema output to challenge the status quo but not so much that he'd be shut down.

Of course the period between the wars was known first for the decadence of the 1920s and then the Depression of the 1930s and, in some ways, Chaplin's political views followed the zeitgeist. When World War II broke out, he contributed by lampooning Hitler, who had at one time been a tramp—and who had in fact modelled his moustache on the Little Tramp's in the belief that it would enhance his popularity. *The Great Dictator* (1940) caused some consternation as the USA was yet to enter the war.

After the war Chaplin hit a snag by underestimating the aggressive paranoia of the McCarthy era. Attacks on Chaplin had been growing in the USA since the end of the war. He was particularly vulnerable to government sanction since he had never become an American citizen. In 1952, when he left for the English premier of *Limelight*, he learnt that his re-entry permit would not be renewed. Chaplin was forced to settle instead in Switzerland, where he remained for the rest of his life. Soon after this, he embarked on a film, *A King in New York*. Shot on London sets made to resemble New York, it was the first film to directly criticise the paranoia of the McCarthy era. While it received warm criticism in London, it wouldn't be shown in America for 15 years.

CURTAINS Chaplin only made one more feature film after that, *The Countess from Hong Kong* (1967), a flop starring Marlon Brando and Sophia Loren. Chaplin and Brando had a major clash of egos and the film only covered its production costs because one of the songs Chaplin had written became a hit for British pop star Petula Clark. In the last 20 years of his life, Chaplin wrote a number of autobiographical books which rather gilded the lily. He died in his sleep in 1977 only to become a prop in a real life comedy when Polish and Bulgarian mechanics stole his body and hid it in the hope of selling it back to the family.

LEFTY LINKS

1. It seems there are a disproportionate number of left-handers in the pantheon of successful actors. A possible reason is that lefties naturally developthe facility for adaptation and self-transformation, integral to their engagement with a right-handed world. In some cases it has helped the kind of body awareness necessary for mimicry. Three of the great mimics of the twentieth century—Chaplin, Marcel Marceau and W. C. Fields—were all left-handers. Other famous left-handed actors include Don Adams, Dan Aykroyd, Matthew Broderick, Drew Carey, Tom Cruise, Matt Dillon, Olivia de Havilland, Robert DeNiro, Fran Drescher, Richard Dreyfuss, Peter Fonda, Greta Garbo, Whoopie Goldberg, Betty Grable, Cary Grant, Mark Hamill, Rex Harrison, Goldie Hawn, Rock Hudson, Angelina Jolie, Danny Kaye, Diane Keaton, Nicole Kidman, Lisa Kudrow, Michael Landon, Hope Lange, Joey Lawrence, Peter Lawford, Shirley MacLaine, Harpo Marx, Marilyn Monroe, Kim Novak, Ryan O'Neal, Sarah Jessica Parker, Anthony Perkins, Luke Perry, Richard Pryor, Ronald Reagan, Robert Redford, Keanu Reeves, Julia Roberts, Mickey Rourke, Telly Savalas, Jerry Seinfeld, Christian Slater, Terence Stamp, Rod Steiger, Emma Thompson, Peter Ustinov, Dick Van Dyke and Bruce Willis.

2. One of the things about left-handers is their facility for adaptation and change, which may be why they can be found excelling in the Protean moments of history. Chaplin prospered at the beginning of the film era because an orthodox way of doing things was yet to be established. The same might be said for Jimi Hendrix, Paul McCartney and music, Henry Ford and the automobile industry, as well as Bill Gates in computers. Having less invested in the status quo, the lefty has an innate capacity to seize the moment of change. As the philosopher Walter Benjamin once said, 'all the decisive blows are struck left-handed'.

3. Chaplin's left-handedness probably came from his mother. Spencer Dryden, who was the son of Charlie's half-brother Wheeler Dryden (same mother, different father), was the drummer in Jefferson Airplane and was also left-handed.

Babe Ruth

1895–1948

FROM BIRTH IN THE BALTIMORE SLUMS AND CHILDHOOD IN A reformatory school, George Herman Ruth became the hero of a nation for his phenomenal left-handed hitting of the baseball. Known as the 'the Babe', 'Bambino' or 'the Sultan of Swat', at the peak of his career he hit baseballs out of ballparks all over America. His record of 61 Major League home runs in a season remained unbroken until 1961 and has only been beaten by four players since (three of them with the possible help of performance enhancing drugs). Ruth still holds the record for the third-highest number of home runs in the history of the game. An old school, play-hard—on and off the field—sportsman, he was the greatest American icon of his time, a generous spirit who captured the brash confidence of a nation in the process of becoming the world's most powerful. As his team-mate of the time Lefty Gomez said, 'He was a circus, a play and a movie, all rolled into one. Kids adored him, Men idolised him. Women loved him. There was something about him that made him great.' A considerable part of that something was his amazing amalgam of left-handed talents.

YOUNG BABE Ruth's parents were German-Americans who operated a grocery and saloon in Pigtown, a slum near a slaughterhouse in Baltimore. It wasn't a healthy life. His parents worked hard and probably drank hard too. Only one other of Ruth's seven siblings survived to adulthood. As a child, Ruth was a livewire. His restless energy got him into trouble. When he was seven, his father took him on a street trolley to the outskirts of town and left him at St Mary's Industrial School for Boys. It was run by the Xaverian Brothers and was a combination of school, reformatory and workhouse, specialising in the training of delinquent boys. The atmosphere was disciplinarian, and conformity was enforced by use of the strap. Although a natural left-hander, Ruth was forced to learn to write with his right hand and would continue to do so for the rest of his life. As such he

Yours Truly "Babe" Ruth #6

never really went for books or writing. His literacy wasn't helped by being forced to write with his right hand, and his sentiments towards school were in line with the famous boys in the tales of lefty author Mark Twain. Today, Ruth would have been diagnosed with attention deficit hyperactivity disorder (ADHD) and dosed with Ritalin. Ruth was a natural rebel and the strictures and emotional shortfalls of his boyhood meant there was something coiled up inside his spirit that was busting to be unleashed. He may well have turned to crime, were it not for baseball.

A terrible place to spend a childhood in many ways, St Mary's had the singular advantage of being an excellent place to shine on the baseball diamond—except for the fact they had no right-handed mitts for lefty fielders. Academic studies were not taken too seriously and the Xaverian Brothers were often young men from poor families who had joined the church because it offered three square meals a day. Many of them were young enough to still be playing baseball. With so many boys around, it was always possible to put together a team. As a result, Ruth played baseball every day, 10 months a year. Since his parents never visited on Sundays, he played baseball. Since he never got to go home for holidays, he played it too. And well. Brother Matthias, 1.98 metres and a good batter of both boys and balls, noticed Ruth's talent and encouraged it. The school had its own baseball league, which borrowed the names of major teams, and played each other. Ruth became the school's star pitcher and hitter. He became a hero to his fellow residents, a status he would retain for the rest of his life.

STARTING OUT On 14 February 1914, acting on information from a brother coaching a baseball team from a competition Xaverian Brothers school, Jack Dunn, owner and manager of the minor league Baltimore Orioles, went down to St Mary's to take a look at Ruth and came back having signed him as a left-handed pitcher for US$250 a month. For Ruth it was an unfathomable amount of money. At Spring training in Fayetteville, North Carolina, where he rode in a train and elevator for the first time in his life, he acquired his nickname and hit the longest home run the local ground had ever seen.

After Ruth's first season pitching for the Orioles, Dunn had financial problems and sold him to the major league Boston Red Sox. Ruth didn't want to leave his friends but he took the raise (US$625 a month)—and the train. He showed his lefty impulsiveness by picking up the 16-year-old waitress in the Back Bay station diner he breakfasted in when he got off the train. She would later become his wife. He then went to Fenway Park, home of the Red Sox, and was fitted for a uniform before playing that afternoon and pitching his first seven innings in major league baseball for a win.

In a game where those who reach the top echelons usually have been playing since they were young, a left-handed pitch forces a batter to adapt his pre-conditioned responses. In other words, a left-hander's pitches take a few micro-seconds to adjust to, but only if they remain in the minority. This is a pure example of the left-hander's enhanced capacity to surprise an

OPPOSITE: AS A PITCHER, 'THE BABE' WAS FORCED TO WEAR A RIGHT-HANDED GLOVE AS LEFTY GLOVES WERE NOT YET AVAILABLE.

PAGE 187: KNOWN AS THE 'SULTAN OF SWAT' AND THE 'COLOSSUS OF CLOUT', RUTH PLAYED FOR THE YANKEES FROM 1920–34.

RUTH'S LEFTY TRAITS

INTUITIVE The Babe was a man of instinct and appetites. The reflexes required to put bat against ball had nothing to do with the rational mind. Nor did the rest of his life.

EMPATHETIC One of the reasons why Ruth was so loved was due to his generosity, and his willingness to spend hours on end signing autographs for kids. He knew what it was like having nothing and, while he enjoyed his money, he never acquired airs and graces.

VISUAL-SPATIAL ABILITY The Babe had some of the best instinctive eye-hand coordination one is ever likely to see.

HOT-TEMPERED Ruth abused umpires and threatened to punch them. He did the same to opponents, his team-mates and sometimes team management. But after the heat had gone out of his temper, he always apologised and rarely bore a grudge.

ICONOCLASTIC Rules were something Ruth had no respect for and, while he loved baseball, he was often in conflict with its administrators. Adultery, boozing his way through prohibition, speeding and crashing cars also brought him to the attention of the law.

SELF-TAUGHT Ruth was an instinctive player and, when he was a kid, he honed his instincts by just playing and playing.

opponent. Having established himself in the Red Sox line-up, Ruth became a crucial part of a highly successful team, helping them to League Pennants and the World Series in 1915, 1916 and 1918. The record he set for scoreless innings, pitched in World Series games, would last until 1961. However, it was his hitting ability that would take him (and innumerable baseballs) into the stratosphere of fame.

THE SULTAN OF SWAT Ruth's emergence as a home-run hitter in 1919 was to change the whole complexion of the game and make him one of the most famous people in America. Before Ruth, baseball was concentrated on the inside game, the high-speed subtleties of bunts, singles and steals. Even in this old-school mode of playing, the left-hander is gifted an advantage by the asymmetry of the baseball field. When the ball is hit, the batter runs counter-clockwise towards first base on the right. The left-handed hitter is already facing this way after their swing, while the right-hander has to turn from facing in the opposite direction, giving the lefty a fraction of a head start off the plate.

Ruth had this advantage, but he often neglected to use it by hitting the ball right out of the park. His hitting created excitement wherever he went. People were astonished at the power of a man who could hit a baseball, according to some accounts, over 180 metres. In these swings there was something akin to a moment of perfect self-expression which added a sense of poetry to their brutality. In 1919, Ruth set the record of 29 for most home runs in a major league season and was sold to the Yankees as a fully fledged star for a record fee. The Boston Red Sox would long regret this. In what became known as 'the Curse of the Bambino', following success in 1919, they wouldn't win another pennant until 2004.

The conditions in baseball were ideally suited for the emergence of a left-handed slugger like Ruth. In addition to the advantage of the lefty's game demanding adaptation from pitchers, recent changes in the game also worked in Ruth's favour. A variety of trick balls had been banned, such as the 'spit ball' and 'emery ball', where the surface of the ball was changed by spit, vaseline or scratching to change its path through the air. The balls had also been made harder by using the superior toughness of an Australian wool yarn, which meant it could be wound tighter without breaking. This created a harder ball that travelled further when it was hit. New concrete technologies also saw a rash of stadium construction, where distances between the plate and the fence were shortened. The lefty was even further advantaged in that the right-field fence, the natural destination for a lefty hit, tended to be shortened more than either centre or left-field.

When Ruth began playing for the Yankees in 1920, crowd attendance increased from 619,000 the year before, to over 1,300,000. That year, he exploded the home run record, hitting 54. His slugging average of .849 would remain a record until 2001. Overnight, he was a national phenom-enon, not just a great pitcher, but the best hitter baseball had ever seen. The next year he went five better, hitting 59. That year the Yankees won their first American League Pennant and the right to play their more established rivals and landlords, the New York Giants, in their first World Series. Ruth's arm became infected after sliding into first base during Game Two. He scraped it again during Game Three, hit his first home run with it heavily bandaged in Game 4, then played with a tube coming out of his arm to drain the pus in Game Five, before being ordered to rest by the doctor. At this point the Yankees were up 3–2 but, with Ruth out, the Giants won the rest of the games to take the best of nine series 5–3.

THE COLOSSUS OF CLOUT
Throughout his life, Ruth had a classically left-handed problem with authority. After the World Series loss of 1922, he embarked on an exhibition tour that had been banned by the Baseball Commissioner, Judge Landis. Despite knowing of the ban, the Babe did it anyway and was suspended for the first seven weeks of the 1922 season. Ruth also had a left-handed temper. That season he called an umpire a coward and threatened to wallop him, and he also had fights with other ball players from both the opposition and his own team.

In 1922, having missed more than 20 per cent of the season, Ruth still hit 35 home runs, which ranked third for the year. The Yankees made the World Series and were beaten again by the Giants, even though Ruth played in all games. Ruth finished the 1923 season with a career-high .393 batting average and major-league leading 41 home runs. This time Ruth starred as they defeated the Giants 4–2 in the World Series. He batted .368, walked eight times, scored eight runs, hit three home runs and slugged 1.000 during the series. The Babe had another fine year in 1924. He hit .378, with 46 home runs and 121 runs batted in, but the Yankees missed the Pennant finishing two games behind Washington. In 1925, Ruth was ill and finished the season with only 25 home runs having missed a chunk of games. The Yankees finished second last.

After 1925, people began to wonder whether Ruth, with his high-living ways, had reached his peak and was on the slide. Not so. In 1926, he hit 47 home runs and batted .372. The Yankees made the World Series only to lose to the St Louis Cardinals, although Ruth set a World Series record by hitting three home runs in one game. He set a less enviable record in the last game with a wild lefty gamble that went wrong. In the final innings, with the series still at stake he attempted a steal and was the last man out, making him the only person to finish a World Series with a failed attempt at a steal.

In 1927, Ruth hit his career high 60 home runs and the Yankees won the World Series against the Pittsburgh Pirates. The next year, he hit 54 and the Yankees again won the World Series, this time against the St Louis Cardinals. Ruth was also top home-run scorer for the next three years, though the Yankees didn't make it to the World Series. All in all, Ruth was equal or top home-run hitter in the American League for 12 seasons. In 1932 the Yankees beat the Chicago Cubs. It was Ruth's last World Series and it became clear that his star was on the wane. The Yankees sold him in 1934, and he spent his final season in major league baseball playing for the Boston Braves.

LEFTY LINKS

1. Baseball is a sport where lefties have proportionally out-performed righties, both in batting and pitching. Ruth's team-mate Lou Gehrig was a fellow lefty great. When Ruth's record for most home runs in a season fell, it was to left-handed hitter Roger Maris. (At the time of writing, the record is held by lefty, Barry Bonds.) Another great lefty hitter is former Boston Red Sox figure Ted Williams. The last man to average over .400 in a season, he is considered by some to be the greatest hitter of all time. Five of the top 10 in the all-time home-run list are lefties, as are nine of the top 20 and 35 of the top 100. Another four from the top 100 were switch hitters, such as Micky Mantle, who batted both left- and right-handed.

2. Left-handed pitchers are valued for their unpredictability. Most Major League teams have at least one left-handed pitcher in their rotation. Of the eight players to win the rare Major League Triple Crown for pitching, four of them were left-handed. Only southpaw, Sandy Koufax, has landed the Triple Crown three times. Between 1956–2006, the Cy Young Award for Best Pitcher in the National League went to a left-hander 18 times, a hugely disproportionate 36 per cent. In the American League between 1958 and 2006, it went to a lefty 12 times, making for a less spectacular but still impressive 25 per cent.

3. Baseball is where the term 'southpaw' originated. Because games were played in the afternoon, the best seats were in the west of the ground so patrons wouldn't have to deal with the glare of the sun. As a consequence a left-handed pitcher had his arm facing south when he pitched, hence the nickname.

4. In the game of cricket, which bears some resemblance to baseball, there also seems to be an advantage to being left-handed, particularly in batting. In the recent Australian Test Cricket team, rated one of the greatest ever, five of the seven recognised batsmen have been left-handers. In the history of Australian test cricket, 17 per cent of bowlers and 20 per cent of batsmen have been left-handed. Other great left-handers include West Indians, Sir Garfield Sobers and Brian Lara (the highest run scorer in Test cricket), South African Graeme Pollock and Pakistani all-rounder Wasim Akram.

BAD BOY BABE With his prodigious talent, for most of his career Ruth lived beyond the rules. His instinctive ability, appetite for life and generous spirit were his only operational principles. Having grown up in deprived circumstances, his popularity and the money he was earning saw him leading his life like a kid let loose in a candy store. It was a land of plenty, where he could escape the strict discipline of St Mary's, which had made him use his right hand and tried to beat him into conformity with the exception of playing ball. Ruth's hyperactivity meant he never stopped except to sleep and apparently he didn't do a lot of that. Everything else, he pretty much did to excess. Although he had married the waitress he met on his first day in Boston, on the road he behaved much as a single man, albeit one with a phenomenal libido. According to team-mates it was not unusual for him to sleep with more than three women in a night. There was a line of women waiting for him in every town. Unusually, this never seemed to inspire male jealousy to the extent that the Babe had to be careful where he went. He was also a man's man and, when on tour, was known to stay up all night boozing, playing cards and carousing, then going out the next afternoon to hit home runs. His capacity for booze matched the one he had for the ladies and was made all the more interesting by the fact that his career coincided with the farce of Prohibition which began in 1920 and would last until 1933. During his heyday, it was nothing for him to drink more than a bottle of Scotch during an evening session. Considering the prevalence of performance enhancing drugs in baseball today, it makes his achievements all the more impressive. Added to these sensual appetites was Ruth's gluttony. He would eat two huge steaks, a dozen hotdogs or a massive plate of ribs at one sitting and, in his prime, was capable of eating 10 meals in a day. Of course, all this excess meant he was at constant risk of falling out of his prime. A well-built 1.88 metres, Ruth had serious problems with his weight and used to rely on catching the flu in the pre-season to bring him back to ideal playing weight. In the latter part of his career, faced with a major form slump in 1925, he became one of the first sportsmen to get a personal trainer in the form of former boxer and gymnasium entrepreneur, Artie McGovern, whose interventions were largely responsible for keeping him in the game till the ripe old age of 39.

CODA After retiring from baseball, Ruth looked for coaching opportunities, but his reputation for fractiousness and ill discipline put most owners off. He was first base coach for the Brooklyn Dodgers for a season, but that was it. The remainder of his life was an anti-climax given the previous dizzying pinnacle of his fame. Still, the Babe remained a hero to many Americans and, when he died from cancer in 1948, more than 200,000 people came to pay their respects as he lay in state at Yankee Stadium, also known as the House that Babe Built, arguably the greatest folk hero baseball has ever known.

OPPOSITE: THE BABE SIGNING AN AUTOGRAPH FOR TWO PAGEBOYS ON THE ROOF OF THE SAVOY HOTEL, DURING HIS VISIT TO LONDON, FEBRUARY 1935.

1912–54 ALAN TURING WAS PERHAPS ONE OF THE MOST ORIGINAL AND ECCENTRIC mathematical minds the world has ever known. His early career involved elegant intuitive solutions to problems in pure mathematics. Although despised by military leaders for his creative anarchy, he became an unheralded national hero with his pivotal work in breaking the German's Enigma codes during World War II. Via his esoteric desire to explore the free will determinism debate, he became the effective inventor of what we now refer to as the computer, and set the scene for the information revolution that shapes our world today. A classic left-handed maverick with a great capacity for lateral and intuitive mathematical thinking, Turing's homosexuality compounded his natural apartness from the world. When he admitted to it, while explaining to Lancashire police who he thought had robbed his house, he was arrested, charged and forced to go on hormone therapy in order to 'cure' his deviancy. Two years later he was found dead in his house after eating an apple laced with cyanide. To this day it remains unclear whether it was an accident, suicide or something more sinister based on information he may have known. It was definitely a tragic end to the life of a largely unrecognised national hero.

EARLY TURING Turing was born the youngest son of Julius and Sarah Turing. His father was an Indian Civil Servant and, for much of his childhood, he lived with friends of the family while his parents were at work in India. From an early age Turing showed signs of the left-handed auto-didact. For instance, in 1917, at the age of five, he taught himself to read in three weeks, and his facility with figures was even greater. With his parents away, his highly independent, individualistic intelligence developed relatively unfettered.

When his father returned from India, having resigned from the service in 1919, his son refused to accept his authority. He was smart, cheeky and by

ALAN TURING'S LEFTY TRAITS

INTUITIVE Turing's mathematical method was brilliantly intuitive and he often came to conclusions without relying on prior research in the field.

VISUAL-SPATIAL ABILITY This was seen in Turing's ability to visualise concrete solutions to abstract mathematical problems.

LATERAL THINKING Similar to the above, Turing had the mental ability to transform the abstract into the concrete and vice versa.

SOLITARY As a mathematician, Turing was famous for solving problems on his own and, with the exception of his boyhood friend Christopher, his emotional life remained solitary, even if he was capable of being a convivial companion.

ICONOCLASTIC Turing was unashamed of his homosexuality, and the creative anarchy of his Bletchley Park days demonstrated his contempt for mindless authority.

SELF-TAUGHT Turing taught himself to read in three weeks at the age of five, and many of his adult ideas sprung from the way science books had affected his imagination as a child. Never one for the formalities of the classroom, he achieved his mathematical breakthroughs with an unusual degree of independence from the thoughts of others.

EXPERIMENTAL From an early age Turing loved to perform chemical experiments, and his interest in engineering the actual technology that proved his mathematical conclusions, showed that there was an empirical side to this mathematical genius.

all accounts phenomenally messy as a child. Around 1924, he discovered chemistry and was attracted by the simplicity of the way atoms were put together. Yet being a child of the English upper middle classes, chemistry was viewed by his parents as a sideline of the main game, which was a public school education, with the requisite emphasis upon the classics. Rescued from the deeply conservative Marlborough College by his older brother's observation that it would squash him, Turing was sent to the slightly less repressive Sherbourne College. In this nonetheless highly conformist environment, Turing was soon conspicuous as a friendless solitary. His mind was already committed to maths and science and his report cards noted his lack of effort in the subjects he wasn't interested in. Even in math, his masters were ambivalent. While his teacher was sufficiently amazed at his ability to solve complex equations to remark that he was a genius, he also wrote on his report card, 'Not very good. He spends a good deal of time apparently in investigations in advanced mathematics to the neglect of elementary work. A solid groundwork is essential in any subject. His work is dirty.' His form master in 1927, A. H. Trelawny Ross, believed that Germany's defeat in World War II was due to the fact that Germany 'thought that science and materialism were stronger than religious thought and observance'. A teacher of English and Latin, he was fond of saying, 'This room smells of mathematics! Go out and fetch a disinfectant spray.' Such a mediocre education had little effect on Turing, other than to consolidate the independence of his left-handed mind. It gave him the impression that thinking was a solitary activity practised by relatively few, and learning was a thing you did by yourself. Ignoring his lessons, he spent his time instead reading and 'improving' upon Einstein's Theory of Relativity.

Turing's isolation was breached that same year, when he fell in love with Christopher Morcom, a small and slight boy a year older than him. Socially awkward and incapable of small talk, Turing was able to form a bond with Christopher through their shared fascination with science. They applied for Trinity scholarships together, and Turing was disappointed when Christopher got one and he didn't. He was even more devastated soon after when, in February 1930, Christopher was admitted to hospital with complications from childhood bovine tuberculosis and died six days after. His only real friend was gone.

CAMBRIDGE The death of Christopher proved to be a motivation in Turing's subsequent mathematical career for a number of reasons. In his grief he determined that he would continue his scientific career on behalf of Christopher as well. His innate facility and fascination with science now had a powerful emotional underpinning.

The following year, Turing won a scholarship to his second-choice college at Cambridge, King's. It was serendipitous. A small college with a tolerance both of eccentricity and homosexuality and some excellent scientists, it was an ideal place for Turing's unique talents to prosper.

In 1935, Turing was elected a Fellow of King's College with the backing of the great economist, John Maynard Keynes. It provided a stipend, rooms, High Table dining privileges and no duties, and was the perfect job for a lefty individualist such as Turing.

Christopher's death also provoked Turing to existential musings. One of the mathematical expressions of this, which displayed his capacity for lateral thought, was his engagement with the decision problem. The decision problem asks whether the human faculty of reasoning can be reduced to computation. The seventeenth-century German mathematician, Gottfried Leibniz (famous for inventing calculus independently of Isaac Newton and also for the binary number system on which computers are based), had envisioned a calculus of reason, whereby debates between men could be solved by calculation. Turing's approach to the problem showed striking originality. He invented an idealised machine which consisted of a tape divided into squares (like toilet paper) over which a scanner passes writing and/or erasing a succession of binary zeros and ones. Such a simple machine was able to do all sorts of complicated mathematical calculations. It became known as a 'Turing machine'. A particular feature of the Turing machine was that each machine's function could be encapsulated in a single number which could be fed into another machine. What this meant is that when a machine was fed the number of another machine it would imitate its functions perfectly. This became known as a 'universal Turing machine' and was the precursor to the digital computers in use today. In answer to the decision question, Turing concluded that in certain cases, such as when a machine was fed its own number and worked on itself, there would be insoluble logical conundrums, similar to the paradox 'I am lying'. Leibniz's dream of a calculus of reason was proven impossible, yet the computer age had been born. Its progenitor, Turing, was only 23 years old.

Just as he was putting the finishing touches to his work on the decision problem, Turing discovered it had also been solved by a Princeton University mathematician Alonzo Church using a technique called lambda calculus. Even though Turing's solution was more elegant, he decided to take a PhD at Princeton under Church. He graduated in 1938 and returned to Cambridge, where he argued with Wittgenstein over math and philosophy. One of their major bones of contention was that Wittgenstein believed that no one had ever been hurt by a logical contradiction. Turing had shown by his machines that he considered the abstract in concrete ways. It's a propensity often found in left-handers, one he shared for instance with Marie Curie, whose experiments preceded theory. As a mathematician this wasn't so easy to do, though Turing passionately believed that mathematics had an effect on the real world. He replied to Wittgenstein that a logical contradiction in an equation used to design a bridge might cause it to fall down. However, the true, real world value of his mathematical genius was about to be manifested in a far more dramatic context.

PAGE 195: CODE-BREAKER ALAN TURING PICTURED IN 1952, DURING THE TIME HE WAS WORKING AT MANCHESTER UNIVERSITY IN ENGLAND.

ENIGMATIC The Nazi invasion of Poland in 1939 saw Britain declare war on Germany. Along with several King's College Fellows, Turing was seconded to Bletchley Park, northwest of London, where the British cipher service had been relocated. The Nazis were using a trumped up version of the Enigma machine to encrypt most of their information. Enigma machines had been used to code information since the 1920s but, during the war, more than 100,000 were used by the Nazis. The machines worked by continually changing the substitution alphabet as a message was encoded. They did this through a combination of keyboard, electric plugboards and rotors, which drastically increased the permutations by which the substitutions could take place. Technically, only someone with an Enigma machine with the same settings would be able to decipher a message sent through them. For Turing, whose task it was to crack the German's naval Enigma code, this was a major mathematical challenge. For his country it was vital. Germany's U-boats were decimating the maritime supply route to Britain, with the consequence that the country was in danger of running out of food. Using fragments of insight provided by Polish mathematicians, who had already made inroads into cracking the Enigma code, Turing and his team went to work.

When Turing first arrived at Bletchley Park, he was one of only two people who believed that the Naval Enigma could be broken. He soon detected a weakness in the code. Within the coded messages there were often fragments of regulation text such as *'Heil Hitler'* or headings such as *'Wetter für die Nacht'*, whose meaning could be guessed. These 'cribs', as they were called, could be used to produce logical chains which corresponded to the billions of possible Enigma settings. If one of these chains produced a contradiction then it and the billions of settings attached to it could be ruled out.

With the task reduced to processing millions of logical chains for contradictions, Turing worked out how to build a machine which would automatically test for logical consistency. The machine, called a Bombe, weighed a tonne and was 2 metres high, 0.6 metres wide and 2.1 metres long. It had dozens of rotating drums, which impersonated the wheels of the Enigma, and massive coils of coloured wire. The machine got its name because, with all its relay switches ticking away as the chains were checked one by one, it sounded something like a bomb.

During the course of the war, 210 such Bombes were built. Turing and his team were able to decipher the German Naval Enigma Code and change the course of the war. On a good day it would take the Bombes little more than an hour to decipher the information. Even when the Germans became aware that the security of their information had been breached, they couldn't believe it was the Enigma machine. They knew it was breakable but didn't believe that anyone would make the effort to go through all the billions of permutations in order to be able to break it. Turing's machine, which was a left-handed masterpiece of transforming abstract mathematical questions into concrete and usable technology, had saved the day.

LEFTY LINKS

1. The longevity of Turing's mourning for Christopher Morcom in some ways resembled the grief of the left-handed Queen Victoria for her consort Prince Albert. For years after his death, Turing would go and stay with Morcom's family and he remained in correspondence with the mother until her death in 1941. This is interesting because, in so many other ways, Turing was an uber-rationalist and devoid of sentimentalism. Both Victoria and Turing seem never to have recovered from the death of their first beloved. It seems unlikely that Victoria ever had another lover. While Turing had other loves in his later life that were physically consummated, it is doubtful whether his relationship with Morcom was. However, none of the later relationships had the same romantic intensity as that with Morcom, who was both Turing's first love and first real friend.

2. Turing is one of the lefties in this book who support a recent Canadian survey that left-handers are more likely to be homosexual. One of the theories for left-handedness is that the right-brain becomes dominant due to exposure to testosterone in the womb. In Turing's day, homosexuality was viewed as a medical condition that could be cured. Hormone therapy was one of the treatments. Interestingly, attempts in America to treat homosexuals with testosterone, on the basis that they suffered from a lack of masculinity, had failed. The libido of the patients actually increased. Turing was treated using the female hormone oestrogen. The physical effects included gaining weight and growing breasts. A year after he finished the treatment, Turing probably committed suicide. Is it possible that this was linked to some chemical imbalance that affected the brilliance of his testosterone-powered, left-handed mind?

3. Chris McManus offers a brilliant and accessible acocunt of how symmetry and assymmetry are related to handedness in his book *Right Hand, Left Hand*. See particularly Chapters 5 and 6.

OPPOSITE: THE NAZIS DID NOT BELIEVE IT WAS POSSIBLE FOR ANYONE TO CRACK THE CODE OF THEIR ENIGMA MACHINE.

While Turing's left-handed brilliance was saving the British war effort, it was not particularly simpatico with army life. An eccentric figure, Turing had a strong affinity with reason and was relatively immune to social convention. When faced with the problem of hayfever while riding his bicycle to work, he simply wore a gas mask. At Bletchley, his leadership of Hut 8, according to his biographer, Andrew Hodges, resulted in an environment of 'creative anarchy'. This radical, left-handed individualism didn't necessarily mesh well with the bureaucracy. As his colleague of the time Peter Hilton claimed:

> His procedure . . . would be maybe to come in at midday and work until midnight the next day. And then, the problem essentially solved, go off and rest up and not come back for 24 hours perhaps . . . they were getting much more work out of Alan Turing that way. But, as I say, the bureaucrats came along and wanted forms to be filled in and wanted us to clock in, and so on.

More vital was the fact that, due to turf wars in the services, there was always a problem of staffing at Bletchley. Many in the Armed Services hierarchy didn't want to credit breaking the Enigma codes with their true importance, because it meant losing some of their authority to make decisions. The idea of a bunch of ill-disciplined boffins controlling the war effort appalled them. Turing was impatient with fools and failed to deal very well in a world where petty ego, rather than reason, could be responsible for decision making. The situation with staffing became so serious that, in the end, Turing went over the heads of everyone to British Prime Minister, Winston Churchill. The Prime Minister, who was the only official with direct access to all the decoded Enigma messages, ordered that the Bletchley mob be given whatever they needed as a matter of 'extreme priority'.

POST-WAR TURING After the war, Turing contributed to various pioneering computer projects before settling down at Manchester University, where he was the director of the computing laboratory that produced the world's first commercially available computer. But for most of the twilight of his career, Turing's attention branched off into an area which, ultimately, would be related to theories of handedness. Turing became interested in the mathematics of biological structures—such as why, for instance, the heads of broccoli are congruent with the Fibonacci series. His particular interest was on how asymmetry can arise out of symmetric conditions. His answer, a brilliant piece of intuitive scientific thinking, was that a possible cause was the non-linearity of chemical equations of reaction and diffusion. The calculations to test this idea were simply too many to be able to be done by hand but, because he had access to a computer, it was possible for him to test model chemical reactions. It was a founding moment in the kinds of non-linear dynamic theory, that now include Chaos Theory and the complex modelling of financial markets.

Turing's willingness to be different and his indifference to social norms brought him undone in 1952. One day while walking in Manchester he caught the eye of a 19-year-old, working-class youth called Arnold Murray. It became something of a rough trade affair. However, when Turing was invited to appear on the BBC radio debate on the issue 'Can Automatic Calculating Machines Be Said to Think', his lover tipped off a mate, who robbed Turing's house while he was out. Because he was a homosexual, the burglars didn't expect Turing would go to the police, for fear of being outed. Turing, however, did. It was an unwise thing to have done. In the course of explaining to the police who he thought was responsible, he admitted to the affair with Arnold, and gave the police no option but to charge him with gross indecency—the offence Oscar Wilde had been charged with in 1885.

Turing was sentenced to two years' probation and a course of oestrogen therapy, a form of chemical castration. On the surface his life seemed far from shattered. The case hadn't received widespread media attention and, after the effects of the hormone therapy wore off, he travelled to Greece for a romantic liaison. Yet other events were troubling. For a long time after the war, Turing had continued to work for British intelligence. With his conviction, he lost his security clearance, since homosexuals were particularly vulnerable to blackmail. He also became disenchanted with a society that he had done so much to help. In some ways it was a crisis of faith. Turing sought solutions outside of science, immersing himself in the literature of Tolstoy, and having sessions with a Jungian therapist. While there is at least a conspiracy theory case for his assassination, it seems more likely that when he ate the apple laced with cyanide on 7 June 1954, it was a successful suicide attempt.

1942–70

FEW PEOPLE HAVE DEFINED THE WAY A MUSICAL INSTRUMENT IS USED TO the extent that Jimi Hendrix did. Rated by *Rolling Stone* magazine as the greatest guitarist of all time, the combination of his unorthodox left-handed playing, embrace of fledgling electronic sound technologies and obsessive pursuit of his own unique vision, massively expanded the instrument's sonic possibilities. From a poverty-stricken childhood and gruelling musical apprenticeship, Hendrix emerged to become one of the mega-stars of the sixties, the first African-American rock star to cross over to a predominantly white audience with his mixed race intercontinental band, the Jimi Hendrix Experience. In becoming a rock god, Hendrix took the blues and transformed it into a psychedelic experience that was accompanied by outrageous fashion, major-league drug taking, and a stage act that matched the wildness of the music with stunts such as playing the guitar with his teeth, smashing guitars and setting them on fire.

EARLY LIFE Jimi Hendrix was born into a poor but multi-racial district of Seattle, Washington. He was the cause of his parents', Lucille and Al's, shotgun marriage. Knowing he was about to be drafted into World War II, Al Hendrix accelerated his courtship of the 16-year-old Lucille with the consequence that she fell pregnant with Jimi. Al then went off to war. Jimi would be three years old and already in foster care before he met his father.

Lucille and Al were both big drinkers and not very good at holding down jobs. They fought and broke up on a regular basis and the Hendrix children were frequently shuffled around in a range of official and unofficial foster care arrangements. Genetically, they were not a great match. While Jimi and his brother, Leon, were healthy, their younger siblings were not so lucky: Joe was born with two rows of teeth, a club foot and a cleft palate; Kathy was born blind; Pamela had health problems and died

young; while Alfred had developmental disabilities. The four younger children would spend little, if any, time with their parents and Al refused to admit to the paternity of all of them except Jimi and Leon.

When Jimi's parents finally broke up for good, his mother's lifestyle degenerated into full-blown alcoholism and quasi-prostitution. For most of his childhood Hendrix lived with his father. Al Hendrix was one of those classically hypocritical parents who were strict (often violently) with their kids, while pursuing a wild life of his own. Perhaps as a consequence, Jimi developed into a mostly passive rebel, although he was hyper-competitive as a musician and prone to uncontrollable rages when he had too much to drink.

FIRST GUITARS Hendrix was fascinated by guitars long before he had one. As a kid, one of Hendrix's favourite movies was *Johnny Guitar* (1954), a western where the hero rode into the sunset with a guitar instead of a rifle strapped to his back. According to father Al Hendrix, he would order Jimi to clean his room only to return to find him playing the broom with strands of straw scattered all over the floor. His first guitar was a battered one-string acoustic another kid had thrown out. Although his father would castigate him for spending too much time playing music, he also bought Jimi his first real guitars, a US$5 right-hand acoustic guitar, then a white Super Ozark electric. When he could afford to put strings on these, he played the guitar obsessively—with the strings on upside down. Although he didn't know why, playing guitar right-handed felt instinctively wrong. Left-handed guitars were rarer and more expensive and Jimi had to make do with what he had, so he swapped the strings around, so that the low E string remained on the top and the high strings on the bottom when he played the guitar left-handed.

As with many of the great lefties of history, Hendrix's lack of formal education was perhaps a crucial factor in the development of his unique talent. A daydreaming child, he was forced to write with his right-hand by his school and father. His grades got worse and worse as he skipped school just to wander around the neighbourhood or play guitar. From a B and C grade student in elementary school, he deteriorated to the point where he had to repeat ninth grade. His father blamed it on his guitar playing and Jimi often had to hide his guitar at friends' houses in case his father would get mad and smash it up. When his friends turned up at Hendrix's house with instruments, Al would shout at them that playing music wasn't going to get them a job. After repeating ninth grade, Jimi pretty much stopped going to class altogether, and just spent his time travelling round the neighbourhood jamming with all the local musicians, watching and learning by imitation. By this time, his first band, the Velvetones, had played their first professional gigs, but Jimi still couldn't afford to buy himself and his first girlfriend, Betty Jean, a hamburger when they went on a date.

When Jimi began to play the electric guitar, this changed the sound because the strings were located in a different position from the pick-ups that carried the sound to the amplifier. As a result, the low strings were bright and the high strings mellow. Most of the time Hendrix played a Fender Stratocaster. Playing it upside down also made it easier for him to access the tone/volume knobs and tremolo bar, which were intrinsic to the originality of his sound.

Hendrix never learnt to read or write music. He used his ear in the same way Leonardo used his eye. His constant playing and jamming trained his ear by exposing him to a variety of influences. Although he absorbed the sounds of other guitarists easily, he developed an idiosyncratic style which he would remain true to, no matter what the cost. When later serving his apprenticeship as a sideman for musicians such as Little Richard, Ike and Tina Turner and Sam Cooke, for example, he was often fired for his inability to temper his flamboyant guitar style and flashy solos. One of the reasons for his uniqueness, was that Hendrix couldn't learn by pure imitation. Instead, he had to watch how a right-handed player did something and then work out how to do it left-handed. This extra move of translating right into left, and the improvisations that inevitably permeated the process, were a big factor in the originality that, by the time he was 23 years old, would be blowing people away, including world famous guitarists such as Paul McCartney and Eric Clapton.

FROM ARMY DAZE TO PURPLE HAZE
After dropping out of school, Hendrix was unable to support himself as a musician. Following arrests in relation to stolen vehicles, he traded in prison time for the army.

As with many a lefty legend, Hendrix proved incapable of toeing the line when it came to authority. He soon became known as a slack soldier and was eventually discharged. His discharge papers said the 'Recommendation is being submitted because the individual is unable to conform to military rules and regulations. Misses bedcheck; sleeps while supposed to be working; unsatisfactory duty performance. Requires excessive supervision at all times. Was caught masturbating by members of platoon.'

An even more telling insight into his attitude towards life was the observation by one of his superior officers that 'Pvt Hendrix plays a musical instrument during his off-duty hours or so he says. This is one of his faults, because his mind apparently cannot function while performing duties and thinking about his guitar.' Hendrix was so single-minded about his guitar playing that it left him with an attitude of dreamy diffidence toward pretty much everything else. He was a left-handed fantasist and this became increasingly pronounced when the rock 'n' roll lifestyle, with its attendant drug consumption, diminished his engagement with the realities of everyday life. Still, if Hendrix hadn't been such a bad soldier, it's likely his life would have taken a very different turn. Instead of adulation, Marshall stacks, LSD and girls, he might have been deployed

LEFTY LINKS

3. One of the key features of Hendrix's personality was his single-minded devotion towards the guitar. Because of this, he was frequently out of touch with the world. However, when it came to matters of music, he was ruthless, competitive, a perfectionist and, especially as his drug intake increased, prone to rage and paranoia. These personality traits—with the exception of the drug taking (and the women)—resemble those of Isaac Newton.

4. Both Jimi Hendrix's parents were big drinkers and Jimi inherited some of the same proclivities. Put bluntly, he was something of a drug pig. LSD, marijuana, heroin, cocaine, speed, alcohol, downers and uppers were all part of a heavily self-medicated existence. Dr Stanley Coren has shown in his book *The Left-Hander Syndrome* that lefties are more likely to be dyslexic, schizophrenic, substance abusers and die early. His theory is that left-handedness is caused by damage sustained in the womb. It's an interesting theory in the case of the Hendrix family, with its one genius and many genetic misfirings. Unfortunately Hendrix helped the early death argument by choking on his own vomit after taking an accidental overdose of sleeping pills. Some of the other lefties in this book who died an early death include Alexander, Joan of Arc and Raphael. Other left-handed musicians who died young include Kurt Cobain, Mike Bloomfield and blues harmonica great Paul Butterfield. It's been mooted that being a left-hander in a right-handed world is more dangerous, particularly when using machinery. Or perhaps it's a potential side effect of lefty rage. However, not everyone is convinced of the early death statistics for lefties. Other reasons for righties seemingly living longer is that older lefties are more likely to have been forced to become righties, so there are less of them. Another reason is that women tend to live longer than men, and are less likely to be lefties. Many of the left-handers in this book have lived to a ripe old age.

to fight out the Cold War in the jungles of Vietnam—a fate that fell to many of his childhood friends. His innate left-handed inability to conform may well have saved his life (for a while at least).

After leaving the army, Hendrix formed the King Kasuals with army buddy and bassist Billy Cox, who would later play with him in the Band of Gypsys and at Woodstock. For the next three years, Hendrix scraped together a living playing the Chitlin' Circuit (African-American venues in the eastern and southern states of the USA), with his own band and, increasingly, as a sideman for bigger acts. It was a hard life. Most musicians resorted at times to day jobs to keep themselves alive. But Hendrix was far too singular: 'People would say if you don't get a job you'll just starve to death. But I didn't want to take a job outside music. I tried a few jobs, including car delivery, but I always quit after a week or so.' Slowly he began to build a reputation, but it didn't stop him from going hungry most of the time and being forced to rely on the kindness of women for food, accommodation and other favours.

PREVIOUS PAGES: HENDRIX CLAIMED THAT HE PLAYED 'COLORS', RATHER THAN NOTES, AND THAT HE SAW THE MUSIC IN HIS HEAD WHILE HE PLAYED.

PAGE 203: THE YOUNG HENDRIX PLAYED A RIGHT-HANDED GUITAR UPSIDE DOWN, SWAPPING THE POSITION OF THE STRINGS.

Hendrix's real break came in 1966 when he befriended Keith Richard's girlfriend, Linda Keith, who championed his playing to a number of influential figures in the industry. He was introduced to Chas Chandler (former bass player from the Animals, turned manager), who took him to London, where he blew away the local guitar talent and had his first hits. It's as if there was no place for him in the often conservative, heavily hierarchical and racially circumscribed, music scene of early sixties USA, and it took the high and hedonistic individualism of Carnaby Street era London to find an audience where he could fully express his gift.

Another benefit of going to London, was a number of fortunate encounters which helped define his sound. Playing the right-handed guitar left-handed gave Hendrix an edge of difference compared to most other guitarists. It also set him on a path of constant innovation which would change the whole way electric guitar was played. When he first arrived in England he jammed on-stage with the Brian Auger Trinity, whose guitarist, Vic Briggs, was using an early Marshall amplifier. Briggs had never turned the amp above five. When Hendrix plugged in he turned the amp on full bore, with his guitar down, and proceeded to dazzle the audience with the wall of feedback and distortion from the Marshall. Along with The Who and Cream, Hendrix pioneered the use of the Marshall stack and the process of increasing sound volume by daisy-chaining amplifiers. Even more important was his ability to innovate using a variety of effects. When he arrived in England, Hendrix became close with electronics whizz Roger Mayer, inventor of the Octavia and Fuzz Face pedals. They distorted the sound and helped thicken the notes. Combined with his reversed stringing and Marshall these effects were crucial to the creation of his heavy, driving psychedelic sound. For a time in 1967, Mayer worked exclusively with Hendrix and their sonic explorations are the basis for many of the guitar sounds being used today. Hendrix was also the first guitarist to fully harness the potential of the wah-wah pedal. Hendrix's originality with the guitar was a classic case of the lefty adapting objects to suit his unique purposes, something every lefty learns by living in a righty world.

Hendrix's first album *Are You Experienced* was released in 1967 and was only prevented from reaching number one in Britain by the simultaneous release of the Beatles' *Sgt. Pepper's Lonely Hearts Club Band*, which featured another lefty musical genius, Paul McCartney. Hendrix now entered the rock stratosphere, with success as a crossover artist in the United States, appealing to both the white, black and, increasingly, the multi-racial hip market. By the time he played Woodstock in August 1969, Hendrix was its number one drawcard and one of the biggest rock stars in the world.

Being a rock god, however, took its toll on Hendrix, who never really knew how to say no. Little more than a year later, on 18 September 1970, the greatest left-handed guitarist who ever lived was found dead in his London apartment from an overdose of pills and alcohol. He was only 27 years old.

JIMI HENDRIX'S LEFTY TRAITS

INTUITIVE With the exception of classical musicians who play to sheet music, most musicians have to be able to improvise. This demands considerable intuitive ability since they need to anticipate the moves of musicians they are playing with. Hendrix, as a sideman, then as a bandleader, was good at this. He also absorbed other guitar players' styles.

EMPATHY Particular evidence of this faculty can be seen by the fact that, wherever Hendrix went, he always found women who helped him and championed his cause.

HOT-TEMPERED Hendrix was prone to violent, drunken rages. He once beat his girlfriend, Kathy Etchingham, in a London pub with a public telephone because he thought she was calling another man. On another occasion he threw a vodka bottle that smashed when it hit her in the head. In 1968 he was arrested for trashing a Stockholm hotel room after a night on the sauce.

ICONOCLASTIC Hendrix lived in an era where rebellion seemed to be the norm, but he still was largely responsible for making the electric guitar a unique instrument rather than merely an electrified acoustic guitar. The amazing distorted version of *Stars and Stripes,* which he played at Woodstock, became the anthem of his generation.

SELF-TAUGHT Hendrix studied by ear and observation and never learnt to read or write music.

EXPERIMENTAL Hendrix was known particularly for his experiments with pedals and new sounds for the guitar. He was also a perfectionist and innovator in the studio, where he was at the cutting edge of recording techniques such as stereophonic sound. In his later career he tuned his guitar a semi-tone down to the unusual key of E flat, which further enhnaced the originality of his sound.

FANTASIST Always keen on escapism, often with good reason, this tendency in Hendrix was magnified by a rock 'n' roll lifestyle, with its constant touring, girls, booze and drugs.

1942–

IT'S IMPOSSIBLE TO IMAGINE POP MUSIC WITHOUT THE BEATLES OR Paul McCartney. According to *Guinness World Records*, McCartney has sold more records (400 million) and penned more number one hits (50) than any other songwriter in history. His song 'Yesterday' remains the song most broadcast by radio stations worldwide. It has been played more than 7 million times on American radio and TV alone and, with more than 3000 versions, is probably the most covered song ever. The Beatles were the runaway number one in *Rolling Stone* magazine's 2004 ranking of the Best Hundred Artists of all time.

McCartney is the first pop music billionaire to have graced the planet with his presence. His public image has largely remained as the 'nice guy' of the Beatles, particularly in comparison to his long-time song-writing partner, John Lennon. Yet this fails to fully capture the output of a complex, creative, experimental and, at times, difficult man. Not only has McCartney written timeless standards with melodies that have stuck in the brains of millions, he was a pioneer of psychedelia, the use of electronics in pop music and even wrote the world's first heavy-metal song, 'Helter Skelter'. Not content to rest on his laurels, when the Beatles folded he went on to found the band Wings with his wife, Linda, which also had a stack of hits throughout the 1970s. A restlessly creative innovator, with a wide range of left-handed traits and talents, he has since engaged in a variety of musical ventures with people ranging from Michael Jackson to Super Furry Animals and has also extended his creative reach to painting and poetry.

LIVERPOOL DAYS Paul McCartney was born in 1942 in Liverpool, England, to working class parents of Irish heritage. His mother, Mary, was a midwife. His father, Jim, had moonlighted as a trumpet player, pianist and jazz band leader in the 1920s, but primarily worked for a company of cotton brokers. Jim had learnt his instruments by ear and encouraged his two sons

to play music. McCartney once claimed that his uncanny ear for a harmony had been developed during family sing-a-longs around the piano.

McCartney's father gave his son a trumpet to learn but, after being exposed to skiffle music—a British derivation of early American rhythm and blues—McCartney traded the trumpet in for a guitar. At first he found the instrument cumbersome. However, when he saw a poster advertising American country star Slim Whitman, who played right-handed guitar left-handed because of injury, McCartney reversed the strings and his subsequent improvement was dramatic.

Like Hendrix, McCartney demonstrated himself to be a left-handed musician who preferred experiential over theoretical modes of learning music. He once told *The Sunday Times* newspaper that:

> At school, in terms of musical education, I got zero. We'd all go into the classroom and the teacher would put on a record, then he'd leave the room. So of course we took it off, posted a guard on the door, got the ciggies and the cards out, and when he came back, we put the record back on for the last couple of bars. He'd go 'What did you think of that?' And we were like, 'Oh, really good, sir. Fabulous.'

McCartney was never a great formal student. While he was smart enough to be one of three children from his elementary school to make it to the academically selective grammar school, he only finished with one A level in English.

Although not a wealthy childhood, it was a happy one until the death of McCartney's mother from breast cancer when he was 14. He was close to her, and he remained deeply affected by this tragedy until much later in life. The title track from the Beatles' final album, *Let it Be*, was about the death of his mum.

BEATLES When he was 15, McCartney met John Lennon and his band the Quarrymen at a church fair. Interestingly, one reason for their connection may have been that both their mothers had died in close proximity. While the two connected, it was a rebellious relationship. Lennon's Aunt Mimi, who he lived with, thought McCartney was socially beneath them, while McCartney's dad thought the older Lennon would get Paul into trouble. McCartney's dad relented, however. After McCartney joined the Quarrymen, they were allowed to rehearse in their loungeroom.

McCartney convinced Lennon to let his younger friend George Harrison join the band as lead guitarist in 1958. The name change to the Beatles was suggested by Lennon's art school friend and bass player, Stuart Sutcliffe. Their first overseas tour came undone when McCartney and Pete Best (an early member of the band) were arrested for arson after setting fire to a condom in a nightclub. From the beginning McCartney, who'd also engaged in a bit of shoplifting with Lennon, was far from the well-behaved boy his clean-cut image would later come to suggest.

OPPOSITE: THE BEATLES AT THE EMI STUDIOS IN ABBEY ROAD, LONDON, PREPARING FOR THE LIVE 'OUR WORLD' BROADCAST, TO 24 COUNTRIES AND AN AUDIENCE OF 400 MILLION.

PREVIOUS PAGES: THE BEATLES, FROM LEFT TO RIGHT, PAUL McCARTNEY, RINGO STARR, JOHN LENNON AND GEORGE HARRISON, NOVEMBER 1963.

PAGE 211: McCARTNEY PLAYING BASS WITH THE BEATLES, 1966.

McCARTNEY'S LEFTY TRAITS

INTUITIVE McCartney's facility for music was intuitive rather than theoretical.

EMPATHETIC McCartney is an outspoken vegetarian and animal-rights activist. He and Linda converted to vegetarianism when they saw lambs in a field while they were eating lamb. He also credits the 1942 Disney film *Bambi*, in which the fawn's mother is shot by a hunter, as the initial spur for his interest in animal rights.

VISUAL-SPATIAL ABILITY A latent talent, but evident from McCartney's late-blooming interest in painting. Also one of his classical pieces was ordered around the 'colours' of the orchestra's instruments, suggesting a degree of synesthesia (perhaps a side-benefit of LSD).

LATERAL THINKING McCartney has tremendous creativity, but also the ability to see music in terms of business. Although having a reputation for being a perfectionist, he also has the knack of successful collaborations with an impressive range of other artists.

HOT-TEMPERED Underneath the Mr Nice Guy image may lie the bad temper of a perfectionist lefty. In his messy divorce from Heather Mills McCartney, allegations of domestic violence were aired.

ICONOCLASTIC The Beatles reinvented pop music. McCartney was the first pop muso to admit in public that he took LSD, while he was arrested on a number of other occasions for possession of marijuana and has long been an advocate for its legalisation.

SELF-TAUGHT McCartney learnt music in family sing-a-longs and never paid attention to his formal lessons.

EXPERIMENTAL McCartney has proven himself to be a musician and composer of dazzling originality. The restlessness of his creative genius sees him constantly experimenting across the spectrum of musical genres.

FANTASIST How could the man who wrote 'Yellow Submarine' not be a fantasist?

The Beatles released their first single, 'Love Me Do', in 1962. Their second single, 'Please Please Me', released several months later, became their first number one and, by the time the album of the same name was released in 1963, Beatlemania had begun. Wherever they went they were met by legions of screaming girls who had fallen for their clean-cut, suited looks, rhythm and blues riffs, harmonies and loveable lyrics such as 'I Want to Hold Your Hand'.

Within the band's dominant song-writing team, McCartney came to be known for his fun lyrics and melody while Lennon was more renowned for his wit and introspection. Listening to the Beatles, the melodies are quite astounding for both their originality and catchiness. McCartney's left-handedness may well have had something to do with this, since melody and singing are musical functions that tend to operate in the right hemisphere of the brain, while rhythm and pitch are functions that tend to be located in the left hemisphere.

Following problems during a tour of the Philippines, frustration at the quality of available stage equipment and exhaustion at the logistics of dealing with the constant crowds of screaming fans, the Beatles quit touring in 1966 and became a studio band. *Revolver*, recorded in 1966, began a shift towards experimentation in Beatles' albums, in terms of both music and production. McCartney contributed songs such as 'Eleanor Rigby' and the psychedelic anthem 'Yellow Submarine'. *Sgt. Pepper's Lonely Hearts Club Band* was begun in December the same year and, over a 129-day recording period, evolved to become what is widely considered the greatest pop album of all time. Like fellow lefty Jimi Hendrix, McCartney and the other members of the band were great technical innovators. McCartney was the first to record his bass using a direct input (DI) instead of through an amplifier. The band used effects such as the wah-wah and the fuzz box and experimented with putting voices through the rotary Leslie speakers normally used for the Hammond organ. Other innovations included automatic double tracking, which allowed effects such as chorus and flange to be created by speeding up or slowing down one of the two tracks. They also used guitar parts played backwards.

These technical innovations were matched by radical changes to the song forms, which no longer seemed related to the simple tunes which had first taken the Beatles to the top of the charts. Esoteric, eccentric and enigmatic lyrics were matched with structures that were far more complex than the verse, chorus, middle-eight structure of the conventional pop song. This increased complexity was augmented by instrumentation which included classical sitar, a mouth organ quartet, string sections and a range of keyboards including the Mellotron, a kind of primitive sampler.

The experimentation continued with *The Beatles*, more commonly known as the 'White Album'. While the album contained McCartney's melodic masterpieces such as 'Blackbird', he was also responsible for many of the harder-edged songs on the album such as 'Birthday' and 'Helter Skelter'.

One of the false stereotypes of the Beatles era is that Lennon was the serious avant-garde figure, while McCartney was the ballad writer. In many ways McCartney was the most experimental of the four Beatles, none of whom could be fairly described as conventional. As the Beatles became famous, John, George and Ringo all bought mansions in the stockbroker belt outside of London, while only Paul remained in the centre, where he engaged fully in the cultural offerings of the swinging sixties, often disguising himself and going out to late-night cabaret clubs. It was McCartney, not Lennon, who first became involved in the avant-garde art scene. He launched and supported the Indica Gallery, where Yoko Ono exhibited and first met John Lennon. He became a friend of leading art dealers and painters such as Willem de Kooning, and explored the world of experimental film and music. In 1966, for instance, McCartney rented a basement apartment from Ringo Starr where he set up a small demo studio for poets and avant-garde musicians to record in. He was also the first British pop star to admit openly to using LSD and spent time in jail in Japan after being arrested for possession of cannabis. To a certain extent, Lennon's unfair representation as the radical of the Beatles and McCartney's resentment of this were an element in the friction that caused the band to disintegrate.

McCartney's love of experimenting has persisted throughout his career, even during the 'Mull of Kintyre' phase of Wings, which was his main

McCARTNEY WITH HIS FIRST WIFE, AND SOULMATE, LINDA, WITH WHOM HE FORMED THE BAND WINGS IN 1971.

217

creative valve during the seventies. Like Hendrix, McCartney became famous as a musician without knowing how to read music. However, this hasn't prevented him from branching out into classical works such as *Liverpool Oratorio* (1991; with Carl Davis), *Standing Stone* (1997) and *Ecce Cor Meum* (*Behold My Heart*; 2006). At the same time, McCartney has maintained a steady output of pop, especially in collaborations with an eclectic range of other musicians such as Michael Jackson and Elvis Costello. In 1994, he released an ambient techno album under the pseudonym Fireman, while he's recently collaborated with Welsh psychedelic outfit Super Furry Animals, who contributed two songs to an album of bizarre Beatles remixes, then had McCartney chewing celery and carrots on a rhythm track of their album *Receptacle for the Respectable*.

McCartney is almost Nietzschean in the restless surgings of his creative spirit. Inspired by a 1982 visit to the barn studio of his friend, the artist

Willem de Kooning, he took up painting and had his first exhibition in 1999. In 2001, he went literary, publishing his first books of poems, *Blackbird Singing*, accompanied by a series of public readings. He has published a collaborative children's book since. His entrepreneurial activities under the guise of his MPL Communications has also seen some masterstrokes, most notably the purchase of the musical rights for the off-Broadway musical which became *Grease*, the hit movie whose soundtrack sold millions of copies.

Unlike Nietzsche, however, whose restless genius had physical consequences, McCartney has maintained this frenzy of creativity while pursuing a personal life as close as possible to his ideal of normal, based on the contented marriage of his parents before his mother died of breast cancer. After being engaged to actress Jane Asher, McCartney married American divorcée Linda Eastman. According to an article in the *Independent* newspaper marking McCartney's 64th birthday:

> For all his fame what Paul craved for his family was the happiness and security of his own childhood. He sought out ordinariness, sending his kids to the local comprehensive, eating Linda's home-cooked (and not always very appetising) food and even insisting that she did the family's laundry so that the house would smell of ironing to evoke the memories of his childhood home. Guests invited to lunch might be treated to a personal performance at the piano afterwards, but then they were expected to help to wash up.

Sadly, this happiness was denied to McCartney. In 1998 his soulmate, Linda, died from breast cancer, the same disease which killed his mother. They had been married for almost 30 years, during which time the longest period they ever spent apart was the eight days that McCartney spent in a Japanese jail on drug charges.

In terms of his left-handed traits, McCartney is something of a paradox. His experimental and iconoclastic streaks are balanced by his urge for domestic normality. It's possible to see it as the left-hander wanting to fit into normality. However, a more accurate way to look at it is as an act of creativity in itself. One of McCartney's contemporaries, Bob Dylan, has commented on the fact that, while ordinary people yearn to be rock stars, rock stars dream of a house in the suburbs with a white picket fence. In this sense, McCartney's domestic life was a dream he managed to achieve. To do so would have taken an impressive amount of intuitive intelligence. Even after the assassination of Lennon made the McCartney family more cautious about being in public, the kids still managed to have a fairly normal life in their home in the south of England. On the back of all the drugs, the fame and experimental imperatives of his creative life, successful domesticity is an achievement that can't be underrated. In recent times, McCartney seems to have proved this by example. His 2002 marriage to 32-year-old Heather Mills, with whom he has a daughter, has ended in divorce proceedings that have been played out luridly in the British gutter press.

LEFTY LINKS

1. Paul McCartney wasn't the only left-handed member of the Beatles. The often underrated Ringo Starr was also a lefty. However, he played a right-handed drum kit which gave him a unique sound. On a number of Beatles tracks McCartney played drums instead of Starr, also hitting left-handed on a right-handed kit.

2. One of the Beatles' pop contemporaries, David Bowie, is also a lefty, as are a striking number of other great pop and rock musicians. The list of sixties and seventies pop luminaries who are lefties includes: Bob Dylan, Bob Geldof, Paul Simon and Art Garfunkel, Judy Garland, Natalie Cole, Aretha Franklin, Led Zeppelin's Robert Plant, Isaac Hayes, Don and Phil Everly, Glenn Frey of the Eagles, James Brown, John 'Rotten' Lydon of the Sex Pistols, blues musician Paul Butterfield and Marianne Faithfull. More recent left-handed pop stars include David Byrne of Talking Heads, Annie Lennox, Phil Collins, Eminem, George Michael, Smashing Pumpkins' Billy Corgan, Kurt Cobain, 50 Cent, Billy Ray Cyrus, Michael Stipe of REM, Australian songster Natalie Imbruglia, Coldplay's Chris Martin, and Britney Spears' husband Kevin Federline. Some of these play their instruments right-handed.

3. For a list of great left-handed guitarists see the links in the Jimi Hendrix chapter (page 202), and for the great classical lefties see the links in the Beethoven chapter (page 100).

4. Perhaps it's got something to do with the empathetic capacity of left-handers, but plenty of famous left-handers have been vegetarians, including Leonardo da Vinci, Friedrich Nietzsche, Henry Ford, Mahatma Gandhi, Paul McCartney and Martina Navratilova.

Bill Gates

1955– When I left college in 1985 I had never touched a computer. Twenty years later, life without software such as Microsoft Windows, Word, Excel and Hotmail is pretty much unimaginable. The products created by Bill Gates have arguably had a greater influence on the developed world in that time than any other. They have changed the way business is done, the way people communicate, the way creativity finds its form and culture is disseminated. Although these inventions don't necessarily belong to Gates, he was the first to see the importance of software as opposed to hardware and has operated, for the most part, with uncanny prescience in bundling these technologies into commercially savvy packages. As a consequence of this, Gates has become the richest man in the world, possibly even the richest man in history. Having made billions changing the way we live, he has now become the world's most generous philanthropist, giving back billions to help raise the standard of living through health and education programs for the underprivileged in both the developing and developed world. It's a story of a man who serendipitously landed in a moment and used his left-handed talents to make the most of it.

CHILDHOOD Bill Gates was born in Seattle, Washington, to a wealthy established family. His great-grandfather had been a state legislator and mayor, his grandfather the vice-president of a national bank, and his father a leading attorney, while his mother was a teacher from a socially prestigious family who served on the boards of charitable institutions and a bank. Gates was the middle of three children, the other two girls. From an early age he was intellectually curious and highly competitive. At elementary school, he outstripped his classmates in almost every subject, but showed the special affinity for math and sciences many great left-handers have had.

While an eighth-grade student at the prestigious Lakeside school, a group of mothers decided to invest the proceeds from the school's annual

jumble sale to buy a computer teletype console and a block of time on a General Electric computer. This marked the beginning of Gates' fascination with the computer. It also illustrates his typically left-handed determination to do things his own way. Before long, Gates had managed to get himself excused from his regular maths classes so he could spend time programming in BASIC, a computer language, on the GE computer. When the mother's club money ran out, a group of boys including Gates and Microsoft co-founder, Paul Allen, scored time on a computer owned by Computer Center Corporation. One of the things they did was to hack into the computer, breaking its security system, and alter the files which recorded their time spent using the machine. When the company discovered this, they banned the kids. Soon after, unable to adequately deal with their system's vulnerabilities, they hired the Lakeside boys to help spot the glitches in the system in return for unlimited free time. Gates began to haunt the school's computer lab night and day, often sneaking out of the house while his parents were asleep, to go to and build code.

One of the reasons for Gates' success is that his computer skills have developed in concert with his business acumen. While many programmers see the programming as an end in itself, from the outset Gates had the lateral vision to see the binary code he worked on in terms of profit. At 14, he and Paul Allen embarked on their first software business venture. They started a company called Traf-O-Data, which designed and sold a computer to measure traffic flow, earning them a gross profit of US$20,000. The school then hired Gates and Allen to computerise its scheduling system. Soon after, hearing of their work, defence contractor TRW hired them to find vulnerabilities in their system and fix them. Their programming skills intensified and Gates and Allen began to think seriously of founding their own company.

MICROSOFT With his pedigree and intelligence, it was expected for Gates to go to college and, in 1973, he crossed the country to Harvard. He enrolled in Freshman pre-law in emulation of his father, and also took some hard-core maths. While Gates did well in his studies, he was perennially distracted, not by girls or partying, but by the Harvard Computer Laboratory where he spent long, solitary hours, often staying there all night programming, then sleeping his way through the next day's classes.

During Gates' first year at college, Paul Allen moved to Boston and the two continued to talk about starting a business, though Gates was reluctant to drop out of college. The watershed moment came when Allen was on his way to visit Gates and saw on the cover of *Popular Electronics*, the announcement of the Altair 8800, 'the world's first microcomputer kit to rival commercial models'.

Within days, Gates was on the phone to the makers of the Altair, offering them a BASIC language operating system for the computer. The company agreed to meet them. The only problem was that Gates had taken an intuitive leap of faith in promising this, since they neither had access to the Altair, or its chip, and were yet to write a single line of code. Yet by lying they had gained a jump on any possible competition. For the next two months they worked around the clock to come up with a code that would work. Allen flew down to New Mexico to demonstrate the code. It worked and a deal was struck. Microsoft was effectively born.

Gates later said, 'Back in 1975, we were the first one. We got the best name, Microsoft, because we were the first one to see that software, rather than hardware, was the key to the future in terms of computers.' On the back of the Altair, Gates decided that the moment to start a business had arrived. To his parents' chagrin, he dropped out of college and took on Microsoft as a full-time concern.

BINARY DEALINGS The pioneering days of the personal computer largely belonged to a bunch of idealistic geeks who were primarily interested in expanding the potential of computing (the same sort of people who continue to provide open source software). There was an anarchic and utopian flavour to the early computing community where programs and code

OPPOSITE: BILL GATES AT A PRESS CONFERENCE TO LAUNCH WINDOWS 98, JUNE 1998.

PAGE 221: BILL GATES GIVES AN IMPASSIONED SPEECH ON MAY 18, 1998, WHILE STATING MICROSOFT'S POSITION AGAINST THE US JUSTICE DEPARTMENT'S LAWSUIT.

BILL GATES' LEFTY TRAITS

INTUITIVE Gates' remarkable intuitive understanding of how the market for personal computers would develop, along with immaculate timing, are significant reasons for the success of Microsoft and its products.

LATERAL THINKING Gates is notable for his ability to contextualise technology within a business environment. In his career, he has also shown remarkable flexibility of thought. He evolved when it became clear how vital the Internet was going to become, and also had the wisdom to relinquish control of his corporation. Unlike Henry Ford, he hasn't become fixed in his thinking.

HOT-TEMPERED Gates' aggressive business strategies have often been accused of lacking ethics. He also established an aggressive internal culture in Microsoft, predicated on creative tension and wedded to the quality of ideas.

SOLITARY As an adolescent Gates became obsessed with the solitary activity of computer programming. A classic nerd, he lacked social skills and led an uneventful romantic life until he married at the relatively late age of 39.

ICONOCLASTIC Gates' belief that software should be sold, not shared, offended the idealist atmosphere that pervaded the nascent industry. He has also stood up to governments and has been prepared to defend these beliefs. The Microsoft culture, while competitive, has also been one in which ideas have been preferred to hierarchy.

SELF-TAUGHT Gates taught himself how to write the programming code that was the foundation of his immense wealth.

OPPOSITE: GATES GIVING AN ADDRESS AT THE 'FUTURE FOCUS' CONFERENCE IN COPENHAGEN, DENMARK, 2001.

were shared. Microsoft's BASIC for the Altair proved very popular with computer enthusiasts, yet it wasn't long before a pre-market copy of the program was being copied and distributed for free. Gates wrote an open letter scathing of the practice, arguing that companies couldn't afford to produce high-quality software if they weren't paid. This approach earnt them the ire of the community, but Gates wasn't fazed. Whether or not he was in the right, he had the successful left-hander's ability to stand up to convention and be unapologetically different in the face of considerable enmity.

Gates' approach really paid off when IBM began to look for an operating system for its new personal computers. When the first company Gates suggested to IBM couldn't come up with an agreement, IBM asked Microsoft to come up with an operating system themselves. Rather than make one, as they had for the Altair, Gates chose to license software made by another company, Seattle Computer Products. Somewhat ruthlessly, he neglected to tell the company that IBM was the customer. Because of this, he got the software—nicknamed QDOS (Quick and Dirty Operating System)—for a far cheaper price than if Seattle Computer Products had known.

Of course, it's one thing to deceive a small company, another entirely to stand up to a corporate monolith. Gates showed even greater business acumen at the other end of the deal by refusing to sign the source code for MS-DOS (as QDOS became known) over to IBM. Consequently, when other companies started to produce clones of the IBM personal computer, Gates was in the position to license his operating system to them as well. In contrast, his main competitor at the time, Apple, who were different from IBM in that they also made computers, refused to license its operating system to other manufacturers, preferring to restrict itself to providing an integrated hardware and software package. As the market for PCs exploded, Microsoft products could be found not just on IBMs but Compaqs, Dells, Gateways, Hewlett Packards, Sonys and Toshibas.

One of the reasons why all these companies took up the MS-DOS software was that the licensing fee Microsoft charged wasn't too high. Following his conviction that the future lay in software, Gates had the foresight to see that providing an operating system was only the beginning of the kinds of software Microsoft would be able to sell to the buyers of PCs. By supplying the operating system cheaply, Microsoft would be in a position to make MS-DOS-compatible software for a whole range of uses such as word processing, accounting, databases and games.

WINDOWS The strengths of Microsoft have been to innovate and adapt. These traits are often found in left-handers who are forced from an early age to adapt to a world that hasn't been designed for them. Under Bill Gates, Microsoft has often taken ideas already in existence and adapted them to create some of its most enduring products. Perhaps the most obvious example of this is Microsoft Windows, which first appeared on the market in 1985. While early PCs ran on DOS, Apple had jumped the gun by

introducing a graphical user interface (GUI) which made its Macintosh computers much easier to use, especially for the general consumer. In order to counter this, Microsoft introduced Windows. At first it was an inferior product that survived only because there was no direct DOS-based competition. It wasn't until version 3.1 was released in 1990 that it really began to take off. It sold over 2 million copies in its first six months.

As Windows improved, it made it easier for people to use other Microsoft software, such as Word, instead of competitors' products like Word Perfect. Microsoft's domination of the personal computer was in full swing. By 1993, Windows had become the most widely used GUI operating system in the world. By 2004, it was estimated that over 90 per cent of the world's PCs were running on Windows. For people who weren't interested in computers, only what they could do with them, Windows and its bundled application suites such as Microsoft Office have proved highly attractive. When you buy a PC today, it comes with a version of Windows pre-installed, meaning that Microsoft is perhaps the only company to be making money on the sale of every PC. These days, even if people want to use alternative software, such as Adobe Photoshop, unless they own a Mac or are an OpenSource geek using Linux, they are likely to do it via Windows. From the lie Bill Gates told the makers of the Altair, Microsoft has achieved astonishing penetration of the market. It has extended its share through constant innovation within its main product lines, generating new demand as the market has become more saturated through a combination of improved functionality and built-in obsolescence.

THE CONQUEROR IN THE GATES The business philosophy of Microsoft has been described as 'embrace, extend, extinguish'. They take ideas from the opposition, improve upon them, then eradicate the competition. Under Gates, who was known for his extreme competitiveness even as a child, Microsoft has pursued market share with a ruthlessness worthy of great left-handed conquerors such as Alexander, Caesar and Napoleon (in fact Judge Penfield would characterise Gates as a Napoleon during the 1998 United States versus Microsoft trial).

Business, while often being in love with the language of war, usually plays its battles out in different contexts. Microsoft has been involved in numerous court battles over the years, primarily as defendant, in a series of cases where competitors have alleged the company has abused its monopoly power. Perhaps the most famous example were the browser wars between Netscape and Microsoft in the 1990s. One of Gates' mistakes was that he was slow to recognise the dawning significance of e-mail and the Internet. Until 1995, Windows had no integrated software that could connect it to the Internet. The market leader was Netscape, who had launched their browser the year before. Netscape remained the market leader as the early versions of Microsoft Internet Explorer (IE) were inferior. However, Gates, having realised his mistake, ordered that every product Microsoft made had to be compatible with the Internet. His ability to turn the focus of such a large organisation around so quickly had almost the same effect as the surprise tactics of Alexander the Great in battle over 2,000 years earlier. Successive editions of IE came to match Netscape's Navigator, feature for feature, with the advantage that the platform was more stable. Even better, for the consumer at least, IE was bundled with Windows. Netscape was effectively screwed.

In 1998, the US government sued Microsoft under anti-trust legislation which had been passed to deal with the robber barons from the end of the nineteenth century. At issue was the fact that computer manufacturers were unable to install Windows 95 without Internet Explorer. If they thought Netscape was the superior product then the best they could do was to provide a PC with both. Yet what was the point of selling a PC with two browsers? As a consequence, Netscape was losing market share drastically. When the judge ordered Microsoft to separate IE from Windows, Gates claimed it couldn't be done. He provided an older, inferior version of Windows 95 for those who didn't want to take the version bundled with IE.

GENEROUS GATES Although the initial judgment went against them, in the end Microsoft was able to defuse the problem, which was threatening to split them into two companies—one to manufacture the Windows Operating System, and another to provide software to work in the Windows environment in competition with other companies.

For Gates, Microsoft's anti-trust problems, which were also replicated in Europe, marked a watershed. In the middle of the case he announced his intention to stand down as CEO and hand the reins over to his Harvard friend Steve Ballmer. Gates might have perceived that his unbridled aggression presented an image problem for the company. Instead, he became chief software architect and chairman. In 2006, Gates announced his further intention to move out of a day-to-day role with Microsoft.

Unlike many of the left-handed conquerors in this book, or fellow business mogul Henry Ford, it seems Gates is unusual in knowing when to stop. Perhaps the major reason for Gates' moving on is the Bill and Melinda Gates Foundation, which began in 2000 with assets of US$106 million. Since then it has expanded to possess an endowment of over US$30 billion, which will only grow, since investor Warren Buffet has pledged a further US$30 billion worth of shares in Berkshire Hathaway. When Gates leaves Microsoft it will be to work with the Foundation.

A mark of many of the left-handed geniuses in this book is their ability to think laterally while under the grip of an obsession. Yet many of them have eventually floundered. Gates' conversion, at such an early age, from being being a young nerd with a talent of binary code, to one of the most ruthless businessmen in the game, to one of the world's greatest ever philanthropists is perhaps an indication that in his life choices he has proved more agile than most.

LEFTY LINKS

1. Although it never became his career, Gates is the latest in a long line of lefties whose genius is marked to some extent by mathematical ability. Leonardo, Isaac Newton, Marie Curie, Lewis Carroll and Alan Turing are the other lefties in these pages whose genius has sprung from an innate ability at maths.

2. Bill Gates shares the conqueror mentality with lefties such as Alexander the Great, Caesar and Napoleon. An argument can be made that the intrinsic apartness of left-handers enables them to be ruthless, yet without too strongly perverting their own nature. Unlike many right-handed conquerors, these lefty figures are remembered as much for what they added to the world as what they destroyed in the pursuit of their ambitions. The other great left-hander in this book, with whom Gates shares some similarity, is Henry Ford. Like Gates, Ford created the market for the Model T at the same time as he created the product. Although both men were technology boffins, they had brilliant insight into what the average person wanted from his or her products.

3. Other famous lefties that have emerged from the northwest coast of the United States include Jimi Hendrix—like Bill Gates, also from Seattle—Kurt Cobain, who was born 140 kilometres outside Seattle, and Matt Groening, founder of TV show *The Simpsons*, who hails from Portland, Oregon, and went to school in Washington State.

Navratilova and McEnroe

MARTINA NAVRATILOVA Tennis is a sport where the left-hander has had disproportionate success. There are several reasons for this. In a game where reaction time is measured in milliseconds, and muscle memory and rally patterns are crucial, right-handed opponents are never quite as comfortable with left-handers. Since there are less lefties, the angles they use and the spin they put on the ball are more difficult to read than those deployed by right-handers. According to some tennis experts, the fact that the left-hander's forehand serve is to the right-hander's backhand also confers an advantage. The left-hander's forehand is also the side of the court in which games are usually decided. In a game of spin and angles, it's also easy to see how the superior visual-spatial skills found in left-handed artists, military leaders and some scientists might be a factor in a game where the ball has to be hit over a net into an extremely limited space. Whatever the reasons, the evidence for left-handed tennis success is weighty: Laver, Roche, Connors, McEnroe, Nadal, Navratilova and Seles to name just a few. However, with the advent of improved racquet technology, and the growing importance of physical strength in the game, the artistry of the left-handed tennis player has recently been in decline. But in the 1980s, when tennis was riding a crest of popularity, left-handers were the best in the game.

The career of Martina Navratilova is one of those instances of a left-hander who thrives on being different. Renowned *Sports Illustrated* journalist, Frank Deford, summed it up when he wrote, 'How gratifying it must have been for her to have achieved so much, triumphed so magnificently, yet always to have been the other, the odd one, alone: lefthander in a righthanded universe, gay in a straight world; defector, immigrant; the (last?) gallant volleyer among all those duplicate baseline bytes'. The overweight, teenage Czech defector, who moulded herself into a tennis force whose 58 combined singles and doubles Grand Slam titles (the last of them acquired at 49) are the second highest ever, is one of the great stories of modern sport.

MARTINA NAVRATILOVA 1956–

INTUITIVE Navratilova's play had the speed of pure intuition, and her amazing success in doubles showed her ability to work intuitively as part of a team.

VISUAL-SPATIAL ABILITY Navratilova played a brilliant serve and volley game, and was a genius of the difficult angles.

LATERAL THINKING From a chubby teenager with a hamburger addiction, Navratilova was able to transform herself into an incredibly fit player who was still winning competitions in her forties. She has written fitness books and was a leader in the trend for sportspeople to adopt social causes.

HOT-TEMPERED A typical left-handed hot-head, Navratilova was prone to explosions on court and even smashed a number of racquets. Her relationship break-up with author Rita-Mae Brown was particularly tempestuous.

SOLITARY Tennis players are by nature often solitary—playing alone on one side of the net. While Martina was usually in relationships, these changed according to the primary need of her desire to win. When she needed revitalisation, she changed both her doubles and romantic partners.

ICONOCLASTIC Navratilova defected from Czechoslovakia and was the first sports superstar to be unrepentant about her homosexuality, even though it cost her millions in endorsements and the ire of her beloved stepfather, whose initial reaction was that he would have preferred it if she'd become a prostitute.

CZECHERED START Born in Prague, Martina's father was a ski instructor, but her parents divorced when she was three. This was fortunate for her tennis career, since Miroslav Navratil, her new stepfather, also became her tennis coach, while she in turn took the feminised form of his surname. He spent hours training Martina how to hit the ball and her talent began to grow. At the time, Czechoslovakia was still a communist country and the ruthless singularity required to become a successful tennis champion went against the grain of the powerfully conformist culture. Nonetheless, sports was one area where talent was allowed into the open. On the tennis court Navratilova would be able to exercise the left-hander's typical individuality, which otherwise might have been suppressed.

Having begun hitting the ball against the wall before she was five, Navratilova repaid her stepfather's faith by winning the Czech under 10 and under 12 girls' championships. In her autobiography, Navratilova claims that during this part of her life she was often upset by people mistaking her for a boy. In 1972, still only 15, she won the Czech open women's championship in straight sets, which meant she was good enough to play in international tournaments.

FLYING THE COMMUNIST COOP In 1973, Navratilova went to play in America for the first time and immediately felt at home. She played and lost to the Ice Maiden, Chris Evert Lloyd who, like Ice Man Bjorn Borg for fellow left-hander John McEnroe, would become her right-handed rival in some of the great tennis matches of the 1980s. Like McEnroe, Navratilova made her mark as an aggressive serve and volley player, a style which favours left-handed brilliance over right-handed consistency. Evert Lloyd on the other hand was a model of coolly controlled baseline consistency. Navratilova also resembled McEnroe in that her behaviour on the court tended towards the volatile end of the spectrum, and it would be some years before she would develop the shell of self-control that would make her truly great. Her first year on the circuit was encouraging, if marred by an enthusiasm for newly discovered foods such as hamburgers and popsicles which saw her put on 11 kilograms, to the extent that one commentator dubbed her 'the great wide hope'.

In 1974, Navratilova reached the finals of the Italian Open before losing to Evert Lloyd. In 1975, she made two Grand Slam finals, the Australian and French. Against Chris Evert Lloyd she lost the semi-final of the US Open after losing her cool; the consequence of a suspect line call. She was earning thousands of dollars a week and the ire of the Czech Tennis Federation who didn't appreciate her decadent ways. The night after she lost to Evert Lloyd at Flushing Meadow, she defected.

Three months before she defected, Navratilova also had her first lesbian affair. The press caught on when she began to hang out with lesbian author Rita Mae Brown, who she later lived with. Once her citizenship papers came through, she took the brave step of outing herself. It was the first time

a major sportsperson had done this. Beginning with her left-handedness, Navratilova kept adding to the list of things that marked her out as different. It was a gamble that initially distracted her from her tennis. The year 1976 was a poor one for her and she compensated with conspicuous consumption, celebrating her official freedom by buying expensive cars, jewellery and clothes. Yet the courage to be herself, which began with the left-handed knowledge that she was different anyway, would translate in the long-term to victories in terms of character and on the tennis court.

ON TOP OF THE WORLD The breakthrough came against Evert Lloyd in the 1978 Wimbledon Final when she won 7–5 in the third set. The following Wimbledon she beat Evert Lloyd in straight sets. However, it was in 1981 when her domination of the women's tennis circuit began in earnest. Between 1981 and 1987, she won 15 out of 27 Grand Slam singles tournaments and finished runner-up in seven more. Her worst performance in a Grand Slam tournament during this time was to lose in the fourth round. Her game was helped by the ease with which she adapted to the added power of the new graphite racquets and a training and dietary program initiated by her basketball playing lover, Nancy Lieberman.

With the ascension of Steffi Graf in the late eighties, Martina's dominance, and that of the serve volley game, began to wane. Yet, unlike John McEnroe, who was arguably a more talented player, there was no doubt she had harnessed all her potential. In 1990, she won her final Grand Slam singles tournament against Zina Garrison to give her a record ninth Wimbledon title. She was 37 years old. Even then, she wasn't finished. In 1994, with a remarkable display of grit and persistence against players sometimes half her age, she got as far as the final of Wimbledon before losing it to Conchita Martinez in three sets. She would continue to win in doubles for more than a decade.

ABOVE: NAVRATILOVA RUNS TO HIT THE BALL DURING THE VIRGINIA SLIMS TOURNAMENT, EARLY 1980S.

PAGE 229: NAVRATILOVA GETTING READY TO SERVE AT WIMBLEDON, ENGLAND, 1979.

NAVRATILOVA RECEIVING THE
WIMBLEDON LADIES SINGLES
TROPHY FROM THE DUCHESS
OF KENT, ENGLAND, 1978.

LEFTY LINKS

1. Left-handed male players have accounted for more than their fair share of winners over the last 50 years or so at the US Open, the French Open, the Australian Open and Wimbledon. They won 41 of the 200 singles titles at these events over the period from 1955–2004. Left-handers accounted for 15 of the winners of the men's singles titles at the US Open from 1955–2004 (30 per cent of the total) and 11 at Wimbledon (22 per cent). For an astonishing period of 11 consecutive years, from 1974–84, the winners of the US Open men's singles title were left-handed. As the game changed post-McEnroe, however, the lefty approach to the game suffered as tennis, with its ever bigger racquets, became more of a slugfest, played by people who spent as much time lifting weights in the gym as they did playing shots on the court. McEnroe was the last of the great touch players.

2. The list of great left-handed tennis players is a long one. Lefty men who have won Grand Slam titles include: Norman Brooks, Rod Laver, Neale Fraser, Tony Roche, Jimmy Connors, John McEnroe, Guillermo Vilas, Manuel Orantes, Roscoe Tanner, Thomas Muster, Goran Ivanisevic, Petr Korda and Rafael Nadal. Lefty women include Navratilova, Ann Haydon Jones and Monica Seles.

3. We've all heard of left-handers being forced to write right-handed. It happened to tennis players too. Australian champion Ken Rosewall, who won 10 singles Grand Slam titles, was a natural left-hander whose father taught him to play right. As a consequence he was known for his excellent backhand and suffered from a weak serve. Margaret Court, who won 24 singles Grand Slam titles and was only the second women's player to win a Grand Slam in a calendar year, also suffered from a weak serve for the same reason. She remarked in

an interview on American Cable TV that, 'I wrote with my left hand, and it was at a time when people were being taught to work with their right hand; some of the male players would say that no women played left-handed. So I thought it was probably wrong to play left-handed, and I changed to right. I always think I would've had a better serve if I had been lefty.' American 1950s Maureen 'Little Mo' Connolly was another who was coached to swap hands. More recently, Kimiko Date, one of Japan's most successful female tennis players, was a left-hander who played right-handed because her father forced her to. One wonders how these players might have done if they'd been allowed to preserve their natural advantage.

4. As an emerging tennis player, McEnroe's hero was Rod Laver, the Australian left-hander who is the only player in Open history ever to have won two Grand Slams

(1962 and 1969), a figure all the more impressive because no male player has won the Grand Slam since. In his autobiography, *Serious*, McEnroe had this to say about Laver: 'Laver was the first guy I saw who did everything – hit topspin and slice on both forehand and backhand, serve with different spins. He utilised every possible shot, all the angles. I used to have a poster of him on the back of my bedroom door. The fact that he was a lefty like me was a big deal, and that massive Popeye forearm of his just seemed so cool.'

Similarly, Navratilova remembers that when she heard that Rod Laver had described her as a player to watch, 'she lived off that compliment . . . If Rod Laver thought I was going to be good I figured I better be.'

5. What happens then when left-handers play other left-handers? While McEnroe's hero was a lefty, partly chosen because he was a lefty, he

didn't necessarily get on with all lefties. In the same autobiography, McEnroe talks about the difficult relationship he had with Jimmy Connors and how they used to trash-talk each other while changing ends when they played against each other. It's a rivalry perhaps reminiscent of the animosity Michelangelo felt towards fellow lefty artists such as Leonardo da Vinci and Raphael. In this case both Connors and McEnroe were too much the angry lefty for them to get on together. Part of this animosity may well have been because they each cancelled the other's natural lefty advantage out.

6. Martina Navratilova is not the only talented left-hander in these pages who was gay. Others include Michelangelo, Leonardo and Alan Turing.

7. In his autobiography, McEnroe questions whether his temper tantrums on the court were more of a hindrance than an asset.

He argues that they were just as capable of ruining his game as that of his opponents, and that he would have rather not have had them if he could have helped it. McEnroe claims that for him the fear of losing was a more powerful motivator than the joy of winning, hence the element of self-loathing in his outbursts. In other respects, however, McEnroe's rage was natural, as was his freakish touch with shots such as the drop volley. Like Michelangelo, he was the product of a rage for perfection within himself. It seems that in many lefty geniuses, there is an inseparable connection between their brilliance and their rage, adding weight to the theory that lefties are formed by an exposure to an excess of testosterone in the womb. Certainly Navratilova, who as a child was often mistaken for a boy, also had problems with the self-destructive capacity of her own anger on the court, especially in the earlier part of her career.

A FAMILIAR IMAGE OF McENROE DISPUTING THE UMPIRE'S CALL DURING A CHAMPIONSHIP LAWN TENNIS MATCH AT WIMBLEDON.

JOHN McENROE As a tennis player, John McEnroe was a brilliant left-handed touch player and competitor who became as well known for his hair-trigger temper as his sporting genius. In his era, there was no player so compelling to watch. Compared to his main right-handed rivals, such as Bjorn Borg and Ivan Lendl, who aimed for, and often achieved, mechanistic perfection on the court, McEnroe was the quintessential angry lefty artist, a Michelangelo inside the tramlines, whose battle was as much with his own inner demons as his opponents. His on-court antics would earn him the sobriquet Super Brat for the abuse he heaped on linesmen and umpires who didn't see things his way. His behaviour saw him booed by crowds the world over as if he was a pantomime villain, yet he also left them gasping with his array of mercurial shots. His opponents believed that McEnroe saw angles that nobody else was able to see and was able to change his racquet position at a later moment than anyone else to take advantage of this, a true sign of a lefty genius with the visual-spatial gift. For some people, the end of his career marked the demise of tennis as a game of artistry, in favour of power and fitness.

JUNIOR MAC McEnroe grew up in Queens, New York City, the son of American–Irish parents who were climbing the social ladder and intensely ambitious for their three sons. John McEnroe internalised this energy from a very early age and developed into an extremely competitive boy, handicapped through adolescence by his lack of size, and prone to bursting into tears whenever he lost. He first came to prominence in the big league of tennis in the 1977 Wimbledon Championship where he reached the semi-finals as an 18-year-old, before being beaten by fellow lefty Jimmy Connors. At the 1979 US Open, aged 20, he beat his friend Vitas Gerulaitis in straight sets in the final to win his first Grand Slam event and guarantee his place in the big league.

It was a good time for McEnroe to be coming through. The popularity of tennis had risen greatly and the money to be made playing it had followed. The super cool, long-haired Swede, Bjorn Borg, had become his country's second-most popular export after ABBA, and was being pursued by a tribe of screaming girls. Tennis stars were acquiring rock star status and, with million of dollars in their bank accounts, were able to lead a rock star life. At the same time, the old school snobberies embedded in tournaments such as Wimbledon were being defrayed by the newly created dependency of the game on its celebrity players, much to the chagrin of its stuffy administrators who, of course, as an anti-authoritarian lefty, McEnroe hated.

SUPER BRAT VERSUS THE ICE MAN One of the greatest tennis rivalries of all time, and a big factor in the growing popularity of tennis, was the rivalry between McEnroe and Borg. Their games arguably constituted the greatest battle between left and right in the modern history of single combat sport. McEnroe arrived on the scene when Bjorn Borg was at the peak of his powers. Known as the Ice Man, Borg was a classic right-handed

JOHN McENROE
1959–

INTUITIVE McEnroe's touch play and career-long ability to surprise his opponents were the marks of an intuitive player, as were his emotionalism and capacity to get under their skins.

VISUAL-SPATIAL ABILITY McEnroe's unique shot angles, in particular, showed a superior visual-spatial mind at work.

HOT-TEMPERED Nicknamed Super Brat, McEnroe has one of the most famous tempers in left-handed history.

ICONOCLASTIC In many ways McEnroe brought the punk ethos to tennis. He took on the stuffy administrators of Wimbledon and won, while *The New York Times* once described him as 'the worst advertisement for our system of values since Al Capone'. He used his image as a rebel to make millions through an endorsement deal with Nike.

FANTASIST How else can McEnroe's post-tennis attempt to become a rock star guitarist be explained?

champion: contained, logical, remorseless. On the court he showed no sign of emotion. When he met with McEnroe in the 1980 Wimbledon Final, Borg had won the championship for the previous four years. McEnroe, on the other hand, was already becoming famous for his on-court explosions of rage. When he came on centre court for the final he was booed by the crowd because of his bad behaviour towards officials during his tense semi-final against fellow lefty and hot-head Jimmy Connors.

The quality of play, however, would soon stun the booers into silence. It was the first time McEnroe played Borg on grass and because of Borg's baseline game, he believed he had his measure. In the first set it seemed so. McEnroe, with his fast-reaction serve volley game, cleaned up 6–1. In the second, McEnroe was winning 5–4, with his serve to come, and starting to think he had climbed the mountain and was about to coast home. The idea appealed to him since he was exhausted, having beaten Connors in four sets the day before, and played his delayed doubles semi-final straight after. Borg, however, had other ideas. With McEnroe letting his foot off the pedal just a little, Borg found rhythm with his serve to win the set 7–5. For McEnroe, tennis was about controlling the inner voices of negativity as much as outdoing the opponent. Angry at himself for losing a set he thought he should have won, he proceeded to lose the next one 3–6. Worse still, in the fourth set he was broken by Borg and was down 3–5. If Borg won the next game, the match was over. Yet McEnroe dug deep and held his serve, saving a couple of match points in the process, before bringing the set to a tie-break by breaking Borg then holding serve again. This tie-break became the most famous tie-break in the history of Wimbledon. Lasting for over 20 minutes of supreme tension, McEnroe defended a further five match points before taking the set with a score of 18–16. At this stage, McEnroe was sure he had the game won. Borg, however, was relentless and McEnroe just couldn't break his serve in the final set which Borg won 8–6 to take the match and his fifth successive Wimbledon title.

While he may have lost arguably the greatest final in tennis history, McEnroe learnt much from it and he won all the remaining three Grand Slam finals he played against Borg. In the epic five-setter, he had absorbed the enemy's game and now he knew how to conquer him. At the US Open that year, two months after Wimbledon, he beat Borg in another epic five-setter, in which there were tie-breaks in the first, second and third sets, after also defeating Connors and Ivan Lendl on the way through. Then at Wimbledon in 1981, he beat Borg in four sets, breaking his record 41 match-winning Wimbledon streak and denying him his sixth successive title. McEnroe then beat Borg in a relatively easy four-set game at the US Open, the last Grand Slam final the 11-time Grand Slam tournament winner would ever play in.

In a sense, McEnroe broke Borg. After losing the US Open in 1981, Borg never played in another Grand Slam event and, in 1982, he retired from the game at the young age of 25. McEnroe was bereft. While relationships between tennis players in the upper echelons of the game are often either indifferent or antipathetic, there was a real synergy between these rivals as if in their left versus right rivalry, each player completed what was missing in the other. As such, their rivalry was imbued with the utmost respect. In 2006 when Borg, having fallen into financial difficulties, decided to auction two of his Wimbledon trophies and one of the tennis racquets he'd used to win it, several players rang to ask him what the story was. It was McEnroe, however, according to sources close to Borg, who rang up and said, 'What's up. Have you gone mad?' and was thus able to make Borg change his mind.

McENROE STATISTICS

At 1.8 metres tall, but weighing an average of only 75 kilograms throughout his career, McEnroe preceded the bigger specimens dominating the court today. Yet his record speaks for itself. After turning pro in 1978, he won 869 of his 1063 singles games and 530 of his 629 doubles games, despite playing on for five or six years past his evident peak. McEnroe's peak came in 1984 when he had a record of 82 wins against 3 defeats—a record unmatched by any player before or since. (Federer came closest in 2005 with a 81–3 win.) During his career, McEnroe won 77 singles tournaments and 78 doubles tournaments, an all-time record of 155 at the top level, for a total prize money of US$12,547,797. He was Number 1 in the world for a total of 170 weeks in his career. He also won seven Grand Slam singles tournaments—four US Opens and three Wimbledons; and nine in doubles—five Wimbledons and four US Opens. Unlike many of his contemporaries, McEnroe was sufficiently patriotic to play the Davis Cup, where he had a 59–10 record, and set US records for years played (12), ties (30), singles wins (41), and total wins in singles and doubles (59).

OPPOSITE: McENROE AND FELLOW LEFT-HANDED TENNIS GIANT, JIMMY CONNORS, WIMBLEDON, 1977.

PAGE 235: McENROE HAVING AN ON-COURT TANTRUM, FOLLOWING AN UMPIRE'S CALL AT WIMBLEDON, 1980.

The Lefty White House Cluster

WHILE ONLY 10 PER CENT OF THE POPULATION IS LEFT-HANDED, FOUR out of the last seven US Presidents have been lefties, a remarkable statistic since the task of climbing to the top of the world's major democracy tends to necessitate some smoothing out of the more idiosyncratic lefty traits. The run began when Gerald Ford assumed the presidency in 1974, following the resignation of Richard Nixon in disgrace. After a break for the right-handed Jimmy Carter, the next three Presidents—Reagan, Bush and Clinton—were all lefties. When Ford inherited the Presidency, America was in crisis. By the time he lost narrowly to Carter, the first two problems had largely been solved. After one term tainted by the Iran hostage crisis, Carter lost in a landslide to left-handed Californian former actor, Ronald Reagan. The rise of the left-handed Presidents saw the decline of left-wing politics in the world. America's power increased dramatically under Reagan, through the gradual collapse of the Soviet Empire. After two terms, Reagan was succeeded by his left-handed Vice-President, George Bush, a former World War II fighter pilot, Texas oilman, head of the CIA and the first serving Vice-President to be elected President since Martin Van Buren in 1836. Bush was President in 1989 when the Berlin Wall came down, presided over victory in the First Gulf War and consolidated America's new status as the world's only genuine superpower. However, he fell victim to the fluctuations of the economic cycle and lost after one term, to the charismatic, saxophone-playing, former Governor of Arkansas and fellow left-hander Bill Clinton. With relative peace on the international front, Clinton presided over two terms of prosperity, propelled by the dot-com boom of the nineties. The last years of his Presidency were seriously affected by the disproportionate scandal that spiralled from his sexual relations with White House intern Monica Lewinsky. There are doubts as to whether America has benefited from its shift back to the right-hand during the two terms of George W. Bush.

OPPOSITE, CLOCKWISE FROM TOP LEFT: GERALD FORD, 38TH US PRESIDENT FROM 1974–77; RONALD REAGAN, 40TH US PRESIDENT FROM 1981–89; GEORGE H. W. BUSH, 41ST US PRESIDENT FROM 1989–93; AND BILL CLINTON, 42ND US PRESIDENT FROM 1993–2001.

GERALD FORD After Richard Nixon sullied the American Presidency, Gerald Ford was the man who got the job, in 1974, of trying to clean it up. A man universally known for his negotiating skills and rare political honesty, he tried to undo the damage Nixon had done and was also responsible for extricating the last American troops from Vietnam. Born in Nebraska, but raised in Michigan, Ford was the political embodiment of the upright values of America's midwest. They weren't sufficient, however, to get him elected. Faced with the fallout from his pardoning of Nixon and deteriorating economic circumstances, he narrowly failed to be elected in the Presidential race of 1976.

One of the most intriguing things about the great lefty cluster of US Presidents is that they all came from homes where either violence or alcoholism was a presence. Whether this is related to the statistics for left-handers having hot tempers, or being vulnerable to addiction, is unknown, since the handedness of their parents has not been recorded. In Ford's case the violence, in the form of his biological father, was expunged from the house before the son was really aware of it. Ford's mother, Dorothy, had married Lesley Lynch King, a wool trader and wife-beater. Sixteen days after the birth of Ford, the couple separated after King threatened to kill his wife, the baby and his nanny with a butcher's knife. Ford and his mother moved to Grand Rapids, Michigan, where her parents lived. Soon after, she met and married Gerald Rudolff Ford, a salesman in a paint and varnish company, who Ford believed was his real father until he was 17 years old.

As a child, Ford had a fierce temper and was prone to tantrums. His mum was concerned that he had inherited his father's violent streak and determined to teach him control. When he got angry, she tried to reason with him, or sent him to his room to cool off. This early taming of his temper was central to the kind of politician Ford became; someone whose talents lay in building bridges, negotiation and calming stormy waters.

Ford's most conspicuous talents as a youth were on the sporting field. He is arguably the best athlete ever to become American President. After graduating from high school, he won a football scholarship to the University of Michigan and on graduating he was offered contracts to play professionally with the Chicago Bears and Green Bay Packers. He usually played centre or linebacker, two positions which demanded strategical intelligence and visual-spatial skills. Ford declined offers to become a professional footballer in favour of going to Yale, where he worked as a football and boxing coach while studying law.

During World War II, Ford joined the navy, where his position as assistant navigator on the aircraft carrier USS *Monterey* also utilised his superior visual-spatial skills.

After becoming active in Grand Rapids Republican politics, Ford was elected to the US House of Representatives in 1949. He remained there until 1973 until events catapulted him first to the Vice-Presidency then the

GERALD FORD 1913–2006

INTUITIVE All successful politicians need to have some intuitive know-how, an ability to see what those around them are thinking and be able to think on their feet. Ford had these talents but they don't appear to have been exceptional.

EMPATHETIC Much of Ford's personality was dedicated to keeping people happy, and he was able to empathise with people in order to achieve political compromises and form consensus without getting too many people off-side.

VISUAL-SPATIAL ABILITY Not so much in terms of Ford's political career, but this quality was definitely evident in his sporting and naval careers.

HOT-TEMPERED Ford inherited his father's bad temper, but it was trained out of him by his mother.

FANTASIST Did Ford really think the public would accept him letting Nixon off?

OPPOSITE: AFTER BEING THE CAPTAIN OF THE HIGH SCHOOL FOOTBALL TEAM, FORD WENT ON TO STAR IN THE UNIVERSITY OF MICHIGAN TEAM AS LINEBACKER AND CENTRE. FORD'S SPORTING PROWESS WAS AT ODDS WITH THE PRESIDENT'S LATER REPUTATION FOR CLUMSINESS.

RONALD REAGAN
1911–2004

INTUITIVE Reagan had the actor's intuition of knowing how to present himself and his cause to an audience.

EMPATHETIC Reagan's folksy fatherly political persona made him attractive to the American people.

LATERAL THINKING Reagan possessed the skills for adaptation and transformation, which have seen many left-handers become thespians.

ICONOCLASTIC Reagan was the first divorced President. Also, the timing of his switch from Democrat to Republican during the Kennedy era illustrated his ability to disregard the benefits of conformity in quest of his own truths.

SELF-TAUGHT Although Reagan studied economics at college, he learnt most of the economics of his 'Reaganomics' through his reading in the 1960s. Like many left-handers, he was also strong on learning from experience.

FANTASIST Reagan sold a dream of America as the 'shining city' of liberty and freedom. Like any great salesman, he believed his story.

OPPOSITE: AFTER HE LEFT COLLEGE IN 1932 RONALD REAGAN BECAME A RADIO SPORTS ANNOUNCER, WORKING FOR WARNER BROS FOR SEVEN YEARS. DURING THE HEIGHT OF THE DEPRESSION, HE WAS EARNING $75 PER WEEK.

Presidency. Unlike many of the left-handers in this book, whose success is defined by their stubborn singularity and ability to stand up against status quo, Ford was a consensus kind of guy, known for his empathetic skills as a reconciler and negotiator rather than any bold legislative strokes. It was his reputation for not rocking the boat which saw him foisted upon Nixon as Vice-President by Congress, when Spiro Agnew resigned after being charged with tax evasion and money laundering.

When Nixon was forced to resign over the Watergate tapes on 9 August 1974, Ford was thrown into the Presidency at a time when its reputation had been severely damaged. Ford did his best to mend fences. His granting of a presidential pardon to Nixon, before there was even a trial, caused a scandal, and it was speculated that Ford and Nixon had done a deal. They hadn't. Ford's reasoning was that by pardoning Nixon, the damage to the office of the Presidency would be minimised. Yet the controversy that his pardon created, along with the economic problem of stagflation, was pivotal in Ford losing the 1976 election to Jimmy Carter.

Ford was not your typical lefty by virtue of his seeming normality. Yet in the conspicuous effort of a career devoted towards being a peace-maker, there was something of the left-handed insecurity of being an outsider trying to fit in. Some great lefties manage this by acquiring the authority to make the world fit in with them. This is harder to do in a democratic system and it probably wasn't Ford's way at any rate. He died on Boxing Day, 2006, at the ripe old age of 93.

RONALD REAGAN Although he got to the Presidency via Hollywood, in many ways Reagan was almost the embodiment of the log cabin myth. Born in a flat on top of a bank in an Illinois village, his father was a shoe salesman and the family moved around often before they settled in the town of Dixon, Illinois, when Reagan was nine. Although Reagan often tapped into the sentimental fantasy of small-town American life, romanticising his childhood and the values it apparently taught him, his childhood wasn't always easy. His father was frequently out of work, and prone to getting on the sauce—another case where a left-handed President overcame either the violence or alcoholism in their genes.

At Dixon High, Reagan discovered an ability for storytelling and acting which would open his mind to a larger world and also give him his first taste of how the power of speech can transform it. Upon graduating from high school, he attended Eureka College, a small private college in a town not far from his home, where he majored in economics and sociology. Following college, Reagan began to work in radio. His love of sports and skill for storytelling combined when, between 1932 and 1937, he became baseball announcer for the WHO station based in Des Moines, Iowa. From a telegraph report that showed only the bare bones of the game, Reagan's job was to concoct the story of what was happening out on the pitch. Apparently his skills with this were such that, when the line went down during a game one

LEFTY LINKS

1. At the time of writing it appears possible that the Presidency will once again move to the left in the elections of 2008. With the Republicans in trouble, one of the leading Democrat contenders, Barack Obama, is also a lefty. For the Republicans, Senator John McCain happens to be a lefty too.

2. There is some precedent for an all-lefty Presidential race. In the 1992 Presidential Election all three candidates were lefties: George H. W. Bush, Bill Clinton and independent Texan billionaire Ross Perot. All in all, seven of the 43 (or 16 per cent) of the Presidents of the United States have been left-handed, a higher proportion than the 10 per cent of left-handers in the population. This supports the theory that there are proportionally more left-handers at the high end of the achievement spectrum. The other three are 20th President James Garfield (1831–81), who was assassinated only six months into the job; 31st President Herbert Hoover (1874–1964) who was President between 1929–1933 during the Great Depression; and Harry S. Truman (1884–1972) who became President in 1945 on the death of F. D. Roosevelt, and held on for a second term with an upset election win in 1948.

3. The current cluster of left-handed Presidents is particularly interesting given the relative dearth of famous left-handed politicians in other countries. Perhaps this is because government favours people who belong to majorities. However there are notable exceptions: India's founding President, Mahatma Gandhi, Cuban leader Fidel Castro, Israel's fiery former Prime Minister, Benjamin Netanyahu, current Israeli PM Ehud Ohlmert, US Christian right-winger Pat Robertson, Ireland's long-serving leader, Bertie O'Hearn, Australian Foreign Minister Alexander Downer, Japan's volatile right-wing Mayor of Tokyo Ishihara Shintaro, and F. W. De Klerk who, as President of South Africa, helped bring about the end of the apartheid era. Only one British Prime Minister, James Callaghan, has been left-handed. Winston Churchill has often been credited with being a left-hander, yet this is not true, though he does have many left-handed traits and could possibly be a switched lefty.

day, he made up a sequence of the game composed entirely of batters hitting fouls (to keep the score static) until the telegraph feed resumed.

In 1937, Reagan took a successful screen test with Warner Brothers Pictures and his movie career began as a contract actor. If not quite an A-grade star, he was still a well-known leading man in the pre-war era.

Reagan's personal life demonstrated the gap between Hollywood values and mainstream America at that time. In 1940, he married actress Jane Wyman, who had been his leading lady in a number of films. They had a daughter, adopted a son, then had another daughter who died in infancy. In 1948, they divorced. Four years later Reagan married another actress, Nancy Davis. It was a meeting of soulmates and she remained his partner until death. Nonetheless, Reagan is somewhat iconoclastic, given his conservative politics, in that he remains the only President of the United States to have ever been divorced.

During the war, Reagan volunteered for active service but was deemed unfit because of problems with his eyes. After the war, his career shifted towards politics, when he became President of the Screen Actors Guild (SAG), effectively a union leader. At this stage in his life, Reagan was a self-described 'haemophiliac liberal'.

The strongest influence in Reagan's eventual shift from being a Democrat to a Republican was communism. Reagan was a libertarian, a common stance for lefties forced to live with the tyranny of the majority. It was a position strengthened by his growing antipathy to the collective threat of communism. In his role as President of the Screen Actor's Guild, Reagan testified against some fellow actors to Senator McCarthy's Commission on UnAmerican Activities, and was also a source for the FBI. During the fifties, while still a Democrat, he supported both Eisenhower and Nixon. He also returned to his college major, economics, and became a convert to free market theories advocated by libertarian thinkers such as Friedrich Hayek. Blessed with the left-handed capacity for adaptation and transformation which had graced his acting career, his political conversion coincided with a new job as a television host for a show funded by General Electric.

Reagan's film career ended in 1964 with *The Killers*. Aided by a beneficial land deal organised by Wasserman, Reagan achieved sufficient financial independence to stand for public office. In 1966, he became California Governor, froze hiring and balanced the budget. He also showed an illiberal streak tinged with the ruthlessness of the lefty conqueror in his prepared-ness to use violence to subdue anti-Vietnam protests.

After two terms as Governor, Reagan stood as a conservative against the more moderate Ford in the race for the Republican nomination for the 1976 Presidential elections. He lost this one but won the nomination in 1980 and defeated Jimmy Carter easily. In 1984, he defeated Walter Mondale in a landslide, winning 49 out of 50 states.

As President, Reagan's political attitude was classically liberal: 'The Founding Fathers knew a government can't control the economy without controlling people. And they knew when a government set out to do that, it must use force and coercion to achieve its purpose. So we have come to a time for choosing.' In effect he chose both. While his 'Reaganomics' of cutting taxes and deregulating the domestic economy helped America recover from the recession of the seventies, his expenditure on defence in staring down the crumbling Soviet empire helped America change from being the world's highest creditor nation at the beginning of his Presidency, to the highest debtor nation by its end. Deregulation also fuelled the activities of the financially unscrupulous and the era was marked by controversies such as the Savings and Loans Scandal, the yuppy fever of the Wall Street boom and security scandals such as Contragate, which sanctioned covert American involvement in the drug and gun trade to help fund rebels against the leftist regime in Nicaragua.

Undoubtedly Reagan's major achievement was presiding over the largely peaceful disintegration of the communist bloc. By the time he handed over the Presidency to George Bush, communism, which Reagan abhorred, was finished. It was a victory that Reagan achieved largely through rhetorical means. The skills he had learnt as an actor proved invaluable. As Margaret Thatcher said, 'He took words and sent them out to fight for us'.

GEORGE BUSH If Ford and Reagan came from relatively lowly backgrounds, George H. W. Bush entered the world as an Eastern States blueblood. His father was Prescott Bush—Yale graduate, wealthy merchant banker and US Senator, and his mother's father, Bert Walker, was an old-school robber baron who made his millions on Wall Street largely through insider trading. Perhaps the only quality of Bush's childhood that he shared with Ford, Reagan and Clinton was a problematic father. Despite his superficial success and the millions he made, Prescott Bush was a drunk and prone to over-application of the strap in the pursuit of disciplined children.

From an early age, Bush proved a natural leader. At his exclusive prep school, he was President of his senior year class and captain of the baseball and soccer teams. When he graduated in 1942, he joined the Navy and became a pilot, a job whose three-dimensional navigation demands enhanced visual-spatial skills. In the war, he demonstrated the conspicuous bravery seen in lefty warriors such as Alexander, Caesar, Napoleon and Joan of Arc. In 1944, he was on a raid to bomb installations on a Japanese island when his plane came under heavy anti-aircraft fire. Bush's plane was hit and half his crew killed. Despite the fact that his engine was on fire, Bush continued to head for the target. When he reached it, he dropped his payload of bombs before bailing out and parachuting into the ocean where he was rescued by a submarine four hours later. His other crewmate's parachute had failed to open and Bush was the only survivor. For his bravery, he was awarded the Distinguished Flying Cross, America's highest aerial medal.

With the war over, Bush got married then went to college. He continued the family's Ivy League tradition of attending Yale. Like Ford he was a

GEORGE BUSH
1924–

VISUAL-SPATIAL ABILITY
This shows in Bush's flying and baseball prowess, yet also in his predilection for the chess of geo-political strategy.

LATERAL THINKING As a youngster, Bush was renowned for his practical jokes, while his rise to the top had some unusual diversions. His time in the spy game often involved the transformative skills of making one thing appear like another, an example of which was his involvement in the extremely murky Iran Contra affair, which saw the CIA illegally selling weapons to Iran to fund right-wing guerillas in Nicaragua.

EXPERIMENTAL Instead of entering Wall Street, Bush took the risk of moving to Texas, joining the oil industry and eventually starting his own company.

FANTASIST Bush has shown a life-long love for the behind-the-scenes, cloak and dagger stuff of the CIA.

seriously good sportsman. As a left-handed first baseman, he was not only captain of the Yale team, but played in the first and second College World Series, where his team were consecutive runners-up, the only two times Yale has ever made it to the final.

When Bush graduated from Yale, like Reagan with a degree in economics, he turned down offers to work with his father and grandfather's firms for a chance to work in the developing oil industry. He got a job with a subsidiary of Dresser Industries, a company where his father was a long-standing member of the board. In 1953, he started Zapata Oil with two business partners. By the end of the 1950s all of them were millionaires. Bush also allowed the CIA to use Zapata's off-shore assets as a staging point for raids into Cuba. Even before Bush became Director of the CIA, there seems to have been a clear penchant for the cloak and dagger stuff.

Bush first campaigned for a Texan seat in the US Senate in 1964, but lost in a battle which saw him derided as 'a tool of the eastern kingmakers'. In 1966, he was elected to the House of Representatives and proved the value of his connections by being appointed almost immediately to the Committee of Ways and Means. With its authority over tax and revenue, it is the most powerful committee in the House of Representatives and it was unusual for such an inexperienced politician to get the nod. After being re-elected to Congress in 1968, Bush stood for the senate in 1970 and lost again. As a consolation, Nixon appointed him Ambassador to the United Nations, then in the crucial role as Special Envoy to China. When Gerald Ford became President, he appointed Bush as Director of the CIA, where he proved not to be the reforming outsider that he was made out to be. These jobs reveal Bush's particular interest in the mechanics of big picture, geo-political strategy, a kind of thinking that involves abstracted utilisation of the kinds of visual-spatial skills that made someone like Napoleon such a brilliant general.

In 1980, Bush became Reagan's running mate after Reagan defeated him for the presidential nomination, illustrating Bush's diplomatic skills. As with Ford and Rockefeller it was a double lefty team. He served two terms as Vice-President, then in 1988 won the Republican nomination and was elected President just in time for the Berlin Wall to fall. It was a Presidency concentrated on foreign policy, where Bush's skills of diplomacy, geo-political nous, and CIA insider knowledge proved invaluable. However, following the economic boom of the Reagan era, the end of the eighties saw America slide into recession. As a conspicuous blueblood, Bush couldn't help but look out of touch with the American people. He lacked Reagan's genius for generating the effect of empathy and it cost him. His perceived failure to finish the First Gulf War properly by killing Saddam Hussein, who as CIA Director he had supported, also damaged his chances for re-election, as did his backpedalling on his 'no new taxes' election pledge. In 1993, he handed over the Presidency to his fellow lefty, Bill Clinton.

BILL CLINTON Of all the left-handed Presidents surveyed here, Bill Clinton had the toughest background. His biological father, William Blythe, was a travelling salesman who was married four times (including to a pair of sisters) by the time he was 25. He was killed in a car crash three months before Clinton was born. When Clinton was four, his mother married Roger Clinton, a used car dealer in Hot Springs, Arkansas. If his real father was a philanderer, his stepfather was a violent alcoholic who used to abuse Clinton's mother and his half-brother.

As a kid, Clinton was into playing the saxophone and considered becoming a pro. However, he realised early that, while he was good, he was probably never going to be great. Unlike many left-handers in this book, but like all his fellow lefty Presidents, Clinton excelled academically. Education was his chance at escaping from uninspiring family circumstances. In high school, he was a delegate to Boys Nation, a scheme where two of the best students from each state go to Washington DC to learn about government. While Clinton was there he met President John Kennedy. By the time he came home he'd decided on politics for his career.

Clinton won scholarships to Georgetown University, Washington, where he studied Foreign Service before winning a coveted Rhodes Scholarship to Oxford in 1968, where he joined the educated elites of his generation in toking on joints, protesting against the Vietnam War and, less conventionally for an American, playing rugby. Like his predecessor, George Bush, Clinton headed a Presidency with a strong foreign policy emphasis, which might be related to his left-handed facility for difference and adaptation. Clinton is also one of few American Presidents to have spent time living abroad before entering politics.

Like Ford and Bush, Clinton went to Yale, where he studied law, graduating in 1973, before returning to Arkansas to begin his political career. In 1978, aged 32, Clinton became the youngest Governor in the country. Having benefited from his own education he put money into making educational opportunities available for all. He lost his re-election campaign in 1980, but showed tenacity and won the job back in 1982 and held onto it until resigning it to contest the Presidency in 1992.

Clinton won the 1992 elections and in 1996 became the first Democratic President to be re-elected since Franklin D. Roosevelt. Clinton's time as President was a period of great prosperity in America. He shared with Reagan an empathetic quality that Bush had lacked. They both used their charm to make their way from the boondocks to the centre of the nation. Both had the skillset of great actors, including the ability to narrate fiction with utter conviction. According to some political commentators, Clinton's greatest skill was his ability to adapt his ideas to whatever the electorate was thinking. Unfortunately, his second term was mired in the Monica Lewinsky scandal and the subsequent witch hunt that led to his impeachment. Since leaving politics, Clinton remains an important presence in global issues.

BILL CLINTON
1946–

EMPATHETIC Clinton is one of the most charismatic men to ever grace the stage of American politics. His charm is famous for its quality of total attention, making a person feel like he or she is the only one alive at that given point in time.

LATERAL THINKING In his Presidency and subsequently, Clinton has strongly advocated multi-lateral solutions to the more intractable political problems of international relations.

HOT-TEMPERED Was reported by his aide George Stephanopoulos as responding to the Somalian crisis by saying, 'We're not inflicting pain on these fuckers. When people kill us, they should be killed in greater numbers. I believe in killing people who try to hurt you. And I can't believe we're being pushed around by these two-bit pricks.'

EXPERIMENTAL Clinton toked but didn't inhale.

FANTASIST Clinton was liberal with the truth, often to comic effect, such as classifying oral sex as belonging outside the field of sexual relations.

OPPOSITE: THE YOUNG BILL CLINTON VISITED WASHINGTON IN 1963, AS A BOYS NATION SENATOR, AND MET PRESIDENT KENNEDY.

Further reading

Ackroyd, Peter, *Brief Lives: Newton*, Chatto and Windus, 2006

Adams, Tim, *Being John McEnroe*, Yellow Jersey Press, 2004

Arnstein, Walter L., *Queen Victoria*, Palgrave Macmillan, 2003

Bakewell, Michael, *Lewis Carroll: A Biography*, William Heinemann, 1996

Blue, Adrianne, *Martina Unauthorized*, Gollancz, 1995

Bragg, Melvyn, *On Giants' Shoulders: Great Scientists and their Discoveries from Archimedes to DNA*, Hodder and Stoughton, 1998

Brunskill, Ian (ed.), *Great Lives: A Century in Obituaries*, Times Books, 2005

Calder, Angus, *Gods, Mongrels and Demons, 101 Brief but Essential Lives*, Bloomsbury, 2003

Carroll, Lewis, *Alice's Adventures in Wonderland, Through the Looking-Glass*, and *The Hunting of the Snark*, Bodley Head, 1974

Cohen, Morton N., *Lewis Carroll: A Biography*, Macmillan, 1995

Collier, Peter and Horowitz, David, *The Fords: An American Epic*, Encounter Books, 2002

Coren, Stanley, *The Left-Hander Syndrome*, The Free Press, 1992

Crossen, Cynthia, *The Rich and How They Got That Way*, Crown Publishers, 2000

Dry, Sarah, *Curie*, Haus Publishing, 2003

Fincher, Jack, *Lefties: The Origins and Consequences of Being Left-handed*, Barnes & Noble, 1977

Freedberg, S. J., *Painting in Italy 1500–1600*, Pelican, 1990

Gardner, Howard, *Creative Minds*, Basic Books, 1993

Gergel, Tania (ed.), *Alexander: Selected Texts from Arrian, Curtius and Plutarch*, Penguin, 2005

Gleick, James, *Isaac Newton*, Pantheon, 2003

Goffen, Rona, *Renaissance Rivals: Michelangelo, Leonardo, Raphael, Titian*, Yale University Press, 2002

Gordon, Mary, *Joan Of Arc*, Penguin, 2000

Hodges, Andrew, *Alan Turing: The Enigma*, Simon and Schuster, 1983

Hollingdale, R. J., *Nietzsche: The Man and His Philosophy*, Cambridge University Press, 1999

Kemp, Martin, *Leonardo*, Oxford University Press, 2004

Lamb, Brian, *Booknotes Life Stories: Notable Biographers On the People Who Shaped America*, Three Rivers Press, 1999

Lucie-Smith, Edward, *Joan of Arc*, Allen Lane, 1976

Lynn, Kenneth S., *Charlie Chaplin and his Times*, Simon and Schuster, 1997

McEnroe, John, *Serious*, Little Brown, 2002

McManus, Chris, *Right Hand, Left Hand*, Phoenix, 2003

Menu, Bernadette, *Ramesses the Great: Warrior and Builder*, New Horizons, 1999

Miles, Barry, *Many Years From Now*, Vintage-Random House, 1998

Montville, Leigh, *The Big Bam: The Life and Times of Babe Ruth*, Doubleday, 2006

Nicholl, Charles, *Leonardo da Vinci: Flights of the Mind*, Viking, 2004

Orga, Ates, *Beethoven: His Life and Times*, Midas Books, 1978

Quinn, Susan, *Marie Curie: A Life*, William Heinemann, 1995

Shepherd, Rowena and Rupert, *1000 Symbols*, Thames and Hudson, 2002

Sofri, Gianni, *Gandhi and India*, Windrush Press, 1999

Strachey, Lytton, *Queen Victoria*, Chatto & Windus, 1922

Twain, Mark, *The Adventures of Huckleberry Finn*, Penguin, 1966

Twain, Mark, *The Adventures of Tom Sawyer*, Penguin, 1986

Tyldesley, Joyce, *Ramesses: Egypt's Greatest Pharaoh*, Penguin 2001

Vasari, Giorgio, *Lives of the Painters, Sculptors and Architects*, translated by Gaston de Vere, Everyman, 1996

Wallace, James, *Hard Drive: Bill Gates and the Making of the Microsoft Empire*, HarperCollins, 1993

West, Thomas G., *In the Mind's Eye: Visual Thinkers, Gifted People With Dyslexia and Other Learning Difficulties, Computer Images and the Ironies of Creativity*, Prometheus Books, 1991

Wolman, David, *A Left-Hand Turn Around the World: Chasing the Mystery and Meaning of All Things Southpaw*, Da Capo Press, 2005

Woodcock, George, *Gandhi*, Fontana, 1972

Wright, Ed, *Celebrity Family Trees: The World's Most Celebrated and Scandalous Dynasties*, Pier 9, 2006

Wullschläger, Jackie, *Inventing Wonderland*, Methuen, 1995

Wyn Jones, David, *The Life of Beethoven*, Cambridge University Press, 1998

Ziff, Larzer, *Mark Twain*, Oxford University Press, 2004